100 PROGRAMS
FOR THE
COMMODORE 64

To our parents

John and Mary Gordon

and

Robert and Isabella McLean

without whom none of this would have been possible.

100 PROGRAMS FOR THE COMMODORE 64

John Gordon
Ian McLean
MEDC, Paisley College, Scotland

Englewood Cliffs, NJ London New Delhi Rio de Janeiro
Singapore Sydney Tokyo Toronto Wellington

CBM is a trademark of Commodore Business Machines Inc.

Library of Congress Cataloging in Publication Data

Gordon, John, 1952–
  100 programs for the Commodore 64.

  1. Commodore 64 (Computer) – Programming. 2. Computer programs. I. McLean, Ian, 1946– . II. Title.
  III. Title: One hundred programs for the Commodore 64.
  QA76.8.C64G67 1984   001.64'2   84–17261
  ISBN 0-13-634650-2 (pbk.)

British Library Cataloging in Publication Data

Gordon, John,
  100 programs for the Commodore 64.
  1. Commodore 64 (Computer) – Programming
  I. Title   II. McLean, Ian, 1946-
  001.64'25   QA76.8.C64
  ISBN 0-13-634650-2 (pbk.)

© 1984 by John Gordon and Ian McLean

All rights reserved. No part of this publication may be reproduced, stored in a retrieval system, or transmitted, in any form or by any means, electronic, mechanical, photocopying, recording or otherwise, without the prior permission of Prentice-Hall International, Inc. For permission within the United States contact Prentice-Hall Inc., Englewood Cliffs, NJ 07632.

ISBN 0-13-634650-2

PRENTICE-HALL INTERNATIONAL INC., London
PRENTICE-HALL OF AUSTRALIA PTY., LTD., Sydney
PRENTICE-HALL CANADA, INC., Toronto
PRENTICE-HALL OF INDIA PRIVATE LIMITED, New Delhi
PRENTICE-HALL OF JAPAN, INC., Tokyo
PRENTICE-HALL OF SOUTHEAST ASIA PTE., LTD., Singapore
PRENTICE-HALL INC., Englewood Cliffs, New Jersey
PRENTICE-HALL DO BRASIL LTDA., Rio de Janeiro
WHITEHALL BOOKS LIMITED, Wellington, New Zealand

Printed in the United Kingdom by A. Wheaton & Co Ltd., Exeter
10 9 8 7 6 5 4 3 2 1

Contents

Section 1 – Introduction

P1	Dice	6
P2	Sound Generator	9
P3	Sounds	12
P4	Musak	16
P5	Bouncing Ball	20
P6	Ball and Wall	22
P7	Digital Clock	24
P8	Jimmy	26
P9	Runner 1	30
P10	Runner 2	34
P11	Nitemare	39

Section 2 – Games

P12	Guess the Number	43
P13	Reaction Test	46
P14	Mastermind	48
P15	Destroyer	52
P16	Monster Island	60
P17	Fighter	67
P18	Bat 'n' Moth	74

Section 3 – Business

P19	Loan Repayment Period	82
P20	Depreciation	84
P21	Stock File Creation	89
P22	Transaction File Creation	92
P23	Stock File Update and Report	95
P24	Tax Calculator	101
P25	True Rate of Interest	103
P26	Mailing List Creation	105
P27	Mailing List Maintenance	109

Section 4 – Point of Sale System

P28	PRICELIST – Main Menu Program	118
P29	MAINT – Price List Maintenance Program	120
P30	POS – Point of Sale Program	124
P31	PRINT – Price List Print Program	128
P32	FDUMP – File Dump Utility	130

Section 5 – Programs for the Home

P33	Monthly Accounts	132
P34	Conversion	135
P35	Birthday List	137
P36	Calendar	140
P37	Telephone List	142
P38	Investments	144
P39	Loan Repayment Schedule	146

Section 6 – Programmer's Utilities

P40	Monitor	150
P41	Renumber	154
P42	Delete	156
P43	Tidy	158

Section 7 – Graphics

P44	Hi-res Screen Utility	161
P45	Text on Graphics Screen	165
P46	Worm	169
P47	Colors	171
P48	Graphics Utility	173
P49	Shading	177
P50	Translation	179
P51	Parallelogram	182
P52	Shape Grabber	185
P53	Rotation	187
P54	Transformations	189
P55	General Transformation	192
P56	3D Rotation	195
P57	Perspective	198
P58	Rotating House	202

Contents   vii

P59	Drawing Circles	205
P60	Four-Weekly Moving Average	208
P61	Interfering Circles	211
P62	Zoom	213
P63	Interference	215
P64	Doodle	216

Section 8 – Data Handling

P65	Bar Chart	218
P66	Mean and Standard Deviation	220
P67	Bubble Sort	222
P68	Shell Sort	225
P69	Merge	228
P70	Permutations	232
P71	Combinations	234
P72	Least Squares	236

Section 9 – Recreation

P73	Number of Days	238
P74	Encoder	240
P75	Decoder	243
P76	Dog Race	246
P77	Magic Matrix	249
P78	Shuffle	252
P79	Recipes	254
P80	Kitchen Timer	261

Section 10 – Programs for the School

P81	School Report	264
P82	Language Tutorial	266
P83	Counting	269
P84	Spelling	272

Section 11 – Science Lab

P85	Number Base Conversion	279
P86	Color Codes for Resistors	284
P87	Volumes of Solids	289
P88	Physics Experiment 1	293

P89	Physics Experiment 2	297
P90	Resistors	300
P91	Calculator	303
P92	Coordinate Conversion	306

Section 12 – Mathematics

P93	Vector Multiplication	310
P94	Quadratic Equations	313
P95	Factorization	316
P96	Factorial	320
P97	Greatest Common Divisor	323
P98	Polynomial Multiplication	325
P99	Secant Method	329
P100	Method of Bisections	334
P101	Trapezoidal Rule	338
P102	Simpson's Rule	342

Introduction

It is with a sense of satisfaction that we present to you this selection of computer programs.

We have, in our selection, attempted to answer the question:

"What do you use a microcomputer for?"

You will find routines in this book which cover the use of micros at home, in business, at school and for pleasure.

After you have entered these programs you might like to save them on to tape. To help you, here is a reminder of how to do this.

To save a program

1. Key the program in.
2. Insert cassette into recorder.
3. Type
      SAVE "prog"
   where prog is the name of your program.
   Press the Return key.
4. A message then appears on the screen.
5. Press PLAY and RECORD on the tape recorder.
6. Press the Return key.
7. When the program has been saved, stop the tape.

If you wish, you can rewind the tape and use the VERIFY command to check that you have saved the program correctly. Refer to your User's Manual for the details of how to do this.

Once your program has been recorded successfully, you can reload it at any time by using the following procedure:

1. Load cassette into recorder.
2. Wind cassette on to the start of your program.

3. Type LOAD "prog" and press Return.
4. Press PLAY on your recorder.
5. The CBM-64 will display the message
   READY.
   when the program is loaded.
6. You can then LIST or RUN your program.

That's enough technical detail. Let's return to the task in hand, 100 or so programs for the CBM-64 microcomputer.

Each program is laid out in the following format:

Program commentary.
Program Listing.
On occasion a photograph of the screen or a printout.

Program Design

There are many styles which can be used when writing and presenting programs. You will probably have come across the devotees of structured programming in the computer press and might have met such people in the course of your hobby. One of the common arguments which you can hear is that you should use only structured programming languages such as Pascal or ADA, and that you should keep away from BASIC because it is such a poor programming tool. When, however, you are presented with a machine such as the Commodore-64 all such arguments disappear.

The Commodore-64 is probably the most flexible microcomputer in its class. If you do not like the BASIC on board, then you can replace it with another, or use it as a kernel for your own unique programming system.

The Commodore-64 has a full 64K of RAM available to do with as you wish. This will allow you to keep on expanding your machine as long as you wish to. You can add in another processor, the Zilog Z80, which will give you access to an almost infinite range of software. We may also presume that Commodore will continue to expand the capabilities of the machine.

Introduction

If, however, you are a newcomer to the industry, you will have to start somewhere. As far as we are concerned, the Commodore-64 is one of the best starting points there is.

We present here a broad selection of programs. These programs exhibit more than one style of construction and more than one style of presentation.

We have used two approaches when dealing with the Commodore editing characters. If we had a Commodore printer then we could have used the normal Commodore symbols for them. We have instead, in some programs, used the CHR$(nn) code for the screen positioning characters. Other programs have been filtered through the "TIDY" program to replace the Commodore characters with the following:

> All strings of the screen positioning characters start with the character [and finish with the character].
>
> cursor-home is replaced by CH
> clear-screen is replaced by CS
> cursor-down is replaced by CD
> cursor-up is replaced by CU
> cursor-left is replaced by CL
> cursor-right is replaced by CR
> reverse-on is replaced by RON
> reverse-off is replaced by ROF

Some of the programs are almost totally 'user-friendly' and some are quite terse. Some of the programs are well littered with commentary lines and some are quite sparse.

We have, however, in our programs shown off the machine as far as we could.

We have programs which explore the sound capabilities of the machine; programs which explore the graphics of the machine, using high resolution graphics, sprite graphics, user defined characters and color. But perhaps the greatest number of our programs explore problem solving using the computer.

In the main, we have used only the cassette as our backing storage device, but we have included one suite of programs to show the use of the disk system. This suite can, however, be easily adapted to cassette.

When we were developing our programs we did not sit down at the keyboard and type in a solution. We first laid out our solution in a form of pseudo-BASIC and only later did we implement these programs in CBM-64 BASIC.

We have taken our programs to the stage where the code is complex enough to solve realistic problems but is straightforward enough to remain fairly easy to understand. So if you feel that some of the programs could do with a little beefing up then go ahead, take our routines and make them into something better.

Bugs

It is possible, of course, for things to go wrong; for bugs to be introduced into your code.

Part of the fun of programming is the finding and correction of bugs. Indeed, correcting bugs often contributes to the process of introducing bugs.

Bugs can be introduced in various ways. We might have left a few bugs in the code. Hopefully, through the efforts of Prentice-Hall in carrying out field tests, these will be at a minimum.

Bugs can be introduced when you are keying in your programs.

Introduction

To catch these bugs you have to go through each section of the program in turn, trying to locate them by eye and by testing the section.

Common errors are :

1. Using the letter O rather than the number 0.
2. Using the number one rather than the letter I.
3. Using lower case rather than upper case.
4. Using the wrong dataname.
5. Going beyond the capabilities of the program.

Developing the Programs

In a sense, none of these programs is complete. They could all be expanded in various ways.

One of the joys of programming is to take a simple routine and give it a professional user-friendly appearance. We have not attempted to make our programs complete in this sense. This is left up to you.

Do not feel shy about using the programs as routines within others. Consider this book to be part of your software library.

If, however, you do use a routine within a work of your own, we would be pleased if you were to acknowledge the source.

GO ON ENJOY YOURSELF!

P1 Dice

A gambler's delight, this program rolls three dice.

This could be extended into a game where you bet against the computer.

COMMANDS

Key in the program and RUN.

Press any key to roll the dice.

RUN/STOP key stops program.

```
10 REM DICE
20 REM ****
30 REM
100 PRINT CHR$(147):REM CLEAR SCREEN
110 POKE 53281,0:REM BLACK SCREEN
120 POKE 53280,0:REM BLACK BORDER
130 PRINT CHR$(158):REM YELLOW INK
140 PRINT
150 PRINT TAB(20)"DICE"
160 PRINT:PRINT:PRINT
170 PRINT TAB(12);"THIS PROGRAM ROLLS"
180 PRINT TAB(15);"THREE DICE"
190 FOR N=0 TO 7
200 PRINT
210 NEXT
220 REM***********************
230 S$=CHR$(32)
240 T$=S$:E$=S$+S$+S$+S$
250 FOR N=0 TO 4
260 S$=S$+S$
270 NEXT
280 S$=S$+E$
290 REM S$ CONTAINS 36 SPACES
300 UP$=CHR$(145)
310 FOR N=0 TO 2
320 UP$=UP$+UP$
330 NEXT
340 REM UP$ CONTAINS 8 CURSOR UP CODES
```

```
350 R$=CHR$(188)
360 A$=R$+T$+T$
370 B$=T$+R$+T$
380 C$=T$+T$+R$
390 D$=R$+T$+R$
400 REM DOT PATTERNS IN STRINGS
410 DIM DICE$(2,2)
450 REM********************
500 REM AGAIN
510 PRINT TAB(11)
    "PRESS ANY KEY TO ROLL"
520 GET W$:IF W$="" THEN 520
530 REM WAIT FOR KEY
540 REM NO SPACE BETWEEN INVERTED COMMAS
560 FOR N=0 TO 7
570 PRINT S$
580 NEXT
590 PRINT UP$
600 REM CLEAR PREVIOUS THROW
610 REM********************
620 FOR N=0 TO 2
630 VL%=1+6*RND(1)
640 ON VL% GOSUB 1000,2000,3000,
               4000,5000,6000
650 NEXT
660 REM GENERATE PATTERNS
670 REM********************
680 FOR N=0 TO 2
690 PRINT,
    DICE$(0,N),DICE$(1,N),DICE$(2,N)
700 NEXT
710 PRINT:PRINT
720 REM PRINT PATTERNS
730 REM********************
740 FOR D=0 TO 200:NEXT
750 REM DELAY
760 GOTO 500:REM GO TO 'AGAIN'
780 REM********************
790 REM
900 REM            ****************
910 REM            *
920 REM            *
930 REM            *   SUBROUTINES
940 REM            *
950 REM            *
960 REM            ****************
970 REM
```

```
1000 REM ONE
1010 DICE$(N,0)=E$
1020 DICE$(N,1)=B$
1030 DICE$(N,2)=E$
1040 RETURN
1050 REM********************
1060 REM********************
2000 REM TWO
2010 DICE$(N,0)=A$
2020 DICE$(N,1)=E$
2030 DICE$(N,2)=C$
2040 RETURN
2050 REM********************
2060 REM********************
3000 REM THREE
3010 DICE$(N,0)=A$
3020 DICE$(N,1)=B$
3030 DICE$(N,2)=C$
3040 RETURN
3050 REM********************
3060 REM********************
4000 REM FOUR
4010 DICE$(N,0)=D$
4020 DICE$(N,1)=E$
4030 DICE$(N,2)=D$
4040 RETURN
4050 REM********************
4060 REM********************
5000 REM FIVE
5010 DICE$(N,0)=D$
5020 DICE$(N,1)=B$
5030 DICE$(N,2)=D$
5040 RETURN
5050 REM********************
5060 REM********************
6000 REM SIX
6010 DICE$(N,0)=D$
6020 DICE$(N,1)=D$
6030 DICE$(N,2)=D$
6040 RETURN
6050 REM********************
6060 REM********************
```

P2 Sound Generator

This program lets you experiment with sound by placing selected values in the sound chip registers. The sound duration is set by entering a number when requested. 900 gives approximately one second. The release cycle is initiated two thirds of the way through the duration.

This program could be extended so that dynamic effects such as varying the frequency or waveform during the sound are incorporated.

COMMANDS

Key in the program and RUN.

Enter the numbers when requested. Terminate each entry by pressing the RETURN key.

```
10 REM SOUND GENERATOR
20 REM **************
30 REM
100 CL$=CHR$(147):REM TO CLEAR SCREEN
110 S=54272:REM START OF SID MEMORY
120 DIM A%(24)
130 POKE 53280,4:REM PURPLE BORDER
140 POKE 53281,1:REM WHITE PAPER
150 PRINT CHR$(31):REM BLUE INK
160 REM*********************
170 PRINT CL$
180 PRINT:PRINT
190 PRINT TAB(12) CHR$(18);
    "SOUND GENERATOR"
200 PRINT:PRINT
210 PRINT TAB(4)
    "THIS PROGRAM ALLOWS YOU TO"
220 PRINT TAB(4)
    "EXPERIMENT WITH ALL THE SOUNDS"
230 PRINT TAB(4)
    "OF WHICH THE CBM 64 IS CAPABLE"
240 PRINT TAB(4)
    "BY LOADING ALL OF THE WRITE ONLY"
```

```
250 PRINT TAB(4)
    "SID REGISTERS WITH A NUMBER"
260 PRINT TAB(4)
    "BETWEEN 0 AND 255."
270 PRINT:PRINT
280 PRINT TAB(6) CHR$(18);
    "PRESS ANY KEY TO CONTINUE"
290 GET A$:IF A$="" THEN 290
300 REM**********************
310 PRINT CL$
320 FOR N=0 TO 24
330 POKE S+N,0:A%(N)=0
340 NEXT
350 REM SET ALL WRITE ONLY REGISTERS
        AND ARRAY ELEMENTS TO ZERO
370 RESTORE
380 FOR N=0 TO 24
390 READ A$
400 PRINT TAB(6) A$;:INPUT A%(N)
410 IF A%(N)<0 THEN A%(N)=0
420 IF A%(N)>255 THEN A%(N)=A%(N)-255:
    GOTO 420
430 NEXT
440 PRINT TAB(6):INPUT"DURATION";DU%
450 DU%=ABS(DU%)
460 DK%=DU%/3:DU%=DU%-DK%
470 REM**********************
480 FOR N=0 TO 24:POKE S+N,A%(N):NEXT
490 POKE S+4,0:POKE S+11,0:POKE S+18,0
500 FOR N=0 TO 24:POKE S+N,A%(N):NEXT
510 FOR N=0 TO DU%:NEXT
520 POKE S+4,A%(4) AND 254
530 POKE S+11,A%(11) AND 254
540 POKE S+18,A%(18) AND 254
550 FOR N=0 TO DK%:NEXT
560 POKE S+24,0
570 POKE S+4,0
580 POKE S+11,0
590 POKE S+18,0
600 PRINT CL$:PRINT:PRINT
610 PRINT TAB(4)
    "PRESS SPACE BAR FOR ANOTHER SOUND"
630 PRINT TAB(4)
    "ANY OTHER KEY STOPS PROGRAM"
640 GET A$:IF A$="" THEN 640:
    REM NO SPACE BETWEEN COMMAS
650 IF ASC(A$)=32 THEN 300
```

```
660 END
670 REM**********************
680 REM**********************
1000 DATA VOICE 1 - LO FREQ.
1010 DATA VOICE 1 - HI FREQ.
1020 DATA VOICE 1 - LO PULSE
1030 DATA VOICE 1 - HI PULSE
1040 DATA VOICE 1 - CONTROL
1050 DATA VOICE 1 - ATTACK-DECAY
1060 DATA VOICE 1 - SUSTAIN-RELEASE
1070 DATA VOICE 2 - LO FREQ.
1080 DATA VOICE 2 - HI FREQ.
1090 DATA VOICE 2 - LO PULSE
1100 DATA VOICE 2 - HI PULSE
1110 DATA VOICE 2 - CONTROL
1120 DATA VOICE 2 - ATTACK-DECAY
1130 DATA VOICE 2 - SUSTAIN-RELEASE
1140 DATA VOICE 3 - LO FREQ.
1150 DATA VOICE 3 - HI FREQ.
1160 DATA VOICE 3 - LO PULSE
1170 DATA VOICE 3 - HI PULSE
1180 DATA VOICE 3 - CONTROL
1190 DATA VOICE 3 - ATTACK-DECAY
1200 DATA VOICE 3 - SUSTAIN-RELEASE
1210 DATA FILTER CONTROL LO
1220 DATA FILTER CONTROL HI
1230 DATA RESONANCE/FILTER
1240 DATA MODE/VOLUME
1250 REM*********************
1260 REM*********************
```

P3 Sounds

This program creates some sounds which you might find useful in programs. It extends the technique demonstrated in the Sound Generator program by introducing dynamic techniques such as altering waveform, frequency and pulse rate during a sound and combining the frequencies of two channels.

COMMANDS

Key in the program and RUN.

Keys 1 to 8 select the sound. Key 9 stops the program.

```
10 REM SOUNDS
20 REM ******
30 REM
100 CL$=CHR$(147):REM TO CLEAR SCREEN
110 POKE 53280,3:REM CYAN BORDER
120 POKE 53281,6:REM BLUE SCREEN
130 PRINT CHR$(5):REM WHITE INK
140 S=54272:REM START OF SOUND CHIP
150 REM***************************
160 PRINT CL$:PRINT
170 PRINT TAB(7)
    "SELECT SOUND BY PRESSING:"
180 PRINT:PRINT
190 PRINT TAB(9)CHR$(18)" KEY 1 "
    CHR$(146)" - MACHINE GUN"
200 PRINT
210 PRINT TAB(9)CHR$(18)" KEY 2 "
    CHR$(146)" - EXPLOSION"
220 PRINT
230 PRINT TAB(9)CHR$(18)" KEY 3 "
    CHR$(146)" - SHOT AND RICOCHET"
240 PRINT
250 PRINT TAB(9)CHR$(18)" KEY 4 "
    CHR$(146)" - ALARM BELL"
260 PRINT
270 PRINT TAB(9)CHR$(18)" KEY 5 "
    CHR$(146)" - BOUNCE"
280 PRINT
```

P3 Sounds

```
290 PRINT TAB(9)CHR$(18)" KEY 6 "
    CHR$(146)" - BREAKING WAVE"
300 PRINT
310 PRINT TAB(9)CHR$(18)" KEY 7 "
    CHR$(146)" - SURPRISE"
320 PRINT
330 PRINT TAB(9)CHR$(18)" KEY 8 "
    CHR$(146)" - ALIEN SPACESHIP"
340 PRINT
350 PRINT TAB(9)CHR$(18)" KEY 9 "
    CHR$(146)" - STOP PROGRAM"
370 REM***************************
380 FOR N=0 TO 23:POKE S+N,0:NEXT
390 POKE S+24,15
400 GET A$:IF A$="" THEN 400:REM
    NO SPACE BETWEEN INVERTED COMMAS
410 IF ASC(A$)<49 OR ASC(A$)>57 THEN 400
420 IF ASC(A$)=57 THEN POKE S+24,0:END
430 SL=ASC(A$)-48
440 ON SL GOSUB 1000,2000,3000,4000,
    5000,6000,7000,8000
450 GOTO 380
460 REM***************************
470 REM***************************
1000 REM MACHINE GUN
1010 POKE S,0:POKE S+1,100
1020 POKE S+5,5:POKE S+6,19
1030 FOR N=0 TO 10
1040 POKE S+4,0:POKE S+4,129
1050 FOR DE=0 TO 50:NEXT
1060 POKE S+4,128
1070 FOR DE=0 TO 20:NEXT
1080 NEXT
1090 RETURN
1100 REM***************************
1110 REM***************************
2000 REM EXPLOSION
2010 POKE S,0:POKE S+1,30
2020 POKE S+5,12:POKE S+6,5
2030 POKE S+4,0:POKE S+4,129
2040 FOR DE=0 TO 2000:NEXT
2050 POKE S+4,128
2060 FOR DE=0 TO 400:NEXT
2070 RETURN
2080 REM***************************
2090 REM***************************
3000 REM SHOT AND RICOCHET
```

```
3010 POKE S,0:POKE S+1,100
3020 POKE S+5,9:POKE S+6,0
3030 POKE S+4,0:POKE S+4,129
3040 FOR DE=0 TO 150:NEXT
3050 POKE S+4,128
3060 FOR DE=0 TO 50:NEXT
3070 POKE S+4,33
3080 FOR DE=0 TO 700:NEXT
3090 RETURN
3100 REM**************************
3110 REM**************************
4000 REM ALARM BELL
4010 POKE S,0:POKE S+1,100
4020 POKE S+5,9:POKE S+6,0
4030 POKE S+7,0:POKE S+8,200
4040 POKE S+12,8:POKE S+13,0
4050 POKE S+15,30
4060 FOR N=0 TO 9
4070 POKE S+4,0:POKE S+4,21
4080 POKE S+11,0:POKE S+11,21
4090 FOR DE=0 TO 30:NEXT
4100 POKE S+11,20
4110 FOR DE=0 TO 30:NEXT
4120 POKE S+11,0:POKE S+11,21
4130 FOR DE=0 TO 30:NEXT
4140 POKE S+4,20:POKE S+11,20
4150 FOR DE=0 TO 30:NEXT
4160 NEXT
4170 RETURN
4180 REM**************************
4190 REM**************************
5000 REM BOUNCE
5010 POKE S+1,50
5020 POKE S+5,141:POKE S+6,134
5030 POKE S+4,0:POKE S+4,33
5040 FOR FR=240 TO 0 STEP -10
5050 POKE S,FR
5060 NEXT
5070 POKE S+1,30
5080 FOR FR=240 TO 0 STEP -10
5090 POKE S,FR
5100 NEXT
5110 POKE S+4,32
5120 FOR DE=0 TO 500:NEXT
5130 RETURN
5140 REM**************************
5150 REM**************************
```

P3 Sounds

```
6000 REM BREAKING WAVE
6010 POKE S,0:POKE S+1,80
6020 POKE S+5,205:POKE S+6,17
6030 POKE S+15,20
6040 POKE S+4,0:POKE S+4,131
6050 FOR DE=0 TO 1500:NEXT
6060 POKE S+1,15
6070 FOR DE=0 TO 1000:NEXT
6080 POKE S+1,60
6090 FOR DE=0 TO 1500:NEXT
6100 POKE S+4,130
6110 FOR DE=0 TO 200:NEXT
6120 RETURN
6130 REM***************************
6140 REM***************************
7000 REM SURPRISE
7010 POKE S,0:POKE S+1,50
7020 POKE S+5,12:POKE S+6,70
7030 POKE S+4,0:POKE S+4,65
7040 FOR PL=0 TO 255
7050 POKE S+3,PL
7060 NEXT
7070 POKE S+4,64
7080 FOR DE=0 TO 200:NEXT
7090 RETURN
7100 REM***************************
7110 REM***************************
8000 REM ALIEN SPACESHIP
8010 POKE S+1,45:POKE S+3,2
8020 POKE S+5,193:POKE S+6,133
8030 POKE S+14,200
8040 POKE S+4,0:POKE S+4,65
8050 POKE S+18,0:POKE S+18,16
8060 FOR K=0 TO 150
8070 A%=PEEK(S+27)*5:B%=A%/256
8080 POKE S,A%-B%*256
8090 POKE S+1,45+B%
8100 NEXT
8110 POKE S+4,64
8120 FOR DE=0 TO 300:NEXT
8130 RETURN
8140 REM***************************
8150 REM***************************
```

P4 Musak

This program turns your CBM 64 into a musical instrument. The bottom three rows of keys select three octaves. Each octave uses a different voice, so that chords may be played. Each voice is given its own ADSR envelope, so that you can combine different tone effects. Keys 1 to 9 select note length. Keys f1, f3, f5, and f7 select different sets of tone effects.

The program could be extended to give six octaves through using the shift key. More tone effects could be called up by the use of keys f2, f4, f6, and f8. Special effects could be created by selecting the noise waveform as well as the tone waveforms.

COMMANDS

Key in the program and RUN.

Stop the program by pressing the RETURN key.

```
10 REM MUSAK
20 REM *****
30 REM
100 CL$=CHR$(147):REM TO CLEAR SCREEN
110 POKE 53280,9:REM BROWN BORDER
120 POKE 53281,1:REM WHITE SCREEN
130 PRINT CHR$(31):REM BLUE INK
140 S=54272:REM START OF SOUND CHIP
150 POKE 650,128:REM KEYBOARD REPEAT
160 PRINT CL$:PRINT
170 PRINT TAB(16)CHR$(18)"-------"
180 PRINT TAB(16)CHR$(18)" MUSAK "
190 PRINT TAB(16)CHR$(18)"-------"
200 PRINT:PRINT
210 PRINT TAB(6)
    "THIS PROGRAM LETS YOU PLAY"
220 PRINT TAB(6)
    "MUSIC ON YOUR COMPUTER."
230 PRINT
```

P4 Musak

```
240 PRINT TAB(6)
    "F1 F3 F5 F7 SELECT TONE;"
250 PRINT
260 PRINT TAB(6)
    "1 TO 9 SELECT NOTE LENGTH;"
270 PRINT
280 PRINT TAB(6)
    "Q W E R T Y U I O P  *"
290 PRINT TAB(6)
    "A S D F G H J K L : ; ="
300 PRINT TAB(6)
    "Z X C V B N M , . / CRSR"
310 PRINT TAB(6)"SELECT NOTE."
320 PRINT
330 PRINT TAB(6)
    "RETURN KEY ENDS PROGRAM"
340 REM*************************
350 DIM FR(35,1):
    REM HOLDS NOTE FREQUENCIES
360 FOR N=0 TO 35:READ FR(N,0),FR(N,1):
    NEXT
370 KB$(0)="QWERTYUIOP*"
380 KB$(1)="ASDFGHJKL:;="
390 KB$(2)="ZXCVBNM,./"+CHR$(17)+
           CHR$(29)
400 REM*************************
410 REM INITIAL CONDITIONS
420 POKE S+4,0:POKE S+11,0:
    POKE S+18,0:POKE S+24,15
430 GOSUB 3000:REM DEFAULT WAVEFORMS
440 DR=4:REM DEFAULT NOTE LENGTH
450 TI$="000000"
460 REM*************************
470 REM PLAY
480 FOR N=0 TO 2
490 IF TI>DE(N)+25*DR THEN
    POKE S+4+7*N,0:GOTO 510:REM OFF
500 IF TI>DE(N)+20*DR AND WF(N)>1 THEN
    POKE S+4+7*N,WF(N)-1:REM RELEASE
510 NEXT
520 GET A$:IF A$="" THEN 470:REM
    NO SPACE BETWEEN INVERTED COMMAS
530 F=0
540 IF ASC(A$)>48 AND ASC(A$)<58 THEN
    DR=ASC(A$)-48:GOTO 470:REM LENGTH
550 GOSUB 2000 REM TONE SELECT
560 IF F=1 THEN 470
```

```
570 GOSUB 7000:REM FREQUENCY
580 IF ASC(A$)=13 THEN POKE S+24,0:
    POKE S+4,0:POKE S+11,0:POKE S-18,0
590 IF ASC(A$)=13 THEN END
600 GOTO 470
610 REM************************
620 REM************************
900 REM
910 REM            ********
920 REM            *
930 REM            * DATA
940 REM            *
950 REM            ********
960 REM
970 REM************************
980 REM************************
1000 REM NOTE FREQUENCY DATA
1010 DATA 33,135,35,134,37,162,39,223
1020 DATA 42,62,44,193,47,107,50,60
1030 DATA 53,57,56,99,59,190,63,75
1040 DATA 16,195,17,195,18,209,19,239
1050 DATA 21,31,22,96,23,181,25,30
1060 DATA 26,156,28,49,29,223,31,165
1070 DATA 8,97,8,225,9,104,9,247
1080 DATA 10,143,11,48,11,218,12,143
1090 DATA 13,78,14,24,14,239,15,210
1100 REM************************
1110 REM************************
1900 REM
1910 REM        ***************
1920 REM        *
1930 REM        * SUBROUTINES
1940 REM        *
1950 REM        ***************
1960 REM
1970 REM************************
1980 REM************************
2000 REM TONE SELECT
2010 IF ASC(A$)<133 OR ASC(A$)>136
     THEN 2050
2020 F=1:POKE S+4,0:POKE S+11,0:
     POKE S+18,0
2030 A=ASC(A$)-132
2040 ON A GOSUB 3000,4000,5000,6000
2050 RETURN
2060 REM************************
2070 REM************************
```

P4 Musak

```
3000 REM F1 WAVEFORMS
3010 POKE S+5,88:POKE S+6,195
3020 POKE S+12,88:POKE S+13,89
3030 POKE S+16,0:POKE S+17,8
3040 POKE S+19,10:POKE S+20,32
3050 WF(0)=33:WF(1)=33:WF(2)=65
3060 RETURN
3070 REM***********************
3080 REM***********************
4000 REM F3 WAVEFORMS
4010 POKE S+5,9:POKE S+6,34
4020 POKE S+12,35:POKE S+13,196
4030 POKE S+19,9:POKE S+20,72
4040 WF(0)=33:WF(1)=17:WF(2)=33
4050 RETURN
4060 REM***********************
4070 REM***********************
5000 REM F5 WAVEFORMS
5010 POKE S+5,35:POKE S+6,196
5020 POKE S+12,0:POKE S+13,240
5030 POKE S+19,137:POKE S+20,129
5040 WF(0)=33:WF(1)=33:WF(2)=33
5050 RETURN
5060 REM***********************
5070 REM***********************
6000 REM F7 WAVEFORMS
6010 POKE S+5,9:POKE S+6,9
6020 POKE S+12,88:POKE S+13,89
6030 POKE S+19,144:POKE S+20,115
6040 WF(0)=37:WF(1)=21:WF(2)=33
6050 RETURN
6060 REM***********************
6070 REM***********************
7000 REM FREQUENCY
7010 FOR M=0 TO 2
7020 FOR N=1 TO 12
7030 IF MID$(KB$(M),N,1)=A$ THEN F=1:
     CT=M:NT=N-1:M=2:N=12
7040 REM CT=OCTAVE, NT=NOTE
7050 NEXT:NEXT
7060 IF F=0 THEN 7120
7070 DE(CT)=TI
7080 POKE S+CT*7+1,FR(CT*12+NT,0)
7090 POKE S+CT*7,FR(CT*12+NT,1)
7100 POKE S+CT*7+4,0
7110 POKE S+CT*7+4,WF(CT)
7120 RETURN
```

P5 Bouncing Ball

This program shows a simple method of achieving animation using POKE instructions. Animation is achieved by placing the ball on the screen and then placing a space on top. The ball is then placed one position on.

COMMANDS

Key in the program and RUN.

The RUN/STOP key stops the program.

```
10 REM BOUNCING BALL
20 REM ************
30 REM
100 POKE 53280,6:REM BLUE BORDER
110 POKE 53281,1:REM WHITE PAPER
120 SC=1024:REM START OF SCREEN MEMORY
130 SD=54272:REM START OF SID MEMORY
140 REM SD ALSO EQUALS THE DIFFERENCE
    BETWEEN SCREEN AND COLOR MEMORY.
150 X=1:Y=INT(1+23*RND(1))
160 DY=1:DX=1:IF RND(1)<.5 THEN DY=-1
170 POKE SD,100:POKE SD+1,5:
    POKE SD+5,5
180 PRINT CHR$(147):REM CLEAR SCREEN
190 REM**************************
200 P=SC+40*Y+X:REM POSITION ON SCREEN
210 C=P+SD:REM COLOR MEMORY
220 POKE P,81
230 POKE C,0
240 IF X=0 OR X=39 THEN DX=-DX:
    GOSUB 1000
250 IF Y=0 OR Y=24 THEN DY=-DY:
    GOSUB 1000
260 FOR N=0 TO 2:NEXT:REM REDUCES
    DOUBLE BALL EFFECT
270 REM REMOVE LINES 260 AND 270 IF YOU
       WISH FASTER BALL MOVEMENT
280 X=X+DX:Y=Y+DY
290 POKE SD+24,0:POKE SD+4,0:POKE P,32
```

P5 Bouncing Ball

```
300 GOTO190
310 REM************************
900 REM
910 REM SUBROUTINE
920 REM **********
930 REM
1000 REM BOUNCE
1010 POKE SD+4,0
1020 POKE SD+24,15
1030 POKE SD+4,129
1040 RETURN
1050 REM************************
1060 REM************************
```

P6 Ball and Wall

This is an extension of the Bouncing Ball program. One of two alternative bounce angles may be chosen, depending on whether the ball hits the face or the corner of a brick. You could expand this program by introducing a bat to control the ball and having several layers of wall.

COMMANDS

Key in the program and RUN.

The RUN/STOP key stops the program.

```
10 REM BALL AND WALL
20 REM *************
30 REM
100 POKE 53280,6:REM BLUE BORDER
110 POKE 53281,1:REM WHITE PAPER
120 SC=1024:REM START OF SCREEN MEMORY
130 SD=54272:REM START OF SID MEMORY
140 REM SD IS ALSO DISPLACEMENT BETWEEN
    SCREEN AND COLOR MEMORY.
150 X=1:Y=INT(1+23*RND(1))
160 DY=1:DX=1:IF RND(1)<.5 THEN DY=-1
170 POKE SD,100:POKE SD+1,5:
    POKE SD+5,5
180 GOSUB 2000:REM BUILD WALL
190 REM**************************
200 P=SC+40*Y+X:REM POSITION ON SCREEN
210 C=P+SD:REM COLOR MEMORY
220 POKE P,81:POKE C,0
230 GOSUB 3000:REM TEST
240 IF X=0 OR X=39 OR F=1 THEN DX=-DX:
    GOSUB 1000
250 IF Y=0 OR Y=24 THEN DY=-DY:
    GOSUB 1000
260 X=X+DX:Y=Y+DY
270 POKE SD+24,0
280 POKE SD+4,0
290 POKE P,32
300 GOTO 190
310 REM**************************
```

P6 Ball and Wall

```
 320 REM**************************
 900 REM
 910 REM            ***************
 920 REM            *
 930 REM            * SUBROUTINES
 940 REM            *
 950 REM            ***************
 960 REM
1000 REM BUMP
1010 POKE SD+24,15
1020 POKE SD+4,0
1030 POKE SD+4,129
1040 RETURN
1050 REM**************************
1060 REM**************************
2000 REM WALL
2010 PRINT CHR$(147):REM CLEAR SCREEN
2020 FOR N=0 TO 24
2030 POKE SC+30+N*40,102
2040 POKE SC+30+N*40+SD,2
2050 NEXT
2060 RETURN
2070 REM**************************
2080 REM**************************
3000 REM TEST
3010 F=0
3020 IF X<>29 AND X<>31 THEN RETURN:
     REM BALL NOT NEXT TO WALL
3030 IF X=29 AND DX=-1 THEN RETURN:
     REM BALL MOVING AWAY FROM WALL
3040 IF X=31 AND DX=1 THEN RETURN:
     REM BALL MOVING AWAY FROM WALL
3050 IF PEEK(P+DX)=102 THEN F=1:
     POKE(P+DX),32:RETURN
3060 REM BALL HITS FACE OF BRICK
3070 IF PEEK(P+40*DY+DX)=102 THEN F=1:
     POKE(P+40*DY+DX),32:DY=-DY
3080 REM BALL HITS CORNER OF BRICK
3090 RETURN
3100 REM**************************
3200 REM**************************
```

P7 Digital Clock
24

This program uses the micro's internal timer to run a 24 hour digital clock. It could be extended so that several zone times are displayed simultaneously.

COMMANDS

Key in the program and RUN.

Enter the current time.

```
10 REM DIGITAL CLOCK
20 REM ************
30 REM
100 CL$=CHR$(147):REM TO CLEAR SCREEN
110 UP$=CHR$(145):REM UP CURSOR
120 S$=CHR$(32)
130 FOR N=0 TO 2:S$=S$+S$+S$:NEXT:
    REM S$ CONTAINS 27 SPACES
140 POKE 53280,0:REM BLACK BORDER
150 POKE 53281,0:REM BLACK SCREEN
160 PRINT CHR$(30):REM GREEN INK
170 REM***************************
180 PRINT CL$:PRINT:PRINT
190 PRINT TAB(10)"24 HOUR DIGITAL CLOCK"
200 PRINT TAB(10)"+++++++++++++++++++++"
210 PRINT:PRINT
220 PRINT TAB(11)"ENTER INITIAL TIME"
230 PRINT
240 PRINT TAB(11):INPUT"HOURS";H%
250 IF H%<0 OR H%>24 THEN
    PRINT UP$+S$+UP$:GOTO 240
260 A$=STR$(H%):IF LEN(A$)=2 THEN
    A$="0"+RIGHT$(A$,1)
270 IF LEN(STR$(H%))=3 THEN
    A$=RIGHT$(STR$(H%),2)
280 PRINT
290 PRINT TAB(11):INPUT"MINUTES";M%
300 IF M%<0 OR M%>60 THEN
    PRINT UP$+S$+UP$:GOTO 290
```

P7 Digital Clock

```
310 B$=STR$(M%):IF LEN(B$)=2 THEN
    B$="0"+RIGHT$(B$,1)
320 IF LEN(STR$(M%))=3 THEN
    B$=RIGHT$(STR$(M%),2)
330 PRINT
340 PRINT TAB(11):INPUT"SECONDS";S%
350 IF S%<0 OR S%>60 THEN
    PRINT UP$+S$+UP$:GOTO 340
360 C$=STR$(S%):IF LEN(C$)=2 THEN
    C$="0"+RIGHT$(C$,1)
370 IF LEN(STR$(S%))=3 THEN
    C$=RIGHT$(STR$(S%),2)
380 TI$=A$+B$+C$:REM SET CLOCK
390 PRINT CL$:FOR N=0 TO 10:PRINT:NEXT
400 REM***************************
410 IF LEFT$(TI$,2)="24" THEN
    TI$="000000"
420 D$=LEFT$(TI$,2)+":"+MID$(TI$,3,2)+
    ":"+RIGHT$(TI$,2)
430 PRINT TAB(15)D$:PRINT UP$+UP$
440 GOTO 410
```

P8 Jimmy

This is another animation program. User defined characters are used to create the cartoon character Jimmy.

Lines 580 to 770 draw Jimmy. Lines 790 to 900 make him wave. These lines are merely an example of how Jimmy can be drawn and moved. You can generate different movements using the shapes given, or expand the program further by defining new shapes.

COMMANDS

Key in the program and RUN.

Stop the program by pressing the RUN/STOP and RESTORE keys simultaneously.

Key in your own routines in lines 550 to 4500 to make Jimmy move.

```
10 REM JIMMY
20 REM *****
30 REM
40 POKE 52,48:POKE 56,48:CLR:
   REM RESERVE RAM AREA FOR CHARACTERS
50 REM RAM RESERVED BEFORE MAIN PROGRAM
         STARTS AS VARIABLES ARE CLEARED
60 REM*****************************
100 CL$=CHR$(147):REM TO CLEAR SCREEN
110 RO=53248:REM START OF CHARACTER ROM
120 RA=12288:REM START OF CHARACTER RAM
130 IT=56334:REM INTERRUPT TIMER
140 CC=53272:
    REM CONTROLS CHARACTER LOCATION
150 SC=1024:REM START OF SCREEN MEMORY
160 POKE 53280,6:REM BLUE BORDER
170 POKE 53281,1:REM WHITE SCREEN
180 PRINT CHR$(144):REM BLACK INK
190 REM*****************************
200 PRINT CL$:PRINT:PRINT
210 PRINT TAB(18)"WAIT"
```

```
220 PRINT CHR$(142):REM UPPER CASE
230 POKE IT,PEEK (IT) AND 254:
    REM DISABLE INTERRUPT TIMER
240 POKE 1,PEEK (1) AND 251:
    REM SWITCH FROM I/O TO CHAR. ROM
250 FOR N=0 TO 511:POKE N+RA,PEEK (N+RO)
    :NEXT:REM TRANSFER CHARACTERS
260 POKE 1,PEEK (1) OR 4:
    REM SWITCH FROM CHAR. TO I/O ROM
270 POKE IT,PEEK (IT) OR 1:
    REM ENABLE INTERRUPT TIMER
280 POKE CC,(PEEK (CC) AND 240)+12:
    REM CONTROL OF CHARACTERS TO RAM
290 REM***************************
300 RESTORE
310 FOR N=33 TO 47
320 FOR K=0 TO 7
330 READ A
340 POKE RA+K+N*8,A
350 NEXT:NEXT
360 REM***************************
370 REM DISPLAY POKE CODES 33 TO 47
380 REM (CHR$(33) TO CHR$(47)) ARE NOW
390 REM REDEFINED TO GIVE THE SHAPES
400 REM WHICH MAKE UP JIMMY.
410 REM***************************
420 REM YOU CAN ENTER ANY PROGRAM YOU
430 REM WISH IN LINES 550 TO 4500,
440 REM USING THE SHAPES TO BUILD THE
450 REM CHARACTER.
460 REM***************************
470 REM WE HAVE PUT IN A SIMPLE ROUTINE
490 REM AS AN EXAMPLE. THIS MAKES JIMMY
500 REM WAVE.
510 REM***************************
520 REM***************************
530 REM
540 REM
550 PRINT CL$:PRINT:PRINT
560 PRINT TAB(15)"HELLO JIMMY"
570 CO=54272:REM ADD TO SCREEN LOCATIONS
                  TO POKE COLOR
580 POKE SC+10*40+19,33:REM HEAD
590 POKE SC+10*40+19+CO,10:REM PINK
600 POKE SC+11*40+18,38:REM UPPER ARM
610 POKE SC+11*40+18+CO,2:REM RED
620 POKE SC+11*40+19,34:REM UPPER TRUNK
```

```
630 POKE SC+11*40+19+CO,2:REM RED
640 POKE SC+11*40+20,36:REM UPPER ARM
650 POKE SC+11*40+20+CO,2:REM RED
660 POKE SC+12*40+18,39:REM LOWER ARM
670 POKE SC+12*40+18+CO,2:REM RED
680 POKE SC+12*40+19,35:REM LOWER TRUNK
690 POKE SC+12*40+19+CO,0:REM BLACK
700 POKE SC+12*40+20,37:REM LOWER ARM
710 POKE SC+12*40+20+CO,2:REM RED
720 POKE SC+13*40+18,44:REM FOOT
730 POKE SC+13*40+18+CO,0:REM BLACK
740 POKE SC+13*40+19,42:REM LEGS
750 POKE SC+13*40+19+CO,0:REM BLACK
760 POKE SC+13*40+20,43:REM FOOT
770 POKE SC+13*40+20+CO,0:REM BLACK
780 REM*********************
790 REM MAKE JIMMY WAVE
800 POKE SC+11*40+20,36:REM UPPER ARM
810 POKE SC+12*40+20,37:REM LOWER ARM
820 FOR N=0 TO 200:NEXT
830 POKE SC+12*40+20,32:REM SPACE
840 POKE SC+10*40+20,40:REM ARM WAVE
850 POKE SC+10*40+20+CO,2:REM RED
860 POKE SC+11*40+20,41:REM ARM WAVE
870 FOR N=0 TO 200:NEXT
880 POKE SC+10*40+20,32:REM SPACE
900 GOTO 790
910 REM*********************
920 REM*********************
4510 REM
4520 REM
4530 REM            **********
4540 REM            *
4550 REM            *
4560 REM            *   DATA
4570 REM            *
4580 REM            *
4590 REM            **********
4600 REM
4610 REM
5000 DATA 24,60,90,126,126,102,62,24
5010 REM HEAD
5020 REM*********************
5030 DATA 24,255,255,255,231,126,102,126
5040 REM UPPER TRUNK
5050 REM*********************
5060 DATA 102,60,60,60,126,231,231,231
```

```
5070 REM LOWER TRUNK
5080 REM*********************
5090 DATA 0,128,192,224,112,48,48,48
5100 REM UPPER LEFT ARM
5110 REM*********************
5120 DATA 48,48,48,0,0,0,0,0
5130 REM LOWER LEFT ARM
5140 REM*********************
5150 DATA 0,1,3,7,14,12,12,12
5160 REM UPPER RIGHT ARM
5170 REM*********************
5180 DATA 12,12,12,0,0,0,0,0
5190 REM LOWER RIGHT ARM
5200 REM*********************
5210 DATA 0,0,0,48,48,48,48,48
5220 REM RAISE UPPER LEFT ARM
5230 REM*********************
5240 DATA 112,240,192,128,0,0,0,0
5250 REM RAISE LOWER LEFT ARM
5260 REM*********************
5270 DATA 231,231,231,231,231,231,231,
     231
5280 REM LEGS AT ATTENTION
5290 REM*********************
5300 DATA 0,0,0,0,0,0,192,192
5310 REM LEFT FOOT
5320 REM*********************
5330 DATA 0,0,0,0,0,0,3,3
5340 REM RIGHT FOOT
5350 REM*********************
5360 DATA 0,0,0,36,60,60,255,255
5370 REM HAT
5380 REM*********************
5390 DATA 0,24,60,126,126,60,24,0
5400 REM BALL
5410 REM*********************
5420 DATA 60,126,255,126,60,24,24,24
5430 REM BAT
5440 REM*********************
5450 REM*********************
```

P9 Runner 1

Here is yet another method of producing animation. A single sprite is made to change shape by altering the sprite pointer. At the same time the sprite is moved from left to right. As a result a figure appears to run across the screen.

The sprite is expanded in both the X and Y directions and movement is made fairly slow so that you can see how animation is achieved. More realistic motion can be created by unexpanding the sprite and reducing the delay in line 430.

COMMANDS

Key in the program and RUN.

Stop the program by pressing the RUN/STOP and RESTORE keys simultaneously.

The program could be expanded by enabling several sprites and making the figures race.

```
10 REM RUNNER 1
20 REM ********
30 REM
100 POKE 52,48:POKE 56,48:CLR:
    REM RESERVE MEMORY FOR SPRITES
110 CL$=CHR$(147):REM TO CLEAR SCREEN
120 POKE 53280,0:REM BLACK BORDER
130 POKE 53281,13:REM GREEN SCREEN
140 PRINT CHR$(144):REM BLACK INK
150 PRINT CL$:PRINT:PRINT
160 PRINT TAB(18)"WAIT"
170 REM**************************
180 REM GENERATE SPRITE
190 V=53248:REM START OF VIDEO CHIP
200 POKE V+21,1:REM SPRITE 1 ENABLED
210 POKE V+39,0:REM BLACK SPRITE
220 POKE V+29,1:REM SPRITE EXPANDED
    IN X DIRECTION
230 POKE V+23,1:REM SPRITE EXPANDED
```

```
            IN Y DIRECTION
240 REM*************************
250 REM GET SHAPES FOR SPRITE
260 FOR N=0 TO 511
270 READ A:POKE 12288+N,A
280 NEXT
290 REM*************************
300 REM SPRITE POSITION
310 POKE V+1,150:REM Y POSITION
320 POKE V+16,0:REM MSB REGISTER
330 X=0
340 PRINT CL$
350 REM*************************
360 REM MOVE SPRITE
370 FOR N=0 TO 7
380 POKE 2040,192+N:REM SELECT SPRITE
    SHAPES IN TURN
390 K=X
400 IF X>255 THEN POKE V+16,1:K=X-256
410 IF X<256 THEN POKE V+16,0
420 POKE V,K
430 FOR DE=0 TO 150:NEXT
440 X=X+7:IF X=350 THEN X=0
450 NEXT
460 GOTO360
900 REM
910 REM           **********
920 REM           *
930 REM           * SPRITE
940 REM           *   DATA
950 REM           *
960 REM           **********
970 REM
980 REM*************************
990 REM*************************
1000 REM SHAPE 1
1010 DATA 0,0,0,0,0,0,0,0,0
1020 DATA 0,0,0,0,0,48,0,0,120
1030 DATA 0,60,124,0,124,124,0,236,120
1040 DATA 0,111,128,0,15,0,0,255,28
1050 DATA 1,255,56,29,249,240,61,240,192
1060 DATA 111,224,0,15,224,0,0,228,0
1070 DATA 0,124,0,0,120,0,0,112,0,0
1080 REM*************************
1090 REM*************************
1100 REM SHAPE 2
1110 DATA 0,0,0,0,0,0,0,0,0
```

```
1120 DATA 0,0,0,0,0,0,0,0,0
1130 DATA 0,0,192,0,1,224,0,57,240
1140 DATA 0,109,240,0,237,224,0,15,0
1150 DATA 0,62,0,1,255,96,3,255,224
1160 DATA 3,241,128,3,224,0,7,224,0
1170 DATA 1,192,0,7,224,0,7,192,0,0
1180 REM*************************
1190 REM*************************
1200 REM SHAPE 3
1210 DATA 0,0,0,0,0,0,0,0,0
1220 DATA 0,0,0,0,0,96,0,0,240
1230 DATA 0,0,248,0,0,248,0,0,240
1240 DATA 0,63,128,0,127,0,0,111,0
1250 DATA 0,127,96,0,127,224,0,255,0
1260 DATA 1,255,0,11,252,0,31,56,0
1270 DATA 28,16,0,24,0,0,12,0,0,0
1280 REM*************************
1290 REM*************************
1300 REM SHAPE 4
1310 DATA 0,0,0,0,0,48,0,0,120
1320 DATA 0,0,124,0,0,124,0,0,120
1330 DATA 0,0,192,0,31,140,0,55,188
1340 DATA 0,63,248,0,127,64,0,63,240
1350 DATA 0,63,224,0,124,248,9,225,224
1360 DATA 15,128,0,60,0,0,48,0,0
1370 DATA 96,0,0,0,0,0,0,0,0
1380 REM*************************
1390 REM*************************
1400 REM SHAPE 5
1410 DATA 0,0,0,0,0,96,0,0,240
1420 DATA 0,0,248,0,0,248,0,112,240
1430 DATA 1,253,128,1,143,140,0,31,252
1440 DATA 0,124,248,56,252,0,251,248,0
1450 DATA 191,252,0,12,127,48,0,7,224
1460 DATA 0,1,192,0,0,128,0,0,0
1470 DATA 0,0,0,0,0,0,0,0,0
1480 REM*************************
1490 REM*************************
1500 REM SHAPE 6
1510 DATA 0,0,0,0,0,0,0,0,0
1520 DATA 0,0,0,0,0,24,0,0,60
1530 DATA 0,12,62,0,124,62,0,230,124
1540 DATA 0,70,192,0,7,192,0,31,206
1550 DATA 6,127,252,14,126,112,30,252,0
1560 DATA 7,248,0,3,56,0,0,25,128
1570 DATA 0,15,0,0,14,0,0,12,0,0
1580 REM*************************
```

```
1590 REM************************
1600 REM SHAPE 7
1610 DATA 0,0,0,0,0,0,0,0,0
1620 DATA 0,0,0,0,0,0,0,0,0
1630 DATA 0,0,24,0,0,60,0,6,62
1640 DATA 0,31,62,0,51,60,0,19,224
1650 DATA 0,15,128,0,127,152,1,254,248
1660 DATA 1,252,224,1,248,0,3,240,0
1670 DATA 7,240,0,0,192,0,3,240,0,0
1680 REM************************
1690 REM************************
1700 REM SHAPE 8
1710 DATA 0,0,0,0,0,0,0,0,0
1720 DATA 0,0,0,0,0,48,0,0,120
1730 DATA 0,0,124,0,0,124,0,0,120
1740 DATA 0,31,192,0,63,128,0,15,128
1750 DATA 0,63,176,0,254,240,1,254,224
1760 DATA 3,252,0,31,112,0,60,48,0
1770 DATA 56,24,0,48,0,0,48,0,0,0
1780 REM************************
1790 REM************************
```

P10 Runner 2

This is a variation of the technique demonstrated in the Runner 1 program. Here the running figure remains in the center of the screen and the background is moved from right to left. As a result the figure appears to be running through a forest. Sprite numbers are chosen so that the runner moves in front of one tree and behind the next, giving a three dimensional effect.

COMMANDS

Key in the program and RUN.

Stop the program by pressing the RUN/STOP and RESTORE keys simultaneously.

```
10 REM RUNNER 2
20 REM ********
30 REM
100 POKE 52,48:POKE 56,48:CLR:
    REM RESERVE MEMORY FOR SPRITES
110 CL$=CHR$(147):REM TO CLEAR SCREEN
120 POKE 53280,0:REM BLACK BORDER
130 POKE 53281,1:REM WHITE SCREEN
140 PRINT CHR$(144):REM BLACK INK
150 PRINT CL$:PRINT:PRINT
160 PRINT TAB(18)"WAIT"
170 REM**************************
180 REM GENERATE SPRITES
190 V=53248:REM START OF VIDEO CHIP
200 POKE V+21,63:REM 5 SPRITES ENABLED
210 POKE V+39,5:POKE V+40,11:POKE V+41,4
    :POKE V+42,5:POKE V+43,11
220 POKE V+29,59:REM 4 SPRITES EXPANDED
    IN X DIRECTION
230 POKE V+23,59:REM 4 SPRITES EXPANDED
    IN Y DIRECTION
240 REM**************************
250 REM GET SHAPES FOR SPRITE
260 FOR N=0 TO 639
270 READ A:POKE 12288+N,A
```

P10 Runner 2

```
280 NEXT
290 REM***************************
300 REM SPRITE POSITION
310 POKE V+1,117:POKE V+3,150:POKE V+5,
    150:POKE V+7,87:POKE V+9,120
320 POKE V+16,0:REM MSB REGISTER
330 POKE V+4,155:X(0)=85:X(1)=225
340 PRINT CL$
350 POKE 2040,200:POKE 2041,201
360 POKE 2043,200:POKE 2044,201
370 REM***************************
380 REM MOVE SPRITE
390 FOR J=0 TO 7
400 POKE 2042,192+J:REM SELECT SPRITE
    SHAPES IN TURN
410 FOR N=0 TO 1
420 K=X(N):IF X(N)>255 THEN POKE V+16,
    PEEK(V+16) OR (3+21*N):K=K-255
430 POKE V+6*N,K:POKE 2+V+6*N,K
440 IF X(N)<256 THEN POKE V+16,
    PEEK(V+16) AND (252-21*N)
450 FOR DE=0 TO 50:NEXT
460 POKE V+39,5:POKE V+40,11:
    POKE V+42,5:POKE V+43,11
470 X(N)=X(N)-2:IF X(N)<0 THEN X(N)=340:
    POKE V+39+3*N,1:POKE V+40+3*N,1
480 IF X(N)=340 THEN 420
490 REM REPOSITION SPRITE IMMEDIATELY AT
    SCREEN BOUNDARY TO REDUCE FLICKER
500 NEXT
510 NEXT
520 GOTO 380
530 REM***************************
540 REM***************************
900 REM
910 REM          **********
920 REM          *
930 REM          * SPRITE
940 REM          * DATA
950 REM          *
960 REM          **********
970 REM
980 REM***************************
990 REM***************************
1000 REM SHAPE 1
1010 DATA 0,0,0,0,0,0,0,0,0
1020 DATA 0,0,0,0,0,48,0,0,120
```

```
1030 DATA 0,60,124,0,124,124,0,236,120
1040 DATA 0,111,128,0,15,0,0,255,28
1050 DATA 1,255,56,29,249,240,61,240,192
1060 DATA 111,224,0,15,224,0,0,228,0
1070 DATA 0,124,0,0,120,0,0,112,0,0
1080 REM*************************
1090 REM*************************
1100 REM SHAPE 2
1110 DATA 0,0,0,0,0,0,0,0,0
1120 DATA 0,0,0,0,0,0,0,0,0
1130 DATA 0,0,192,0,1,224,0,57,240
1140 DATA 0,109,240,0,237,224,0,15,0
1150 DATA 0,62,0,1,255,96,3,255,224
1160 DATA 3,241,128,3,224,0,7,224,0
1170 DATA 1,192,0,7,224,0,7,192,0,0
1180 REM*************************
1190 REM*************************
1200 REM SHAPE 3
1210 DATA 0,0,0,0,0,0,0,0,0
1220 DATA 0,0,0,0,0,96,0,0,240
1230 DATA 0,0,248,0,0,248,0,0,240
1240 DATA 0,63,128,0,127,0,0,111,0
1250 DATA 0,127,96,0,127,224,0,255,0
1260 DATA 1,255,0,11,252,0,31,56,0
1270 DATA 28,16,0,24,0,0,12,0,0,0
1280 REM*************************
1290 REM*************************
1300 REM SHAPE 4
1310 DATA 0,0,0,0,0,48,0,0,120
1320 DATA 0,0,124,0,0,124,0,0,120
1330 DATA 0,0,192,0,31,140,0,55,188
1340 DATA 0,63,248,0,127,64,0,63,240
1350 DATA 0,63,224,0,124,248,9,225,224
1360 DATA 15,128,0,60,0,0,48,0,0
1370 DATA 96,0,0,0,0,0,0,0,0
1380 REM*************************
1390 REM*************************
1400 REM SHAPE 5
1410 DATA 0,0,0,0,0,96,0,0,240
1420 DATA 0,0,248,0,0,248,0,112,240
1430 DATA 1,253,128,1,143,140,0,31,252
1440 DATA 0,124,248,56,252,0,251,248,0
1450 DATA 191,252,0,12,127,48,0,7,224
1460 DATA 0,1,192,0,0,128,0,0,0
1470 DATA 0,0,0,0,0,0,0,0,0
1480 REM*************************
1490 REM*************************
```

```
1500 REM SHAPE 6
1510 DATA 0,0,0,0,0,0,0,0,0
1520 DATA 0,0,0,0,0,24,0,0,60
1530 DATA 0,12,62,0,124,62,0,230,124
1540 DATA 0,70,192,0,7,192,0,31,206
1550 DATA 6,127,252,14,126,112,30,252,0
1560 DATA 7,248,0,3,56,0,0,25,128
1570 DATA 0,15,0,0,14,0,0,12,0,0
1580 REM**************************
1590 REM**************************
1600 REM SHAPE 7
1610 DATA 0,0,0,0,0,0,0,0,0
1620 DATA 0,0,0,0,0,0,0,0,0
1630 DATA 0,0,24,0,0,60,0,6,62
1640 DATA 0,31,62,0,51,60,0,19,224
1650 DATA 0,15,128,0,127,152,1,254,248
1660 DATA 1,252,224,1,248,0,3,240,0
1670 DATA 7,240,0,0,192,0,3,240,0,0
1680 REM**************************
1690 REM**************************
1700 REM SHAPE 8
1710 DATA 0,0,0,0,0,0,0,0,0
1720 DATA 0,0,0,0,0,48,0,0,120
1730 DATA 0,0,124,0,0,124,0,0,120
1740 DATA 0,31,192,0,63,128,0,15,128
1750 DATA 0,63,176,0,254,240,1,254,224
1760 DATA 3,252,0,31,112,0,60,48,0
1770 DATA 56,24,0,48,0,0,48,0,0,0
1780 REM**************************
1790 REM**************************
1800 REM TREE LEAVES
1810 DATA 0,248,0,1,252,0,3,254,0
1820 DATA 3,255,0,3,255,19?,7,255,224
1830 DATA 7,255,240,31,255,240,63,255,
          252
1840 DATA 127,255,254,255,255,255,255,
          255,254
1850 DATA 255,255,252,127,255,252,31,
          255,254
1860 DATA 63,255,255,127,255,255,255,
          255,255
1870 DATA 127,192,126,63,128,24,0,0,0,0
1880 REM**************************
1890 REM**************************
1900 REM TREE TRUNK
1910 DATA 0,0,0,3,62,56,3,62,112
1920 DATA 1,190,96,0,255,192,0,127,192
```

```
1930 DATA 0,62,0,0,62,0,0,62,0
1940 DATA 0,62,0,0,62,0,0,62,0
1950 DATA 0,62,0,0,62,0,0,62,0
1960 DATA 0,62,0,0,62,0,0,62,0
1970 DATA 0,119,0,0,227,128,1,193,192,0
1980 REM**************************
1990 REM**************************
```

P11 Nitemare

This program combines the sound and sprite graphics features of the micro. Eight sprites are used, all having the same shape but different colors. The sprites move, expand and contract at random. Meanwhile all three sound channels are used to play random discords.

The program could be expanded to give different shapes to each sprite. It could also be adapted to run in high resolution bit map mode so that the background could contain random patterns. This latter modification would probably require to be implemented in machine code.

COMMANDS

Key in the program and RUN.

Stop the program by pressing any key. Pressing the RUN/STOP and RESTORE keys simultaneously clears the sprites from the screen.

Don't watch alone!

```
10 REM NITEMARE
20 REM ********
30 REM
100 PRINT CHR$(147):REM CLEAR SCREEN
110 POKE 52,48:POKE 56,48:CLR:
    REM RESERVE MEMORY FOR SPRITES
120 POKE 53280,0:REM BLACK BORDER
130 POKE 53281,0:REM BLACK SCREEN
140 V=53248:REM START OF VIDEO CHIP
150 S=54272:REM START OF SOUND CHIP
160 REM*****************************
170 FOR N=0 TO 63:READ A:NEXT:
    REM POINT TO START OF SOUND DATA
180 DIM B(24):FOR N=0 TO 24:READ B(N):
    POKE S+N,B(N):NEXT:REM SOUND
190 POKE S+4,0:POKE S+11,0:POKE S+18,0
200 POKE S+4,B(4):POKE S+11,B(11):
    POKE S+18,B(18)
```

```
210 REM****************************
220 REM DEFINE SPRITES
230 POKE V+21,255:
    REM ALL SPRITES ENABLED
240 FOR N=1 TO 8
250 POKE V+39+N,N+1
260 NEXT:REM SPRITES ALL DIFFERENT
        COLORS
270 POKE V+29,255:REM ALL SPRITES
    EXPANDED IN X DIRECTION
280 POKE V+23,170:REM FOUR SPRITES
    EXPANDED IN Y DIRECTION
290 POKE V+16,0:REM X MSB REGISTER
300 DIM P%(7,1):REM HOLDS POSITIONS
    OF SPRITES ON SCREEN
310 FOR N=0 TO 7
320 POKE 2040+N,N+192:
    REM SET SPRITE POINTERS
330 P%(N,0)=24+271*RND(1):
    P%(N,1)=50+159*RND(1)
340 RESTORE:FOR K=0 TO 63:READ A
350 POKE 12288+N*64+K,A:NEXT:
    REM GENERATE SPRITE SHAPES
360 GOSUB 4000:REM PUT SPRITES ON SCREEN
370 GOSUB 5000:REM CHANGE SOUND
380 NEXT:REM SET INITIAL POSITIONS
390 REM**********************
400 REM MOVE SPRITES
410 FOR N=0 TO 7
420 P%(N,0)=P%(N,0)+15*RND(1)-7
430 IF P%(N,0)>288 THEN
    P%(N,0)=P%(N,0)-8
440 IF P%(N,0)<24 THEN
    P%(N,0)=P%(N,0)+8
450 P%(N,1)=P%(N,1)+15*RND(1)-7
460 IF P%(N,1)>208 THEN
    P%(N,1)=P%(N,1)-8
470 IF P%(N,1)<50 THEN
    P%(N,1)=P%(N,1)+8
480 GOSUB 4000:REM PUT SPRITES ON SCREEN
490 POKE V+2*N+1,P%(N,1):REM Y POSITION
500 NEXT
510 POKE V+29,255*RND(1):REM ALTER
    SPRITE EXPANSION IN X DIRECTION
520 POKE V+23,255*RND(1):REM ALTER
    SPRITE EXPANSION IN Y DIRECTION
530 GOSUB 5000:REM CHANGE SOUND
```

P11 Nitemare

```
540 GET A$:IF A$="" THEN 400:REM NO
    SPACE BETWEEN INVERTED COMMAS
550 REM****************************
560 REM KEY PRESS DETECTED. STOP SOUND
    AND END PROGRAM
570 FOR N=0 TO 24:POKE S+N,0:NEXT:
    REM STOPS THE SOUND
580 END
610 REM****************************
620 REM****************************
900 REM DATA TO DEFINE SPRITE SHAPES
910 REM *****************************
920 REM
1900 REM DATA TO DEFINE SPRITE SHAPES
1910 REM *****************************
1920 REM
2000 DATA 0,255,0,3,255,192,7,255,224
2010 DATA 15,255,240,31,255,248,63,255,
     252
2020 DATA 63,255,252,63,255,252,127,255,
     254
2030 DATA 124,255,62,120,126,30,240,60,
     15
2040 DATA 240,60,15,240,36,15,248,102,
     31
2050 DATA 252,195,63,255,195,255,127,
     255,254
2060 DATA 127,255,254,57,153,156,1,153,
     128,0
2070 REM
2900 REM DATA TO DEFINE SOUND
2910 REM *********************
2920 REM
3000 DATA 210,70,0,0,37,140,199,34,30,
     100,120,65,140,198
3010 DATA 56,4,0,0,17,140,198,0,0,0,15
3020 REM**********************
3030 REM**********************
3900 REM
3910 REM
3920 REM         SUBROUTINES
3930 REM         ***********
3940 REM
3950 REM
4000 REM SPRITES ON TO SCREEN
4010 K=P%(N,0):IF K<256 THEN
     POKE V+16,PEEK(V+16) AND (255-2^N)
```

```
4020 IF K>255 THEN K=K-255:
     POKE V+16,PEEK(V+16) OR 2^N
4030 POKE V+2*N,K:REM X POSITION
4040 POKE V+2*N+1,P%(N,1):REM Y POSITION
4050 RETURN
4060 REM**********************
4070 REM**********************
5000 REM CHANGE SOUND
5010 POKE S+4,0:POKE S+11,0:POKE S+18,0
5020 POKE S+1,180*RND(1)+20
5030 POKE S+8,180*RND(1)+20
5040 POKE S+15,20*RND(1)+5
5050 POKE S+4,B(4):POKE S+11,B(11):
     POKE S+18,B(18)
5060 RETURN
5070 REM**********************
5080 REM**********************
```

P12 Guess the Number

In this game the computer generates a random whole number between 1 and 100 and the player has to guess what it is.

The instuctions for the game are included in the code. Remember to press the RETURN key after typing in your guess.

COMMANDS

Key in the program and RUN.

```
10 REM GUESS THE NUMBER
20 REM ****************
30 REM
100 POKE 53280,14:REM BLUE BORDER
110 POKE 53281,9:REM BROWN SCREEN
120 CL$=CHR$(147):REM TO CLEAR SCREEN
130 PRINT CHR$(158):REM YELLOW INK
140 PRINT CL$
150 PRINT TAB(10)CHR$(18)
    "??????????????????"
160 PRINT TAB(10)CHR$(18)
    "?                ?"
170 PRINT TAB(10)CHR$(18)
    "? GUESS THE NUMBER ?"
180 PRINT TAB(10)CHR$(18)
    "?                ?"
190 PRINT TAB(10)CHR$(18)
    "??????????????????"
200 PRINT:PRINT
210 PRINT TAB(5)
    "IN THIS PROGRAM YOU ARE ASKED"
220 PRINT TAB(5)
    "TO GUESS A NUMBER BETWEEN 1"
230 PRINT TAB(5)"AND 100."
240 PRINT
250 PRINT TAB(5)
    "IF YOU GUESS WRONGLY THE"
260 PRINT TAB(5)
    "COMPUTER WILL TELL YOU WHETHER"
```

```
270 PRINT TAB(5)
    "YOU ARE TOO HIGH OR TOO LOW."
280 PRINT
290 PRINT TAB(5)
    "WHEN YOU ARE FINISHED THE"
300 PRINT TAB(5)
    "COMPUTER WILL TELL YOU THE"
310 PRINT TAB(5)
    "AVERAGE NUMBER OF ATTEMPTS"
320 PRINT TAB(5)"YOU TOOK."
330 PRINT:PRINT
340 PRINT TAB(7)CHR$(18)
    " PRESS ANY KEY TO PLAY "
350 GET A$:IF A$="" THEN 350:REM
    NO SPACE BETWEEN INVERTED COMMAS
360 REM*****************************
370 PRINT CL$:PRINT:PRINT
380 N%=1+100*RND(1)
390 FOR K=1 TO 100
400 AT=AT+1
410 PRINT TAB(6):INPUT
    "WHAT IS YOUR GUESS";G
420 IF G>N% THEN PRINT TAB(6)"TOO HIGH"
430 IF G<N% THEN PRINT TAB(6)"TOO LOW"
440 IF G=N% THEN PRINT TAB(6) CHR$(18)
    "CORRECT":K=100:PL=PL+1
450 PRINT
460 NEXT
470 REM*****************************
480 PRINT
490 PRINT TAB(6):INPUT
    "WANT TO TRY AGAIN (Y/N)";Y$
500 IF ASC(Y$)=89 THEN 360
510 REM*****************************
520 PRINT CL$:PRINT:PRINT:PRINT:PRINT
530 AV=AT/PL
540 AV=(INT(100*AV+.5))/100
550 PRINT TAB(6)
    "YOU TOOK AN AVERAGE OF:"
560 PRINT
570 PRINT TAB(5)AV;"PER SHOT"
580 PRINT:PRINT
590 IF AV<7 THEN PRINT TAB(6) CHR$(18)
    " PRETTY GOOD! "
600 PRINT:PRINT
610 PRINT TAB(6):INPUT
    "WANT TO PLAY AGAIN (Y/N)";Y$
```

P12 Guess the Number

```
620 IF ASC(Y$)=89 THEN AT=0:PL=0:
    GOTO 360
630 END
640 REM*****************************
650 REM*****************************
```

P13 Reaction Test

This program could help develop your keyboard skills. The computer places a random character on the screen and starts to time your response.

The object of the game is to press the required key as quickly as possible.

When the program is complete an average reaction time is displayed on the screen.

COMMANDS

Key in the program and RUN.

```
10 REM REACTION TEST
20 REM ************
30 REM
100 CL$=CHR$(147):REM TO CLEAR SCREEN
110 POKE 53280,0:REM BLACK BORDER
120 POKE 53281,0:REM BLACK SCREEN
130 PRINT CHR$(158):REM YELLOW INK
140 PRINT CL$:PRINT:PRINT
150 PRINT TAB(13)"REACTION TEST"
160 PRINT TAB(13)"-------------"
170 PRINT:PRINT:PRINT:PRINT
180 PRINT TAB(4):INPUT
    "HOW MANY TRIES DO YOU WANT";TR%
190 IF TR%<1 THEN 140
200 TI$="000000":REM INITIAL TIME VALUE
210 REM*****************************
220 FOR N=1 TO TR%
230 PRINT CL$
240 A%=1+26*RND(1)
250 B%=1024+1000*RND(1)
260 POKE B%,A%:POKE 54272+B%,7
280 GET A$:IF A$="" THEN 280:
    REM NO SPACE BETWEEN COMMAS
290 IF ASC(A$)<>A%+64 THEN 280
300 NEXT
310 REM*****************************
```

P13 Reaction Test

```
330 PRINT CL$:PRINT:PRINT:PRINT
340 T%=TI/60:REM TOTAL TIME IN SECONDS
350 PRINT TAB(8)"NUMBER OF ATTEMPTS"TR%
360 PRINT:PRINT
370 PRINT TAB(8)"TOTAL TIME"T%"SECONDS"
390 PRINT:PRINT
400 AT=INT((T%/TR%)*100+.5)/100
410 PRINT TAB(8)
    "AVERAGE REACTION TIME":PRINT
420 PRINT TAB(7)AT"SECONDS"
430 PRINT:PRINT:PRINT
440 PRINT TAB(8):INPUT
    "WANT ANOTHER GO (Y/N)";Y$
450 IF ASC(Y$)=89 THEN 140
460 END
470 REM*****************************
480 REM*****************************
```

P14 Mastermind

This program implements the first version of the popular game by Invicta Ltd.

The object of the game is to determine the color of four rectangles on the screen. The player has up to twenty attempts to work out the code.

When an attempt has been entered, the computer responds by indicating whether you have a correctly colored rectangle in the correct position, or a correctly colored rectangle in the wrong position.

For each correct color in the correct position, the computer places a purple dash to the right of the guess.

For each correct color in the wrong position the computer places a cyan dash to the right of the guess.

COMMANDS

Key in the program and RUN.

Enter your guess as e.g. RGYB. If you enter an invalid color a purple rectangle will result.

```
10 REM MASTERMIND
20 REM **********
30 REM
100 CL$=CHR$(147):REM CLEAR SCREEN
110 H$=CHR$(19):REM HOME CURSOR
120 S$=CHR$(32):REM SPACE
130 FOR N=0 TO 5:S$=S$+S$:NEXT
140 REM S$ CONTAINS 64 SPACES
150 POKE 53281,0:REM BLACK SCREEN
160 POKE 53280,0:REM BLACK BORDER
170 REM*****************************
180 REM INITIAL LINE
190 PRINT CL$:PRINT:PRINT
200 P(0)=156:P(1)=156:P(2)=156:P(3)=156
210 GOSUB 1000:REM PRINT LINE
```

P14 Mastermind

```
220 REM****************************
230 REM SET UP TARGET PATTERN
240 FOR N=0 TO 3
250 T(N)=1+INT(4*RND(1)):C(N)=T(N)
260 NEXT:REM T(N) HOLDS CORRECT ANSWER
270 REM****************************
280 REM PLAY
290 L=L+1:IF L=21 THEN GOSUB 3000:
    GOTO 630:REM PATTERN NOT FOUND
300 FOR N=0 TO 3:C(N)=T(N):NEXT
310 REM****************************
320 REM GET GUESS
330 PRINT CHR$(158)H$
340 INPUT
    "ENTER COLOR PATTERN (E.G. RGYB)";G$
350 IF LEN(G$)<>4 THEN PRINT H$:
    PRINT S$:GOTO 320
360 REM****************************
370 GOSUB 2000:REM SET UP ARRAYS
380 PRINT H$:PRINTS$
390 FOR N=0 TO L-1:PRINT:NEXT
400 GOSUB 1000:REM PRINT LINE
410 REM****************************
430 REM TEST FOR CORRECT COLOR IN
    CORRECT POSITION
440 PC=0
450 FOR N=0 TO 3
460 IF G(N)=C(N) THEN PC=PC+1:G(N)=8:
    C(N)=9
470 REM CHANGE G(N) AND C(N) ON MATCH
    SO THEY DO NOT AFFECT NEXT TEST
480 NEXT
490 REM****************************
500 REM TEST FOR CORRECT COLOR IN
    WRONG POSITION
510 CC=0
520 FOR N=0 TO 3
530 FOR K=0 TO 3
540 IF G(N)=C(K) THEN CC=CC+1:C(K)=9:
    K=3
550 NEXT:NEXT
560 REM****************************
570 REM ACT ON RESULTS
580 IF PC=4 THEN GOSUB 4000:GOTO 630:
    REM GUESS CORRECT
590 IF PC>0 THEN GOSUB 5000
600 IF CC>0 THEN GOSUB 6000
```

```
610 GOTO 280:REM PLAY
620 REM***************************
630 REM FINISH
640 PRINT:PRINT:PRINT CHR$(158)
650 PRINT TAB(9):INPUT
    "ANOTHER GAME (Y/N)";Y$
660 IF ASC(Y$)=89 THEN RUN
670 END
900 REM
910 REM            ***************
920 REM            *
930 REM            * SUBROUTINES
940 REM            *
950 REM            ***************
960 REM
1000 REM GENERATE AND PRINT LINE
1010 A$="":REM NO SPACE
1020 FOR N=0 TO 3
1030 A$=A$+CHR$(P(N))+CHR$(32)+CHR$(184)
1040 NEXT
1050 PRINT TAB(14)A$;
1060 RETURN
1070 REM***************************
1080 REM***************************
2000 REM SET UP ARRAYS
2010 FOR N=0 TO 3
2020 G(N)=0:P(N)=156
2030 IF MID$(G$,N+1,1)="R" THEN G(N)=1:
     P(N)=28
2040 IF MID$(G$,N+1,1)="G" THEN G(N)=2:
     P(N)=30
2050 IF MID$(G$,N+1,1)="B" THEN G(N)=3:
     P(N)=31
2060 IF MID$(G$,N+1,1)="Y" THEN G(N)=4:
     P(N)=158
2070 NEXT
2080 RETURN
2090 REM***************************
2100 REM***************************
3000 REM PATTERN NOT FOUND
3010 PRINT CL$:PRINT:PRINT:PRINT
3020 PRINT CHR$(158):REM YELLOW INK
3030 PRINT TAB(8)
     "THE CORRECT PATTERN WAS"
3040 PRINT:PRINT
3050 FOR N=0 TO 3
3060 IF T(N)=1 THEN P(N)=28
```

```
3070 IF T(N)=2 THEN P(N)=30
3080 IF T(N)=3 THEN P(N)=31
3090 IF T(N)=4 THEN P(N)=158
3100 NEXT
3110 GOSUB 1000
3120 RETURN
3130 REM***************************
3140 REM***************************
4000 REM CORRECT GUESS
4010 PRINT CL$:PRINT:PRINT:PRINT
4020 PRINT CHR$(158):REM YELLOW INK
4030 PRINT TAB(14)"CORRECT"
4040 PRINT:PRINT
4050 PRINT TAB(10)"YOU TOOK";L;"GOES."
4060 RETURN
4070 REM***************************
4080 REM***************************
5000 REM COLOR AND POSITION
5010 FOR N=1 TO PC
5020 PRINT CHR$(156)CHR$(32)CHR$(188);
5030 NEXT
5040 RETURN
5050 REM***************************
5060 REM***************************
6000 REM POSITION
6010 FOR N=1 TO CC
6020 PRINT CHR$(159)CHR$(32)CHR$(188);
6030 NEXT
6040 RETURN
6050 REM***************************
6060 REM***************************
```

P15 Destroyer

This is a fairly straightforward game, although we rather like the graphics. It illustrates some important techniques such as how to control motion with either keyboard or joystick, how to make moving objects reverse direction and how to use the sprite collision register to indicate a hit.

The submarines are at random depths. There is also a random element in their movement, so that hitting them is not as easy as it looks. The destroyers move faster than the submarines, so that if you miss one you can catch it provided it is not too deep. If you give chase, however, there is a danger that you will be left on the wrong side of the screen as a submarine escapes.

You could extend this program by having more than one submarine on the screen, by allowing more than one depth charge at a time to be fired and by devising some means for the submarines to shoot back.

COMMANDS

Key in the program and RUN.

If you are using a joystick ensure it is connected to PORT 1.

Instructions for using the keyboard are included in the code.

```
10 REM DESTROYER
20 REM ********
30 REM
100 POKE 52,48:POKE 56,48:CLR:
    REM RESERVE MEMORY FOR SPRITES
110 CL$=CHR$(147):REM TO CLEAR SCREEN
120 POKE 53280,6:REM BLUE BORDER
130 POKE 53281,14:REM LIGHT BLUE SCREEN
140 V=53248:REM START OF VIDEO CHIP
150 PRINT CHR$(144):REM BLACK INK
160 PRINT CL$:PRINT:PRINT
170 PRINT TAB(18)"WAIT"
180 REM***************************
```

P15 Destroyer

```
190 REM SPRITE COLORS
200 POKE V+39,11:POKE V+40,0:
    POKE V+41,2
210 REM**************************
220 POKE V+29,3:REM TWO SPRITES
    EXPANDED IN X DIRECTION
230 POKE V+23,0:REM NO SPRITES
    EXPANDED IN Y DIRECTION
240 REM**************************
250 REM SET SPRITE POINTER
260 POKE 2042,196
270 REM**************************
280 REM GENERATE SPRITE SHAPES
290 FOR N=0 TO 383
300 READ K:POKE 12288+N,K
310 NEXT
320 REM**************************
330 REM SET UP SOUNDS
340 S=54272:REM START OF SID CHIP
350 POKE S,255
360 POKE S+1,10
370 POKE S+5,72:POKE S+6,0
380 POKE S+7,25
390 POKE S+8,30
400 POKE S+12,12:POKE S+13,0
410 POKE S+24,15
420 REM**************************
430 REM KEYBOARD OR JOYSTICK
440 PRINT CL$:PRINT:PRINT:PRINT
450 PRINT TAB(14)CHR$(18)"***********"
460 PRINT TAB(14)CHR$(18)" DESTROYER "
470 PRINT TAB(14)CHR$(18)"***********"
480 PRINT:PRINT:PRINT:PRINT
490 PRINT TAB(7)
    "SELECT CONTROL BY PRESSING:"
500 PRINT
510 PRINT TAB(10)CHR$(18)
    " KEY F1 "CHR$(146)" - KEYBOARD"
520 PRINT
530 PRINT TAB(10)CHR$(18)
    " KEY F3 "CHR$(146)" - JOYSTICK"
540 GET A$:IF A$="" THEN 540:REM
    NO SPACE BETWEEN INVERTED COMMAS
550 SL=ASC(A$)-132:IF SL<1 OR SL>2
    THEN 540
560 IF SL=1 THEN GOSUB 8000
570 REM**************************
```

```
580 REM SKY
590 PRINT CHR$(5)CL$
600 S$=CHR$(32)
610 FOR N=0 TO 4:S$=S$+S$+S$:NEXT
620 S$=MID$(S$,4):
    REM S$ CONTAINS 240 SPACES
630 PRINT CHR$(18)CHR$(145)S$
640 REM**************************
650 REM INITIAL CONDITIONS
660 POKE V+1,78
670 XD=150:POKE V,XD
680 POKE V+16,0:REM X MSB REGISTER
690 SB=20:HT=0:FR=0:DD=-1
700 POKE 2040,192
710 POKE V+21,1:REM ENABLE SPRITE 1
720 REM**************************
730 REM NEXT SUBMARINE
740 IF SB=0 THEN 950 REM FINISH
750 POKE V+3,100+100*RND(1)
760 T=RND(1):IF T<.5 THEN POKE 2041,194:
    DS=-1:XS=300
770 IF T>=.5 THEN POKE 2041,195:DS=1:
    XS=5
780 GOSUB 6000:REM MOVE SUBMARINE
790 REM**************************
800 REM PLAY
810 ON SL GOSUB 3000,4000
820 IF FB=0 AND FR=0 THEN GOSUB 9000:
    REM FIRE DEPTH CHARGE
830 IF FR=1 THEN YC=YC+10:POKE V+5,YC:
    REM DEPTH CHARGE FALLS
840 IF DX<>0 THEN GOSUB 5000:
    REM MOVE DESTROYER
850 IF FR=1 AND YC>235 THEN FR=0:
    POKE V+21,PEEK(V+21)-4:REM MISS
860 IF FR=1 AND PEEK(V+30) AND 2=2
    THEN GOSUB 7000:GOTO 730:REM HIT
870 IF TI<40 THEN 800
880 REM**************************
890 REM SUBMARINE CONTROL
900 GOSUB 6000:REM MOVE SUBMARINE
910 IF FR=1 AND PEEK(V+30) AND 8=8
    THEN GOSUB 7000:GOTO 730:REM HIT
920 IF XS=0 OR XS=320 THEN POKE V+21,
    PEEK(V+21)-2:SB=SB-1:GOTO 730
930 GOTO 800
940 REM**************************
```

P15 Destroyer

```
950 REM FINISH
960 POKE V+21,0:POKE S+4,0:POKE S+11,0
970 PRINT CHR$(144)
980 PRINT CL$:PRINT:PRINT
990 PRINT TAB(15)"GAME OVER"
1000 PRINT:PRINT
1010 PRINT TAB(16)"KILLS";HT
1020 IF HT>15 THEN PRINT:PRINT:PRINT
     TAB(13)CHR$(18)" PRETTY GOOD "
1030 PRINT:PRINT
1040 GET A$:IF A$<>"" THEN 1040:REM
     NO SPACE BETWEEN INVERTED COMMAS
1050 REM FLUSH KEYBOARD BUFFER
1060 PRINT TAB(10):INPUT
     "ANOTHER GAME (Y/N)";Y$
1070 IF ASC(Y$)=89 THEN 580
1080 POKE S+24,0
1090 END
1100 REM***************************
1110 REM***************************
1900 REM
1910 REM          **********
1920 REM          *
1930 REM          * SPRITE
1940 REM          *   DATA
1950 REM          *
1960 REM          **********
1970 REM
1980 REM***************************
1990 REM***************************
2000 REM DESTROYER 1
2010 DATA 0,0,0,0,0,0,0,0,0
2020 DATA 0,0,0,0,0,0,0,128,0
2030 DATA 0,128,0,0,128,0,0,128,0
2040 DATA 1,160,128,1,160,128,1,160,128
2050 DATA 1,160,128,19,241,128,19,241,
     128
2060 DATA 255,249,152,255,249,152,127,
     255,255
2070 DATA 127,255,255,63,255,254,63,255,
     254,0
2080 REM***************************
2090 REM***************************
2100 REM DESTROYER 2
2110 DATA 0,0,0,0,0,0,0,0,0
2120 DATA 0,0,0,0,0,0,0,1,0
2130 DATA 0,1,0,0,1,0,0,1,0
```

```
2140 DATA 1,5,128,1,5,128,1,5,128
2150 DATA 1,5,128,1,143,200,1,143,200
2160 DATA 25,159,255,25,159,255,255,255,
      254
2170 DATA 255,255,254,127,255,252,127,
      255,252,0
2180 REM*************************
2190 REM*************************
2200 REM SUBMARINE 1
2210 DATA 0,0,0,0,0,0,0,0,0
2220 DATA 0,0,0,0,0,0,0,64,0
2230 DATA 0,64,0,0,64,0,0,64,0
2240 DATA 0,112,0,0,112,0,0,112,0
2250 DATA 0,112,0,3,255,0,3,255,0
2260 DATA 127,255,247,127,255,247,255,
      255,255
2270 DATA 255,255,255,127,255,247,127,
      255,247,0
2280 REM*************************
2290 REM*************************
2300 REM SUBMARINE 2
2310 DATA 0,0,0,0,0,0,0,0,0
2320 DATA 0,0,0,0,0,0,0,2,0
2330 DATA 0,2,0,0,2,0,0,2,0
2340 DATA 0,14,0,0,14,0,0,14,0
2350 DATA 0,14,0,0,255,192,0,255,192
2360 DATA 239,255,254,239,255,254,255,
      255,255
2370 DATA 255,255,255,239,255,254,239,
      255,254,0
2380 REM*************************
2390 REM*************************
2400 REM DEPTH CHARGE
2410 DATA 0,0,0,0,0,0,0,0,0
2420 DATA 0,0,0,0,0,0,0,0,0
2430 DATA 0,0,0,0,0,0,0,0,0
2440 DATA 0,0,0,0,0,0,0,0,0
2450 DATA 0,0,0,0,0,0,0,0,0
2460 DATA 0,126,0,0,126,0,0,255,0
2470 DATA 0,255,0,0,126,0,0,126,0,0
2480 REM*************************
2490 REM*************************
2500 REM EXPLOSION
2510 DATA 240,56,8,240,60,24,48,62,120
2520 DATA0,0,120,51,18,120,49,146,0
2530 DATA 1,216,192,1,249,131,31,255,7
2540 DATA 15,254,7,7,255,227,97,255,128
```

P15 Destroyer

```
2550 DATA 97,191,0,103,63,131,6,89,131
2560 DATA 0,88,192,0,152,96,94,152,33
2570 DATA 194,17,147,224,17,131,224,0,0,
     0
2580 REM*************************
2590 REM*************************
2900 REM
2910 REM          ***************
2920 REM          *
2930 REM          * SUBROUTINES
2940 REM          *
2950 REM          ***************
2960 REM
2970 REM*************************
2980 REM*************************
3000 REM KEYBOARD
3010 DX=0:FB=1
3020 T=PEEK(197)
3030 IF T=23 THEN DX=16
3040 IF T=12 THEN DX=-16
3050 IF T=3 THEN FB=0
3060 RETURN
3070 REM*************************
3080 REM*************************
4000 REM JOYSTICK
4010 DX=0:DY=0
4020 T=PEEK(56321)
4030 JS=15-(T AND 15)
4040 IF JS>7 THEN DX=16
4050 IF JS<7 AND JS>3 THEN DX=-16
4060 REM FIRE BUTTON
4070 FB=T AND 16:REM FIRE BUTTON
4080 RETURN
4090 REM*************************
4100 REM*************************
5000 REM MOVE DESTROYER
5010 IF SGN(DX)<>SGN(DD) THEN DD=-DD:
     DX=0
5020 IF DD=-1 THEN POKE 2040,192
5030 IF DD=1 THEN POKE 2040,193
5040 XD=XD+DX
5050 IF XD<40 THEN XD=40
5060 IF XD>280 THEN XD=280
5070 K=XD

5080 IF K<256 THEN
     POKE V+16,PEEK(V+16) AND 254
```

```
5090 IF K>255 THEN K=K-255:
     POKE V+16,PEEK(V+16) OR 1
5100 POKE V,K
5110 RETURN
5120 REM**************************
5130 REM**************************
6000 REM MOVE SUBMARINE
6010 XS=XS+DS*(10*RND(1)+6)
6020 IF XS<0 THEN XS=0
6030 IF XS>320 THEN XS=320
6040 K=XS
6050 IF K<256 THEN
     POKE V+16,PEEK(V+16) AND 253
6060 IF K>255 THEN K=K-255:
     POKE V+16,PEEK(V+16) OR 2
6070 POKE V+2,K
6080 POKE V+21,PEEK(V+21) OR 2
6090 RETURN
6100 REM**************************
6110 REM**************************
7000 REM HIT
7010 HT=HT+1:SB=SB-1:FR=0
7020 POKE S+11,0:POKE S+11,129
7030 POKE 2041,197:POKE V+40,2
7040 POKE V+21,PEEK(V+21)-4
7050 FOR DE=0 TO 300:NEXT
7060 POKE V+21,1:POKE V+40,0
7070 RETURN
7080 REM**************************
7090 REM**************************
8000 REM KEY INSTRUCTIONS
8010 PRINT CL$:PRINT:PRINT:PRINT:PRINT
8020 PRINT TAB(5)CHR$(18)" KEY Z "
     CHR$(146)" - MOVES DESTROYER LEFT"
8030 PRINT
8040 PRINT TAB(5)CHR$(18)" KEY X "
     CHR$(146)" - MOVES DESTROYER RIGHT"
8050 PRINT
8060 PRINT TAB(5)CHR$(18)" KEY F7 "
     CHR$(146)" - FIRES DEPTH CHARGE"
8070 PRINT:PRINT:PRINT:PRINT
8080 PRINT TAB(6)CHR$(18)
     " PRESS ANY KEY TO CONTINUE "
8090 GET A$:IF A$="" THEN 8090:REM
     NO SPACE BETWEEN INVERTED COMMAS
8100 RETURN
8110 REM**************************
```

P15 Destroyer

```
8120 REM************************
9000 REM FIRE DEPTH CHARGE
9010 DC=-DD:FR=1
9020 T=XD-10:IF DC=1 THEN T=T+40
9030 POKE S+4,0:POKE S+4,129
9040 FOR N=0 TO 16 STEP 2
9050 XC=T+DC*N
9060 YC=70-10*SIN(N* /16)
9070 POKE V+5,YC
9080 K=XC
9090 IF K<256 THEN
     POKE V+16,PEEK(V+16) AND 251
9100 IF K>255 THEN K=K-255:
     POKE V+16,PEEK(V+16) OR 4
9110 POKE V+4,K
9120 POKE V+21,PEEK(V+21) OR 4
9130 NEXT
9140 RETURN
9150 REM************************
9160 REM************************
```

P16 Monster Island

In this program you have landed on a volcanic island and are being pursued by voracious monsters. Your only hope is to lead them into pits over which you can jump.

The monsters always move in your direction; so with thought you should survive.

The monsters do not notice you until you move.

This program employs user defined characters rather than sprites. It also demonstrates how movement both across and up and down the screen can be controlled by keyboard or joystick. It could be made into one episode of a larger adventure game.

COMMANDS

Key in the program and RUN.

If you are using a joystick, ensure it is connected to PORT 1.

Instructions for using the keyboard are included in the code.

```
10 REM MONSTER ISLAND
20 REM *************
30 REM
40 POKE 52,48:POKE 56,48:CLR:
   REM RESERVE RAM AREA FOR CHARACTERS
50 REM RAM RESERVED BEFORE MAIN PROGRAM
        STARTS AS VARIABLES ARE CLEARED
60 REM***************************
100 CL$=CHR$(147):REM TO CLEAR SCREEN
110 RO=53248:REM START OF CHARACTER ROM
120 RA=12288:REM START OF CHARACTER RAM
130 IT=56334:REM INTERRUPT TIMER
140 CC=53272:
    REM CONTROLS CHARACTER LOCATION
150 SC=1024:REM START OF SCREEN MEMORY
```

P16 Monster Island

```
160 D=54272:REM COLOR DISPLACEMENT,ALSO
    START OF SOUND CHIP
170 POKE 53281,12:POKE 53280,14:REM
    GRAY SCREEN,LIGHT BLUE BORDER
180 PRINT CHR$(31):REM BLUE INK
190 REM**************************
200 PRINT CL$:PRINT:PRINT
210 PRINT TAB(18)"WAIT"
220 PRINT CHR$(142):REM UPPER CASE
230 POKE IT,PEEK (IT) AND 254:
    REM DISABLE INTERRUPT TIMER
240 POKE 1,PEEK (1) AND 251:
    REM SWITCH FROM I/O TO CHAR. ROM
250 FOR N=0 TO 511:POKE N+RA,PEEK (N+RO)
    :NEXT:REM TRANSFER CHARACTERS
260 POKE 1,PEEK (1) OR 4:
    REM SWITCH FROM CHAR. TO I/O ROM
270 POKE IT,PEEK (IT) OR 1:
    REM ENABLE INTERRUPT TIMER
280 POKE CC,(PEEK (CC) AND 240)+12:
    REM CONTROL OF CHARACTERS TO RAM
290 REM**************************
300 FOR N=27 TO 29
310 FOR K=0 TO 7
320 READ A:POKE RA+8*N+K,A
330 NEXT:NEXT:REM REDEFINE CHARACTERS
340 REM**************************
350 PRINT CL$:PRINT:PRINT TAB(10)
    "*****************"
360 PRINT TAB(10)"                 "
370 PRINT TAB(10)"  MONSTER ISLAND "
380 PRINT TAB(10)"                 "
390 PRINT TAB(10)"*****************":
    PRINT:PRINT
400 PRINT TAB(4)
    "HARD LUCK-YOU HAVE LANDED ON"
410 PRINT TAB(4)
    "MONSTER ISLAND. YOUR ONLY CHANCE"
420 PRINT TAB(4)
    "IS TO LURE THE MONSTERS INTO"
430 PRINT TAB(4)
    "VOLCANIC PITS OVER WHICH YOU CAN"
440 PRINT TAB(4)"JUMP."
450 PRINT:PRINT
460 PRINT TAB(10)"SELECT CONTROL DEVICE"
```

```
470 PRINT:PRINT TAB(11)
    "KEY 1 - KEYBOARD"
480 PRINT:PRINT TAB(11)
    "KEY 2 - JOYSTICK"
490 GET A$:IF A$="" THEN 490:REM
    NO SPACE BETWEEN INVERTED COMMAS
500 IF A$<>"1" AND A$<>"2"THEN 490
510 DIM MN(5,1)
520 SL=VAL(A$)
530 REM***************************
540 REM ANOTHER
550 ON SL GOSUB 3000,4000
560 PRINT:PRINT
570 PRINT TAB(4)
    "ENTER LEVEL OF DIFFICULTY-"
580 PRINT TAB(4)
    "0 (EASY) TO 5 (HARD)."
590 GET A$:IF A$="" THEN 590:REM
    NO SPACE BETWEEN INVERTED COMMAS
600 IF ASC(A$)<48 OR ASC(A$)>53 THEN
    590:REM INVALID ENTRY
610 DF=6-VAL(A$)
620 M%=1+5*RND(1):REM NUMBER OF MONSTERS
630 P%=6+5*RND(1):REM NUMBER OF PITS
640 PRINT CL$
650 REM***************************
660 REM PRINT MONSTERS
670 FOR N=1 TO M%
680 X%=40*RND(1):Y%=25*RND(1):
    IF PEEK(SC+40*Y%+X%)=27 THEN 680
690 MN(N,0)=X%:MN(N,1)=Y%
700 POKE(SC+40*Y%+X%),27
710 POKE(SC+40*Y%+X%+D),2
720 NEXT
730 REM***************************
740 REM PRINT PITS
750 FOR N=1 TO P%
760 X%=1+38*RND(1):Y%=1+23*RND(1)
770 K=SC+40*Y%+X%:IF PEEK(K)=27 OR
    PEEK(K)=28 THEN 760
780 POKE K,28:POKE K+D,6
790 NEXT
800 REM***************************
810 REM PRINT FIGURE
820 FX=INT(40*RND(1))
830 FY=INT(25*RND(1))
```

P16 Monster Island

```
840 K=SC+40*FY+FX:IF PEEK(K)=27 OR
    PEEK(K)=28 THEN 820
850 POKE K,29:POKE K+D,0
860 DX=0:DY=0:ON SL GOSUB 5000,6000
870 IF DX=0 AND DY=0 THEN 860: REM
    MONSTERS WAIT FOR YOU TO MOVE
880 TI$="000000"
890 REM***************************
900 REM PLAY
910 DX=0:DY=0
920 ON SL GOSUB 5000,6000
930 IF FX+DX=-1 OR FX+DX=40 THEN DX=0
940 IF FY+DY=-1 OR FY+DY=25 THEN DY=0
950 REM TEST FOR PIT
960 REM***************************
970 K=PEEK(SC+40*(FY+DY)+FX+DX)
980 IF K=28 AND DX>0 THEN DX=DX+1:
    GOTO 970
990 IF K=28 AND DX<0 THEN DX=DX-1:
    GOTO 970
1000 IF K=28 AND DY>0 THEN DY=DY+1:
    GOTO 970
1010 IF K=28 AND DY<0 THEN DY=DY-1:
    GOTO 970
1020 REM***************************
1030 REM TEST FOR MONSTER
1040 IF K=27 THEN FLG=1:GOSUB 7000:
    GOTO 1300:REM EATEN
1050 REM***************************
1060 REM MOVE FIGURE
1070 IF DX<>0 OR DY<>0 THEN
    POKE SC+40*FY+FX,32
1080 FX=FX+DX
1090 FY=FY+DY
1100 POKE SC+40*FY+FX,29
1110 POKE D+SC+40*FY+FX,0
1120 IF TI<3*DF THEN 900
1130 REM***************************
1140 REM MOVE MONSTER
1150 FOR N=1 TO M%
1160 CX=SGN(FX-MN(N,0))
1170 CY=SGN(FY-MN(N,1))
1180 IF PEEK(SC+40*(MN(N,1)+CY)+MN(N,0)+
    CX)=28 THEN GOSUB 8000:GOTO 1250
1190 POKE SC+MN(N,1)*40+MN(N,0),32
1200 MN(N,0)=MN(N,0)+CX
1210 MN(N,1)=MN(N,1)+CY
```

```
1220 POKE SC+MN(N,1)*40+MN(N,0),27
1230 POKE D+SC+MN(N,1)*40+MN(N,0),2
1240 IF FX=MN(N,0) AND FY=MN(N,1) THEN
     GOSUB 7000:GOTO 1300:REM EATEN
1250 IF M%=0 THEN GOSUB 9000:GOTO 1300:
     REM ESCAPED
1260 NEXT
1270 TI$="000000"
1280 GOTO 900:REM PLAY
1290 REM**************************
1300 REM FINISH
1310 PRINT:PRINT
1320 GET A$:IF A$<>"" THEN 1320:REM
     WAIT UNTIL NO KEY PRESSED
1330 REM NO SPACE BETWEEN INVERTED
     COMMAS
1340 PRINT TAB(9):INPUT
     "ANOTHER GAME (Y/N)";Y$
1350 IF ASC(Y$)=89 THEN 540
1360 END
1900 REM
1910 REM           ********
1920 REM           *
1930 REM           * DATA
1940 REM           *
1950 REM           ********
1960 REM
2000 REM DATA FOR SHAPES
2010 DATA 31,124,200,248,248,120,60,31:
     REM MONSTER
2020 DATA 60,126,255,254,254,62,30,28:
     REM PIT
2030 DATA 28,28,8,127,28,20,20,54:
     REM FIGURE
2900 REM
2910 REM           **************
2920 REM           *
2930 REM           * SUBROUTINES
2940 REM           *
2950 REM           **************
2960 REM
3000 REM KEY INSTRUCTIONS
3010 PRINT CL$:PRINT:PRINT
3020 PRINT TAB(4)
     "KEY A: UP","KEY Z: DOWN"
3030 PRINT TAB(4)
     "KEY N: LEFT","KEY M: RIGHT"
```

P16 Monster Island

```
3040 RETURN
3050 REM**************************
3060 REM**************************
4000 REM JOYSTICK INSTRUCTION
4010 PRINT CL$:PRINT:PRINT
4020 PRINT TAB(4)
     "ENSURE YOUR JOYSTICK IS CONNECTED"
4030 PRINT TAB(4)"TO PORT 1."
4040 RETURN
4050 REM**************************
4060 REM**************************
5000 REM GET KEYBOARD ENTRY
5010 T=PEEK(197)
5020 IF T=10 THEN DY=1:REM KEY A
5030 IF T=10 THEN DY=-1:REM KEY A
5040 IF T=12 THEN DY=1:REM KEY Z
5050 IF T=36 THEN DX=1:REM KEY M
5060 IF T=39 THEN DX=-1:REM KEY N
5070 RETURN
5080 REM**************************
5090 REM**************************
6000 REM GET JOYSTICK POSITION
6010 T=PEEK(56321)
6020 JS=15-(T AND 15)
6030 IF JS>7 THEN DX=1
6040 IF JS<7 AND JS>3 THEN DX=-1
6050 IF JS=2 OR JS=6 OR JS=10 THEN DY=1
6060 IF JS=1 OR JS=5 OR JS=9 THEN DY=-1
6070 RETURN
6080 REM**************************
6090 REM**************************
7000 REM EATEN
7010 IF FLG=1 THEN POKE SC+40*FY+FX,32:
     FLG=0
7020 POKE D,100:POKE D+1,190:
     POKE D+24,15:POKE D+5,45
7030 POKE D+4,0:POKE D+4,17
7040 FOR N=0 TO 5
7050 POKE 53281,N
7060 FOR K=0 TO 50:NEXT
7070 NEXT
7080 POKE D+4,33
7090 FOR N=7 TO 12
7100 POKE 53281,N:POKE D+1,40-2*N
7110 FOR K=0 TO 50:NEXT
7120 NEXT
7130 POKE D+4,0:POKE D+24,0
```

```
7140 PRINT CL$:PRINT:PRINT:PRINT
7150 PRINT TAB(9)"OOPS - MUNCHED BY A"
7160 PRINT TAB(9)"MONSTER."
7170 PRINT:PRINT
7180 PRINT TAB(9)"YUMMY, THAT WAS"
7190 PRINT TAB(9)"TASTY!!!"
7200 RETURN
7210 REM**************************
7220 REM**************************
8000 REM MONSTER FALLS INTO PIT
8010 POKE D,100:POKE D+1,20:POKE D+5,45:
     POKE D+24,15
8020 POKE D+4,0:POKE D+4,129
8030 POKE SC+MN(N,1)*40+MN(N,0),32
8040 IF N=M% THEN 8090
8050 FOR K=N TO M%-1
8060 MN(K,0)=MN(K+1,0)
8070 MN(K,1)=MN(K+1,1)
8080 NEXT
8090 M%=M%-1
8100 POKE D+4,0:POKE D+24,0
8110 RETURN
8120 REM**************************
8130 REM**************************
9000 REM ESCAPED
9010 PRINTCL$:PRINT:PRINT:PRINT
9020 POKE D,52:POKE D+1,122:POKE D+5,7:
     POKE D+24,15
9030 POKE D+4,0:POKE D+4,33
9040 PRINT TAB(10)"WELL DONE,THE"
9050 PRINT TAB(10)"MONSTERS ARE ALL"
9060 PRINT TAB(10)"DEAD."
9070 PRINT
9080 PRINT TAB(10)"BET YOU WON'T GET"
9090 PRINT TAB(10)"AWAY NEXT TIME."
9100 FOR N=0 TO 14
9110 POKE D+1,122-6*N:POKE 53280,N
9120 FOR K=0 TO 100:NEXT
9130 POKE D+4,0:POKE D+4,33
9140 NEXT
9150 POKE D,141:POKE D+1,30
9160 POKE D+4,0:POKE D+4,33
9170 FOR K=0 TO 300:NEXT
9180 POKE D+4,0:POKE D+24,0
9190 RETURN
9200 REM**************************
9210 REM**************************
```

P17 Fighter

In this game you are the pilot of a First World War aircraft. You have to shoot down the Red Baron and two of his henchmen. If you don't succeed within a certain time they will get you.

An interesting feature of this program is that your gunsight does not actually move. It appears to do so because the clouds and enemy aircraft move relative to it as you operate the controls.

Your guns are set for the nearer aircraft. The cunning Baron knows this and stays at long range. You can hit him, but not if he is in the dead center of your sights. See if you can work out why this is.

You could make the motion in this program smoother by moving the aircraft and clouds in smaller steps. This, however, slows down the game. The program could be expanded by adding a section at the start where you take off and a section at the end where you land.

This program requires a joystick. Not even First World War planes could fly without one.

COMMANDS

Key in the program and RUN.

Ensure your joystick is connected to PORT 1.

Good shooting!

```
10 REM FIGHTER
20 REM *******
30 REM
100 POKE 52,48:POKE 56,48:CLR:
    REM RESERVE MEMORY FOR SPRITES
110 CL$=CHR$(147):REM TO CLEAR SCREEN
120 POKE 53280,11:REM BROWN BORDER
130 POKE 53281,14:REM BLUE SCREEN
140 V=53248:REM START OF VIDEO CHIP
```

```
150 PRINT CHR$(144):REM BLACK INK
160 PRINT CL$:PRINT:PRINT
170 PRINT TAB(18)"WAIT"
180 REM***************************
190 REM SPRITE COLORS
200 POKE V+39,0:POKE V+40,1:POKE V+41,1
210 POKE V+42,2:POKE V+43,2:POKE V+44,2
220 REM***************************
230 POKE V+29,31:REM FIVE SPRITES
    EXPANDED IN X DIRECTION
240 POKE V+23,11:REM THREE SPRITES
    EXPANDED IN Y DIRECTION
250 REM***************************
260 REM SET SPRITE POINTERS
270 POKE 2040,192:POKE 2041,193:
    POKE 2042,193
280 POKE 2043,194:POKE 2044,194:
    POKE 2045,194
290 REM***************************
300 REM GENERATE SPRITE SHAPES AND SET
    INITIAL POSITIONS
310 FORN=0 TO 255
320 READ K:POKE 12288+N,K:NEXT
330 DIM P%(5,1):REM HOLDS POSITIONS
    OF SPRITES ON SCREEN
340 FOR N=1 TO 5
350 P%(N,0)=24+271*RND(1)
360 P%(N,1)=50+159*RND(1)
370 NEXT:REM SET INITIAL POSITIONS
380 POKE V+16,0:REM X MSB REGISTER
390 REM***************************
400 REM SET UP SOUNDS
410 S=54272:REM START OF SID CHIP
420 POKE S,255:POKE S+1,10:POKE S+5,72
430 POKE S+7,25:POKE S+8,30:
    POKE S+12,12
440 REM***************************
450 REM INITIAL CONDITIONS
460 POKE S+14,10:POKE S+15,1:
    POKES+19,7:POKE S+20,192
470 POKE S+18,0:POKE S+24,15:
    POKE S+18,129
480 POKE V,155:POKE V+1,125:
    REM POSITION GUNSIGHT
490 H(0)=0:H(1)=0:H(2)=0:HT=0
500 PRINT CL$:TI$="000000"
510 POKE V+21,63:
```

P17 Fighter

```
     REM SIX SPRITES ENABLED
520  REM**************************
530  REM PLAY
540  GOSUB 6000
550  GOSUB 3000
560  GOSUB 6000
570  GOSUB 4000
580  GOSUB 5000
590  FOR N=3 TO 5
600  IF H(N-3)=1 THEN 630
610  FG=0:IF FR=0 AND P%(N,0)>135
     AND P%(N,0)<165 THEN FG=1
620  IF FG=1 AND P%(N,1)>115 AND
     P%(N,1)<135 THEN GOSUB 7000:REM HIT
630  NEXT
640  IF HT=3 THEN GOSUB 8000:
     GOTO 680:REM WON
650  IF TI>5000 THEN GOSUB 9000:
     GOTO 680:REM LOST
660  GOTO 530
670  REM**************************
680  REM FINISH
690  POKE S+4,0:POKE S+11,0:
     POKE S+18,0:POKE S+24,0
700  PRINT:PRINT
710  GET A$:IF A$<>"" THEN 710:REM
     NO SPACE BETWEEN INVERTED COMMAS
720  FOR DE=0 TO 500:NEXT
730  GET A$:IF A$<>"" THEN 710:REM
     NO SPACE BETWEEN INVERTED COMMAS
740  REM ENSURE KEYBOARD BUFFER EMPTY
750  PRINT TAB(7):INPUT
     "WANT ANOTHER GO (Y/N)";Y$
760  IF ASC(Y$)=89 THEN 450
770  END
780  REM**************************
790  REM**************************
1900 REM
1910 REM          **********
1920 REM          *
1930 REM          * SPRITE
1940 REM          *   DATA
1950 REM          *
1960 REM          **********
1970 REM
1980 REM**************************
1990 REM**************************
```

```
2000 REM GUNSIGHT
2010 DATA 0,127,0,1,136,192,6,8,48
2020 DATA 8,8,8,8,8,8,16,8,4
2030 DATA 16,8,4,32,28,2,32,42,2
2040 DATA 32,73,2,63,255,254,32,73,2
2050 DATA 32,42,2,32,28,2,16,8,4
2060 DATA 16,8,4,8,8,8,8,8,8
2070 DATA 6,8,48,1,136,192,0,127,0,0
2080 REM************************
2090 REM************************
2100 REM CLOUD
2110 DATA 0,248,0,1,252,0,3,254,0
2120 DATA 3,255,0,3,255,192,7,255,224
2130 DATA 7,255,240,31,255,240,63,255,
     252
2140 DATA 127,255,254,255,255,255,255,
     255,254
2150 DATA 255,255,252,127,255,252,31,
     255,254
2160 DATA 63,255,255,127,255,255,255,
     255,255
2170 DATA 127,192,126,63,128,24,0,0,0,0
2180 REM************************
2190 REM************************
2200 REM FIGHTER
2210 DATA 0,0,0,0,0,0,0,0,0
2220 DATA 0,24,0,0,24,0,255,255,255
2230 DATA 68,24,34,68,189,34,68,126,34
2240 DATA 79,231,242,79,219,242,68,219,
     34
2250 DATA 255,231,255,0,126,0,0,189,0
2260 DATA 0,36,0,0,102,0,0,66,0
2270 DATA 0,0,0,0,0,0,0,0,0
2280 REM************************
2290 REM************************
2300 REM EXPLOSION
2310 DATA 240,56,8,240,60,24,48,62,120
2320 DATA0,0,120,51,18,120,49,146,0
2330 DATA 1,216,192,1,249,131,31,255,7
2340 DATA 15,254,7,7,255,227,97,255,128
2350 DATA 97,191,0,103,63,131,6,89,131
2360 DATA 0,88,192,0,152,96,94,152,33
2370 DATA 194,17,147,224,17,131,224,0,0,
     0
2380 REM************************
2390 REM************************
2900 REM
```

```
2910 REM          ***************
2920 REM          *
2930 REM          * SUBROUTINES
2940 REM          *
2950 REM          ***************
2960 REM
2970 REM*************************
2980 REM*************************
3000 REM JOYSTICK
3010 DX=0:DY=0
3020 T=PEEK(56321)
3030 JS=15-(T AND 15)
3040 IF JS>7 THEN DX=-2
3050 IF JS<7 AND JS>3 THEN DX=2
3060 IF JS=2 OR JS=6 OR JS=10 THEN DY=2
3070 IF JS=1 OR JS=5 OR JS=9 THEN DY=-2
3080 RETURN
3090 REM*************************
3100 REM*************************
4000 REM MOVE CLOUDS
4010 FOR N=1 TO 2
4020 P%(N,0)=P%(N,0)+7*(RND(1)+DX)
4030 IF P%(N,0)>339 THEN P%(N,0)=0
4040 IF P%(N,0)<0 THEN P%(N,0)=320
4050 P%(N,1)=P%(N,1)+7*DY
4060 IF P%(N,1)>255 THEN P%(N,1)=12
4070 IF P%(N,1)<0 THEN P%(N,1)=243
4080 GOSUB 6000:REM FIRE BUTTON
4090 K=P%(N,0)
4100 IF K<256 THEN
     POKE V+16,PEEK(V+16) AND (255-2^N)
4110 IF K>255 THEN K=K-255:
     POKE V+16,PEEK(V+16) OR 2^N
4120 POKE V+2*N,K:REM X POSITION
4130 POKE V+2*N+1,P%(N,1):REM Y POSITION
4140 GOSUB 6000:REM FIRE BUTTON
4150 NEXT
4160 RETURN
4170 REM*************************
4180 REM*************************
5000 REM MOVE FIGHTERS
5010 FOR N=3 TO 5
5020 P%(N,0)=P%(N,0)+15*RND(1)+7*(DX-1)
5030 IF P%(N,0)>319 THEN P%(N,0)=300
5040 IF P%(N,0)<0 THEN P%(N,0)=12
5050 P%(N,1)=P%(N,1)+15*RND(1)+7*(DY-1)
5060 IF P%(N,1)>255 THEN P%(N,1)=243
```

```
5070 IF P%(N,1)<0 THEN P%(N,1)=12
5080 GOSUB 6000:REM FIRE BUTTON
5090 K=P%(N,0)
5100 IF K<256 THEN
     POKE V+16,PEEK(V+16) AND (255-2^N)
5110 IF K>255 THEN K=K-255:
     POKE V+16,PEEK(V+16) OR 2^N
5120 POKE V+2*N,K:REM X POSITION
5130 POKE V+2*N+1,P%(N,1):REM Y POSITION
5140 GOSUB 6000:REM FIRE BUTTON
5150 NEXT
5160 RETURN
5170 REM************************
5180 REM************************
6000 REM FIRE BUTTON
6010 T=PEEK(56321)
6020 FR=T AND 16:REM FIRE BUTTON
6030 POKE S+4,0:IF FR=0 THEN
     POKE S+4,129
6040 RETURN
6050 REM************************
6060 REM************************
7000 REM HIT
7010 HT=HT+1:H(N-3)=1
7020 POKE S+11,0:POKE S+11,129
7030 POKE 2040+N,195
7040 FOR DE=0 TO 500:NEXT
7050 POKE V+21,PEEK(V+21)-2^N
7060 POKE 2040+N,194
7070 RETURN
7080 REM************************
7090 REM************************
8000 REM WON
8010 POKE V+21,0:
     REM NO SPRITES ENABLED
8020 PRINT CL$:PRINT:PRINT
8030 PRINT TAB(11)"CONGRATULATIONS"
8040 PRINT
8050 PRINT TAB(11)"MISSION COMPLETE"
8060 PRINT
8070 PRINT TAB(11)"NEW RANK IS ";
8080 IF TI<2500 THEN PRINT "ACE":
     GOTO 8110
8090 IF TI<3750 THEN PRINT:PRINT TAB(11)
     "PILOT CLASS 1":GOTO 8110
8100 PRINT"PILOT"
8110 RETURN
```

P17 Fighter

```
8120 REM*************************
8130 REM*************************
9000 REM LOST
9010 POKE S+11,0:POKE S+11,129
9020 POKE S+15,200:POKE S+18,0:
     POKE S+18,65
9030 FOR N=0 TO 14
9050 POKE 53281,N:POKE S+17,10*N
9060 FOR DE=0 TO 40:NEXT
9070 NEXT
9080 POKE V+21,0:
     REM NO SPRITES ENABLED
9090 PRINT CL$:PRINT:PRINT
9100 PRINT TAB(14)"TOUGH LUCK"
9110 PRINT
9120 PRINT TAB(13)"THEY GOT YOU"
9130 PRINT
9140 PRINT TAB(10)"POSTHUMOUS RANK IS"
9150 IF HT=0 THEN PRINT TAB(14)
     "PASSENGER"
9160 IF HT=1 THEN PRINT TAB(14)
     "ROOKIE"
9170 IF HT=2 THEN PRINT TAB(14)
     "NOVICE"
9180 RETURN
9190 REM*************************
9200 REM*************************
```

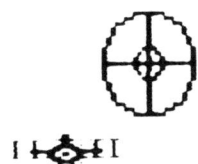

P18 Bat'n'Moth

You've heard of bat'n'ball – well here's bat'n'moth. This program was developed from an idea by Theresa Gordon, who also designed the characters used.

The object of the game is to control a bat and make it eat a set of moths which flit across the screen.

You can specify the level of difficulty. This controls the speed of the moths and the range of the bat. There is a random element in the former. As a result of this, catching the last moth, even at lower difficulty levels can drive you to distraction. You have been warned!

You can use either joystick or keyboard control. If you use the joystick, pressing the fire button makes the bat attempt to eat the moth. The instructions for using the keyboard are included in the code.

COMMANDS

Key in the program and RUN.

Enter level of difficulty (1 is easy – 9 is hard).

If you are using a joystick, ensure it is connected to PORT 1.

```
10 REM BAT'N'MOTH
20 REM **********
30 REM
100 POKE 48,64:POKE 56,48:CLR:
    REM RESERVE MEMORY FOR SPRITES
110 CL$=CHR$(147):REM TO CLEAR SCREEN
120 POKE 53281,11:REM BROWN SCREEN
130 POKE 53280,6:REM BLUE BORDER
140 V=53248:REM START OF VIDEO CHIP
150 PRINT CHR$(159):REM CYAN INK
160 PRINT CL$:PRINT:PRINT
170 PRINT TAB(18)"WAIT"
180 REM**************************
190 REM SPRITE COLORS
```

P18 Bat 'n' Moth

```
200 POKE V+39,0
210 FOR N=40 TO 46:POKE V+N,3:NEXT
220 REM***************************
230 POKE V+29,255:REM ALL SPRITES
    EXPANDED IN X DIRECTION
240 POKE V+23,255:REM ALL SPRITES
    EXPANDED IN Y DIRECTION
250 POKE 2040,192
260 FOR N=1 TO 7:POKE 2040+N,193:NEXT:
    REM SET SPRITE POINTERS
270 REM***************************
280 REM GENERATE SPRITE SHAPES
290 FOR N=0 TO 191
300 READ K:POKE 12288+N,K
310 NEXT
320 REM***************************
330 REM SET UP SOUNDS
340 S=54272:REM START OF SID CHIP
350 POKE S,255
360 POKE S+1,75
370 POKE S+5,73:POKE S+6,68
380 POKE S+7,25
390 POKE S+8,50
400 POKE S+12,12:POKE S+13,70
410 POKE S+15,7:POKE S+24,15
420 REM***************************
430 REM KEYBOARD OR JOYSTICK
440 PRINT CL$:PRINT:PRINT:PRINT
450 PRINT TAB(13)CHR$(18)"*************"
460 PRINT TAB(13)CHR$(18)" BAT 'N MOTH "
470 PRINT TAB(13)CHR$(18)"*************"
480 PRINT:PRINT:PRINT:PRINT
490 PRINT TAB(7)
    "SELECT CONTROL BY PRESSING:"
500 PRINT
510 PRINT TAB(10)CHR$(18)
    " KEY F1 "CHR$(146)" - KEYBOARD"
520 PRINT
530 PRINT TAB(10)CHR$(18)
    " KEY F3 "CHR$(146)" - JOYSTICK"
540 GET A$:IF A$="" THEN 540:REM
    NO SPACE BETWEEN INVERTED COMMAS
550 SL=ASC(A$)-132:IF SL<1 OR SL>2
    THEN 540
560 IF SL=1 THEN GOSUB 8000
570 REM***************************
580 REM INITIAL CONDITIONS
```

```
590 DIM P%(7,1):
    REM HOLDS SPRITE POSITIONS
600 REM***************************
610 REM NEW GAME
620 PRINT CL$:FOR N=0 TO 16:PRINT:NEXT
630 FOR N=1 TO 7:MT(N)=0:NEXT
640 P%(0,0)=150:P%(0,1)=125:REM INITIAL
    POSITION OF BAT
650 POKE V,P%(0,0):POKE V+1,P%(0,1):
    REM BAT POSITION IN MEMORY
660 POKE V+21,1:REM ENABLE SPRITE 1
670 REM***************************
680 REM INITIAL MOTH POSITIONS
690 POKE V+16,0:REM X MSB REGISTER
700 FOR N=1 TO 7
710 P%(N,0)=50+240*RND(1)
720 P%(N,1)=50+100*RND(1)
730 T=0:IF P%(N,0)>120 AND P%(N,0)<180
    THEN T=1
740 IF T=1 AND P%(N,1)>95
    AND P%(N,1)<155 THEN 710
750 K=P%(N,0):IF K>255 THEN K=K-255:
    POKE V+16,PEEK(V+16)+2^N
760 POKE V+2*N,K:POKE V+2*N+1,P%(N,1)
770 POKE V+21,PEEK(V+21)+2^N
780 NEXT
790 REM***************************
800 PRINT TAB(5)
    "LEVEL OF DIFFICULTY (1 TO 9)?"
810 FOR N=1 TO 7:GOSUB 9000:NEXT
820 GET A$:IF A$="" THEN 810:REM
    NO SPACE BETWEEN INVERTED COMMAS
830 IF ASC(A$)<49 OR ASC(A$)>57
    THEN 810
840 REM***************************
850 DF=ASC(A$)-48
860 PRINT CL$
870 POKE V+29,0:REM ALL SPRITES
    UNEXPANDED IN X DIRECTION
880 POKE V+23,0:REM ALL SPRITES
    UNEXPANDED IN Y DIRECTION
890 MS=7:REM NUMBER OF MOTHS
900 TI$="000000"
910 REM***************************
920 REM PLAY
930 IF MS=0 THEN 1040:REM FINISH
940 FOR N=1 TO 7
```

P18 Bat 'n' Moth

```
 950 IF MT(N)=1 THEN 1010:REM DEAD MOTH
 960 GOSUB 5000:REM MOVE MOTH
 970 GOSUB 9000:REM FLUTTER
 980 ON SL GOSUB 3000,4000:REM KEYBOARD
     OR JOYSTICK CONTROL
 990 IF DX<>0 OR DY<>0 THEN GOSUB 6000:
     REM MOVE BAT
1000 IF FR=0 THEN GOSUB 7000:REM TRY
     TO EAT MOTH
1010 NEXT
1020 GOTO 930
1030 REM**************************
1040 POKE V+21,0
1050 PRINT:PRINT:PRINT
1060 PRINT TAB(14)CHR$(18)" GAME OVER "
1070 TM=INT(TI*100/60/7+.5)/100
1080 PRINT:PRINT
1090 PRINT TAB(4)
     "AVERAGE TIME PER MOTH";TM;"SECS"
1100 PRINT:PRINT
1110 GET A$:IF A$<>"" THEN 1110:REM
     NO SPACE BETWEEN INVERTED COMMAS
1120 REM FLUSH KEYBOARD BUFFER
1130 PRINT TAB(9):INPUT
     "ANOTHER GAME (Y/N)";Y$
1140 IF ASC(Y$)=89 THEN 610
1150 FOR N=0 TO 24:POKE S+N,0:NEXT
1160 END
1170 REM**************************
1180 REM**************************
1900 REM
1910 REM         *********
1920 REM         *
1930 REM         * SPRITE
1940 REM         *   DATA
1950 REM         *
1960 REM         *********
1970 REM
1980 REM**************************
1990 REM**************************
2000 REM BAT
2010 DATA0,0,0,0,0,0,8,36,16
2020 DATA 8,36,16,8,24,16,12,60,48
2030 DATA 12,126,48,12,60,48,14,24,112
2040 DATA 14,24,112,14,126,112,15,255,
     240
```

```
2050 DATA 15,255,240,14,255,112,14,126,
          112
2060 DATA 12,90,48,8,153,16,9,195,144
2070 DATA 0,0,0,0,0,0,0,0,0,0
2080 REM**************************
2090 REM**************************
2100 REM MOTH 1
2110 DATA 0,0,0,0,0,0,0,0,0
2120 DATA 0,0,0,0,0,0,0,0,0
2130 DATA 0,129,0,0,129,0,0,195,0
2140 DATA 0,231,0,0,255,0,0,231,0
2150 DATA 0,195,0,0,129,0,0,0,0
2160 DATA 0,0,0,0,0,0,0,0,0
2170 DATA 0,0,0,0,0,0,0,0,0
2180 REM**************************
2190 REM**************************
2200 REM MOTH 2
2210 DATA 0,0,0,0,0,0,0,0,0
2220 DATA 0,0,0,0,0,0,0,0,0
2230 DATA 0,36,0,0,102,0,0,102,0
2240 DATA 0,102,0,0,126,0,0,102,0
2250 DATA 0,102,0,0,36,0,0,0,0
2260 DATA 0,0,0,0,0,0,0,0,0
2270 DATA 0,0,0,0,0,0,0,0,0
2280 REM**************************
2290 REM**************************
2900 REM
2910 REM         ***************
2920 REM         *
2930 REM         *  SUBROUTINES
2940 REM         *
2950 REM         ***************
2960 REM
2970 REM**************************
2980 REM**************************
3000 REM KEYBOARD
3010 DX=0:DY=0:FR=1
3020 T=PEEK(197)
3030 IF T=36 THEN DX=25:REM RIGHT
3040 IF T=39 THEN DX=-25:REM LEFT
3050 IF T=10 THEN DY=-25:REM UP
3060 IF T=12 THEN DY=25:REM DOWN
3070 IF T=60 THEN FR=0
3080 RETURN
3090 REM**************************
3100 REM**************************
4000 REM JOYSTICK
```

P18 Bat 'n' Moth

```
4010 DX=0:DY=0
4020 T=PEEK(56321)
4030 JS=15-(T AND 15)
4040 IF JS>7 THEN DX=25:REM RIGHT
4050 IF JS<7 AND JS>3 THEN DX=-25:
     REM LEFT
4060 IF JS=1 OR JS=5 OR JS=9 THEN
     DY=-25:REM UP
4070 IF JS=2 OR JS=6 OR JS=10 THEN
     DY=25:REM DOWN
4080 FR=T AND 16:REM FIRE BUTTON
4090 RETURN
4100 REM*************************
4110 REM*************************
5000 REM MOVE MOTHS
5010 MX%=15*RND(1)+3*DF
5020 IF RND(1)>.5 THEN MX%=-MX%
5030 P%(N,0)=P%(N,0)+MX%
5040 IF P%(N,0)<24 THEN P%(N,0)=24
5050 IF P%(N,0)>320 THEN P%(N,0)=320
5060 MY%=15*RND(1)+3*DF
5070 IF RND(1)>.5 THEN MY%=-MY%
5080 P%(N,1)=P%(N,1)+MY%
5090 IF P%(N,1)<50 THEN P%(N,1)=50
5100 IF P%(N,1)>229 THEN P%(N,1)=229
5110 K=P%(N,0)
5120 IF K<256 THEN
     POKE V+16,PEEK(V+16) AND (255-2^N)
5130 IF K>255 THEN K=K-255:
     POKE V+16,PEEK(V+16) OR 2^N
5140 POKE V+2*N,K:POKE V+2*N+1,P%(N,1)
5150 RETURN
5160 REM*************************
5170 REM*************************
6000 REM MOVE BAT
6010 P%(0,0)=P%(0,0)+DX
6020 IF P%(0,0)<21 THEN P%(0,0)=21
6030 IF P%(0,0)>320 THEN P%(0,0)=320
6040 P%(0,1)=P%(0,1)+DY
6050 IF P%(0,1)<50 THEN P%(0,1)=50
6060 IF P%(0,1)>232 THEN P%(0,1)=232
6070 K=P%(0,0)
6080 IF K<256 THEN
     POKE V+16,PEEK(V+16) AND 254
6090 IF K>255 THEN K=K-255:
     POKE V+16,PEEK(V+16) OR 1
6100 POKE V,K:POKE V+1,P%(0,1)
```

```
6110 RETURN
6120 REM**************************
6130 REM**************************
7000 REM DINNER TIME
7010 POKE S+4,0:POKE S+4,21:T=0
7020 FOR J=1 TO 7
7030 IF MT(J)=1 THEN 7120:REM DEAD MOTH
7040 LET RN=10+2*(9-DF):REM BAT'S RANGE
7050 IF ABS(P%(J,0)-P%(0,0))>RN OR
     ABS(P%(J,1)-P%(0,1))>RN THEN 7120
7060 REM**************************
7070 REM BAT CATCHES MOTH
7080 T=1:POKE S+11,0:POKE S+11,65:
     REM MUSIC AIDS DIGESTION
7090 MT(J)=1:MS=MS-1
7100 POKE V+21,PEEK(V+21)-2^J:
     REM MOTH DELETED
7110 REM**************************
7120 NEXT
7130 POKE S+4,20
7140 IF T=1 THEN FOR J=128 TO 0 STEP-1:
     POKE S+10,J:NEXT
7150 POKE S+11,64
7160 RETURN
7170 REM**************************
7180 REM**************************
8000 REM KEY INSTRUCTIONS
8010 PRINT CL$:PRINT:PRINT:PRINT:PRINT
8020 PRINT TAB(8)CHR$(18)" KEY M "
     CHR$(146)" - MOVES BAT RIGHT"
8030 PRINT
8040 PRINT TAB(8)CHR$(18)" KEY N "
     CHR$(146)" - MOVES BAT LEFT"
8050 PRINT
8060 PRINT TAB(8)CHR$(18)" KEY A "
     CHR$(146)" - MOVES BAT UP"
8070 PRINT
8080 PRINT TAB(8)CHR$(18)" KEY Z "
     CHR$(146)" - MOVES BAT DOWN"
8090 PRINT
8100 PRINT TAB(8)CHR$(18)" SPACE BAR "
     CHR$(146)" - BAT EATS MOTH"
8110 PRINT:PRINT:PRINT:PRINT
8120 PRINT TAB(6)CHR$(18)
     " PRESS ANY KEY TO CONTINUE "
8130 GET A$:IF A$="" THEN 8130:REM
     NO SPACE BETWEEN INVERTED COMMAS
```

P18 Bat 'n' Moth

```
8140 POKE 650,128:REM KEY REPEAT
8150 RETURN
8160 REM**************************
8170 REM**************************
9000 REM FLICKER
9010 FOR FL=0 TO 2
9020 POKE 2040+N,194:POKE 2040+N,193
9030 NEXT
9040 RETURN
9050 REM**************************
9060 REM**************************
```

P19 Loan Repayment Period

This program uses the formula

where T=Period in years
P=Principal
R=Rate of interest
N=Number of payments each year
A=Amount of each payment.

This could be calculated by using a calculator, but it is far quicker to allow the computer to do the work for you.

This program could be improved by designing a more robust input routine, to check for bad keyboard input.

COMMANDS

Key in the program and type RUN.

Follow instructions.

```
10 REM PROGRAM  - LOAN REPAYMENT PERIOD
20 PRINT "[CS ]":PRINT:PRINT:PRINT
30 PRINT "IF YOU ARE ABOUT TO TAKE OUT A LOAN"
40 PRINT "IT COULD BE USEFUL TO CONSIDER HOW LONG"
50 PRINT "IT WILL BE BEFORE THE LOAN IS REPAID."
60 PRINT :PRINT :PRINT
70 PRINT "TO USE THIS PROGRAM YOU MUST INPUT"
80 PRINT:PRINT
90 PRINT TAB(5);"AMOUNT BORROWED"
100 PRINT TAB(5);"NUMBER OF PAYMENTS PER YEAR"
110 PRINT TAB(5);"AMOUNT OF REPAYMENTS"
120 PRINT:PRINT:PRINT
130 PRINT "PRESS ANY KEY TO CONTINUE"
140 GET A$:IF A$="" THEN GOTO 140
150 PRINT "[CS ]"
160 FOR Z=1 TO 9:PRINT:NEXT Z
170 PRINT TAB(5);"AMOUNT BORROWED   $"
180 PRINT TAB(5);"ANNUAL INTEREST RATE(%)"
190 PRINT TAB(5);"NUMBER OF PAYMENTS PER YEAR"
200 PRINT TAB(5);"AMOUNT OF PAYMENTS $"
```

P19 Loan Repayment Period

```
210 Y=10:X=24:GOSUB 5000
220 INPUT P
230 Y=11:X=28:GOSUB 5000
240 INPUT R:R=R/100
250 Y=12:X=32:GOSUB 5000
260 INPUT N
270 Y=13:X=25:GOSUB 5000
280 INPUT A
290 TM=-LOG(1-P*R/N/A)/LOG(1+R/N)/N
300 YR=INT(TM)
310 MT=INT(12*(TM-YR))+1
320 PRINT:PRINT:PRINT
330 PRINT "LOAN WILL BE PAID OFF IN "
340 PRINT YR;" YEARS AND "
350 PRINT MT;" MONTHS"
360 END
4990 REM SUBROUTINE TO PLACE CURSOR AT X,Y
5000 PRINT "[CH ]";:REM CURSOR HOME
5010 FOR I=1 TO Y
5020 PRINT "[CD ]";
5030 NEXT I
5040 FOR I=1 TO X
5050 PRINT "[CR ]";
5060 NEXT I
5070 RETURN
```

P20 Depreciation

This program may be used to calculate the depreciation in the value of an article arising from normal use through time.

The program shows the effect of two common methods of calculating this depreciation.

1. The straight line method

    Under this method a fixed amount (a percentage of the initial value) is written off annually. The resultant graph shows a linear relationship between value and year. If, for example, the initial value was $8000, and 25% of this original value was written off each year, then we have:

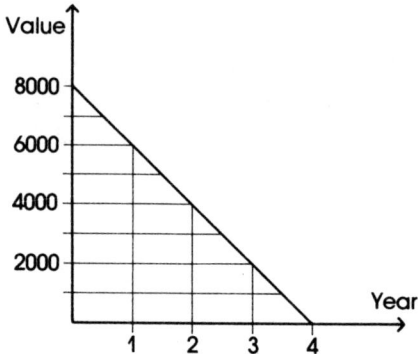

P20 Depreciation

2. The diminishing balance method

Under this method a percentage of the residual value at the beginning of each year is written down at the end of that year. This gives a curve like:

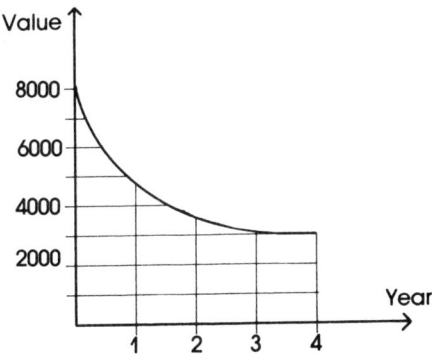

The program presents the two depreciation methods in the form of a table showing the amount to be written off over a period of years.

COMMANDS

Key in the program and RUN.

Follow the instructions.

Enter amounts as numbers only. This program works with any currency.

```
10 REM DEPRECIATION
20 REM ************
30 REM
100 PRINT CHR$(147):REM CLEAR SCREEN
110 POKE 53280,15:REM GRAY BORDER
```

```
120 POKE 53281,15:REM GRAY SCREEN
130 PRINT CHR$(28):REM RED   INK
140 PRINT TAB(7)
    "DEPRECIATION CALCULATIONS"
150 PRINT TAB(7)
    "*************************"
160 PRINT:PRINT
170 PRINT TAB(5)
    "THERE ARE TWO COMMON METHODS OF"
180 PRINT TAB(5)
    "CALCULATING THE DEPRECIATION OF"
190 PRINT TAB(5)
    "THE VALUE OF AN ASSET OVER A"
200 PRINT TAB(5)
    "GIVEN PERIOD. THESE ARE:"
210 PRINT
220 PRINT TAB(5)
    "1. THE STRAIGHT LINE METHOD."
230 PRINT
240 PRINT TAB(5)
    "2. THE DIMINISHING BALANCE"
250 PRINT TAB(8)"METHOD."
260 PRINT:PRINT
270 PRINT TAB(5)
    "THIS PROGRAM SHOWS DEPRECIATION"
280 PRINT TAB(5)
    "OVER A FIXED PERIOD USING BOTH"
290 PRINT TAB(5)"METHODS."
300 PRINT:PRINT
310 PRINT TAB(5)
    "PRESS ANY KEY TO CONTINUE"
320 GET A$:IF A$="" THEN 320
330 REM NO SPACE BETWEEN INVERTED COMMAS
340 REM WAIT FOR A KEY
350 REM***********************
360 REM***********************
370 PRINT CHR$(147):REM CLEAR SCREEN
380 PRINT:PRINT
390 INPUT
    "VALUE OF ASSET ON ACQUISITION";IV
400 PRINT:PRINT
410 PRINT
    "IF YOU WROTE OFF A FIXED AMOUNT"
420 INPUT
    "EACH YEAR, HOW MUCH WOULD IT BE";A
430 PRINT:PRINT
```

P20 Depreciation

```
440 PRINT
    "IF YOU WROTE OFF A PERCENTAGE"
450 INPUT
    "EACH YEAR, WHAT WOULD IT BE";PR
460 PRINT:PRINT
470 PRINT
    "NUMBER OF YEARS TO BE PRESENTED"
480 INPUT"(1 TO 20)";YR%
490 REM NO TRAPS ON ENTRIES
500 REM SILLY ENTRIES WILL GIVE SILLY
    RESULTS
510 PRINT:PRINT
520 PRINT "PRESS ANY KEY TO CONTINUE"
530 GET A$:IF A$="" THEN 530
540 REM NO SPACE BETWEEN INVERTED COMMAS
550 REM WAIT FOR A KEY
560 REM*************************
570 REM*************************
580 PRINT CHR$(147):REM CLEAR SCREEN
590 PRINT"YEAR","STR. LINE",,"DIM. BAL."
600 PRINT,"VALUE",,"VALUE"
610 PRINT
620 VA=IV
630 FOR N=1 TO YR%
640 VL=IV-A*N
650 REM VALUE=INITIAL VALUE MINUS (FIXED
    AMOUNT TIMES NUMBER OF YEARS)
660 IF VL<0 THEN VL=0
670 VA=VA*(100-PR)/100
680 IF VA<0 THEN VA=0
690 REM REDUCE VALUE BY A PERCENTAGE
    EACH YEAR
700 DEF FNR(X)=(INT(X*100+.5))/100
710 REM FIGURES CORRECT TO 2 DECIMAL
    PLACES AFTER THE POINT
720 PRINTN,FNR(VL),,FNR(VA)
730 NEXT
740 GET A$:IF A$="" THEN 740
750 REM "PRESS ANY KEY TO END PROGRAM
760 END
```

Stock Control System

The next three programs form a rudimentary stock control system. As they are written they use the tape cassette for information storage, but they could easily be amended to use floppy disks instead. If you intend using your computer extensively for file handling of this type you would be well advised to consider floppy disks.

The first program lets you set up the stock file initially. In its present form it allows only ten different types of stock item. We are sure the reader will be able to amend the program to increase this number if necessary.

The next program is used to record all transactions, both additions to and withdrawals from stock. At present the program does not verify the data as it is entered. This would be a useful extension.

The third program updates the stock file with the information held in the transaction file. This is a fairly complicated program, which we have tried to make self explanatory by the use of PRINT and REM statements. This program also produces a list of items to be reordered.

The full stock control system is:

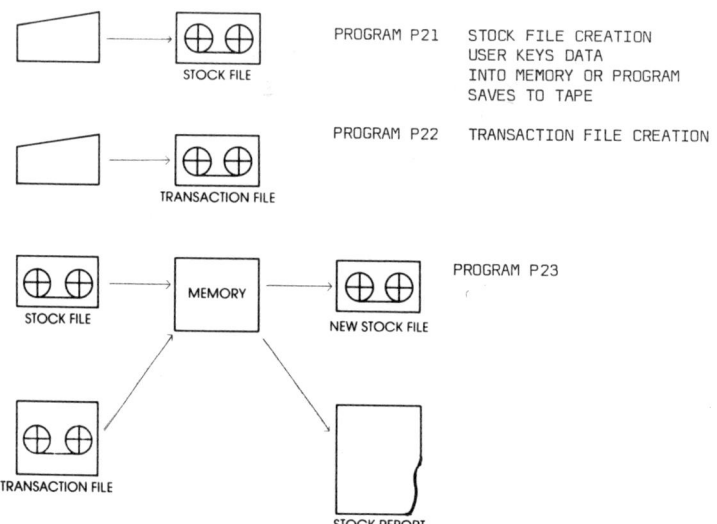

P21   Stock File Creation

This program creates the stock file.

COMMANDS

Key in the program and RUN.

Have some blank tapes ready.

```
10 REM STOCK FILE CREATION
20 REM *******************
30 REM
100 CL$=CHR$(147):REM TO CLEAR SCREEN
110 POKE 53280,9:REM BROWN BORDER
120 POKE 53281,1:REM WHITE SCREEN
130 PRINT CHR$(31):REM BLUE INK
140 PRINT CL$
150 PRINT:PRINT
160 PRINT TAB(10)"STOCK FILE CREATION"
170 PRINT TAB(10)"==================="
180 PRINT:PRINT
190 PRINT TAB(4)
    "THIS PROGRAM SETS UP A STOCK FILE"
200 PRINT TAB(4)
    "ON TAPE. THE STRUCTURE OF EACH"
210 PRINT TAB(4)"STOCK LINE IS:"
220 PRINT
230 PRINT TAB(9)"STOCK NUMBER (1 TO 10)"
240 PRINT TAB(9)
    "DESCRIPTION (UP TO 30 CHRS)"
250 PRINT TAB(9)"NUMBER IN STOCK"
260 PRINT TAB(9)"REORDER LEVEL"
270 PRINT TAB(9)"REORDER QUANTITY"
280 PRINT
290 PRINT TAB(4)
    "PLEASE ENTER DATA WHEN PROMPTED"
300 PRINT:PRINT
310 PRINT TAB(6)CHR$(18);
    "PRESS ANY KEY TO CONTINUE"
320 GET A$:IF A$="" THEN 320
330 REM NO SPACE BETWEEN INVERTED COMMAS
```

```
340 REM***************************
350 DIM N%(10,3):DIM J%(10,3)
360 FOR K=1 TO 10
370 D$(K)="NONE":REM COMPLETELY EMPTY
    STRING ELEMENTS PREVENT VERIFY
380 PRINT CL$:PRINT:PRINT
390 PRINT TAB(12)"STOCK NUMBER =";K
400 PRINT
410 PRINT TAB(9)"DESCRIPTION?":PRINT:
    INPUT D$(K)
420 PRINT
430 PRINT TAB(9):INPUT
    "NUMBER IN STOCK";N%(K,1)
440 PRINT
450 PRINT TAB(9):INPUT
    "REORDER LEVEL";N%(K,2)
460 PRINT
470 PRINT TAB(9):INPUT
    "REORDER QUANTITY";N%(K,3)
480 NEXT
490 REM***************************
500 PRINT CL$:PRINT:PRINT
510 PRINT TAB(4)
    "ENSURE THERE IS A TAPE IN THE"
520 PRINT TAB(4)
    "CASSETTE RECORDER READY FOR SAVING"
530 PRINT:PRINT
540 PRINT TAB(4)
    "WHAT IS THE NAME OF THE FILE"
550 PRINT TAB(4):INPUT N$
560 REM***************************
570 PRINT:PRINT TAB(4);:
    REM FILE SAVE STARTS HERE
580 OPEN 1,1,1,N$
590 FOR K=1 TO 10
600 PRINT# 1,D$(K)
610 PRINT# 1,N%(K,1)
620 PRINT# 1,N%(K,2)
630 PRINT# 1,N%(K,3)
640 NEXT:CLOSE 1
650 REM***************************
660 PRINT CL$
670 PRINT:PRINT
680 PRINT TAB(4)
    "REWIND CASSETTE RECORDER TO START"
690 PRINT TAB(4)"OF FILE"
700 PRINT:PRINT
```

P21 Stock File Creation

```
710 PRINT TAB(4)
    "PRESS ANY KEY WHEN READY"
720 GET A$:IF A$="" THEN 720
730 REM NO SPACE BETWEEN INVERTED COMMAS
740 PRINT:PRINT
750 OPEN 1,1,0,N$
760 FOR K=1 TO 10
770 INPUT# 1,E$(K)
780 INPUT# 1,J%(K,1)
790 INPUT# 1,J%(K,2)
800 INPUT# 1,J%(K,3)
810 NEXT:CLOSE 1
820 PRINT CL$:PRINT:PRINT:F=0
830 FOR K=1 TO 10
840 IF D$(K)<>E$(K) THEN K=10:F=1
850 IF N%(K,1)<>J%(K,1) THEN K=10:F=1
860 IF N%(K,2)<>J%(K,2) THEN K=10:F=1
870 IF N%(K,3)<>J%(K,3) THEN K=10:F=1
880 NEXT:IF F=1 THEN 940
890 PRINT TAB(7)CHR$(18);
    " VERIFICATION CHECK PASSED "
900 PRINT:PRINT
910 PRINT TAB(9)"STOP CASSETTE RECORDER"
920 END
930 REM****************************
940 PRINT TAB(7)CHR$(18);
    " VERIFICATION CHECK FAILED "
950 PRINT:PRINT
960 PRINT TAB(5)
    "REWIND TAPE TO INITIAL POSITION"
970 PRINT:PRINT
980 PRINT TAB(8)
    "PRESS ANY KEY WHEN READY"
990 GET A$:IF A$="" THEN 990:
    REM NO SPACE
1000 GOTO 570
1010 REM****************************
1020 REM****************************
```

P22 Transaction File Creation

This program allows you to record up to 100 transactions.

COMMANDS

Key in the program and RUN.

Have a blank tape ready.

```
10 REM TRANSACTION FILE CREATION
20 REM *************************
30 REM
100 CL$=CHR$(147):REM TO CLEAR SCREEN
110 POKE 53280,9:REM BROWN BORDER
120 POKE 53281,1:REM WHITE SCREEN
130 PRINT CHR$(31):REM BLUE INK
140 PRINT CL$
150 PRINT
160 PRINT TAB(8)
    "TRANSACTION FILE CREATION"
170 PRINT TAB(8)
    "========================="
180 PRINT
190 PRINT TAB(4)
    "THIS PROGRAM ALLOWS THE USER TO"
200 PRINT TAB(4)
    "RECORD A SET OF TRANSACTIONS"
210 PRINT TAB(4)
    "AGAINST A STOCK FILE."
220 PRINT
230 PRINT TAB(4)
    "THE TRANSACTION FILE STRUCTURE IS"
240 PRINT TAB(4)"AS FOLLOWS:"
250 PRINT
260 PRINT TAB(9)"STOCK NUMBER"
270 PRINT TAB(9)"CODE [1 - WITHDRAWAL"
280 PRINT TAB(9)"     [2 - ADDITION"
290 PRINT TAB(9)"QUANTITY"
300 PRINT
310 PRINT TAB(4)
    "UP TO 100 ITEMS CAN BE HANDLED."
```

P22 Transaction File Creation

```
320 PRINT
330 PRINT TAB(4)
    "ENTER DETAILS WHEN PROMPTED."
340 PRINT TAB(4)
    "ENTER A NEGATIVE STOCK NUMBER TO
350 PRINT TAB(4)"FINISH."
360 PRINT
370 PRINT TAB(6) CHR$(18);
    "PRESS ANY KEY TO CONTINUE"
380 GET A$:IF A$="" THEN 380:
    REM NO SPACE BETWEEN COMMAS
390 REM*************************
400 DIM T%(100,3):DIM W%(100,3)
410 FOR N=1 TO 100
420 PRINT CL$:PRINT
430 PRINT TAB(9):INPUT
    "STOCK NUMBER(1 TO 10)";T%(N,1)
440 IF T%(N,1)<0 THEN 540:
    REM ENTRIES COMPLETE
450 IF T%(N,1)<1 OR T%(N,1)>10 THEN
    PRINT TAB(9)"INVALID":GOTO 430
460 PRINT
470 PRINT TAB(9):INPUT
    "CODE(1 OR 2)";T%(N,2)
480 IF T%(N,2)<1 OR T%(N,2)>2 THEN
    PRINT TAB(9)"INVALID":GOTO 470
490 PRINT
500 PRINT TAB(9):INPUT
    "QUANTITY";T%(N,3)
510 IF T%(N,3)<1 THEN
    PRINT TAB(9)"INVALID":GOTO 500
520 NEXT
530 REM*************************
540 PRINT CL$:PRINT
550 PRINT TAB(4)
    "ENSURE TAPE IS READY THEN PRESS"
560 PRINT TAB(4)"ANY KEY."
570 GET A$:IF A$="" THEN 570:
    REM NO SPACE BETWEEN COMMAS
580 PRINT:PRINT TAB(4)
    "WHAT IS THE NAME OF THE FILE?"
590 PRINT TAB(4):INPUT N$
600 R$=CHR$(13):REM RETURN CHARACTER
610 PRINT:PRINT TAB(4);:
    REM FILE SAVE STARTS HERE
620 OPEN 1,1,1,N$
630 FOR K=1 TO 100
```

```
640 PRINT# 1,T%(K,1) R$ T%(K,2) R$
    T%(K,3)
650 NEXT:CLOSE 1
660 REM***************************
670 PRINT CL$
680 PRINT:PRINT
690 PRINT TAB(4)
    "REWIND CASSETTE RECORDER TO START"
700 PRINT TAB(4)"OF FILE."
710 PRINT:PRINT
720 PRINT TAB(4)
    "PRESS ANY KEY WHEN READY."
730 GET A$:IF A$="" THEN 730:
    REM NO SPACE BETWEEN COMMAS
740 PRINT:PRINT
750 OPEN 1,1,0,N$
760 FOR K=1 TO 100
770 INPUT# 1,W%(K,1)
780 INPUT# 1,W%(K,2)
790 INPUT# 1,W%(K,3)
800 NEXT:CLOSE 1
810 PRINT CL$:PRINT:PRINT:F=0
820 PRINT TAB(15) CHR$(18);"VERIFYING"
830 FOR K=1 TO 100
840 IF T%(K,1)<>W%(K,1) THEN K=100:F=1
850 IF T%(K,2)<>W%(K,2) THEN K=100:F=1
860 IF T%(K,3)<>W%(K,3) THEN K=100:F=1
870 NEXT:IF F=1 THEN 940
880 PRINT CL$:PRINT:PRINT
890 PRINT TAB(8)CHR$(18);
    "VERIFICATION CHECK PASSED"
900 PRINT:PRINT
910 PRINT TAB(8)"STOP CASSETTE RECORDER"
920 END
930 REM***************************
940 PRINT CL$:PRINT:PRINT:PRINT TAB(8)
    CHR$(18);"VERIFICATION CHECK FAILED"
950 PRINT:PRINT
960 PRINT TAB(4)
    "REWIND TAPE TO INITIAL POSITION"
970 PRINT:PRINT
980 PRINT TAB(4)
    "PRESS ANY KEY WHEN READY"
990 GET A$:IF A$="" THEN 990:
    REM NO SPACE
1000 GOTO 610:REM SAVE FILE AGAIN
1010 REM***************************
```

P23   Stock File Update and Report

This program updates the stock file and produces a list of items to be ordered.

The program can output to the screen or to a printer. As it stands it will work with the Commodore MPS801 and most other printers. If your printer does not have an automatic line feed on carriage return then modify the printer control instructions to use a file number greater than 128.

COMMANDS

Key in the program and RUN.

Have your stock file tape, your transaction file tape and a blank tape handy.

```
10 REM STOCK FILE UPDATE AND REPORT
20 REM ***************************
30 REM
100 CL$=CHR$(147):REM TO CLEAR SCREEN
110 POKE 53280,9:REM BROWN BORDER
120 POKE 53281,1:REM WHITE SCREEN
130 PRINT CHR$(31):REM BLUE INK
140 PRINT CL$
150 PRINT:PRINT
160 PRINT TAB(6)
    "STOCK FILE UPDATE AND REPORT"
170 PRINT TAB(6)
    "==========================="
180 PRINT:PRINT
190 PRINT TAB(4)
    "THIS PROGRAM UPDATES A STOCK FILE"
200 PRINT TAB(4)
    "OF TEN ITEMS AND THEN SAVES IT"
210 PRINT TAB(4)
    "BACK TO TAPE. THE PROGRAM ALSO"
220 PRINT TAB(4)
    "PRODUCES A REPORT OF ALL ITEMS TO"
230 PRINT TAB(4)"BE REORDERED."
240 PRINT:PRINT:PRINT
```

```
250 PRINT TAB(6)CHR$(18)
    " PRESS ANY KEY TO CONTINUE "
260 GET A$:IF A$="" THEN 260:REM
    NO SPACE BETWEEN INVERTED COMMAS
270 REM*****************************
290 PRINT CL$:PRINT:PRINT
300 DIM N%(10,3)
310 DIM J%(10,3)
320 DIM T%(100,3)
330 PRINT TAB(4)
    "WHAT IS THE NAME OF THE STOCK"
340 PRINT TAB(4):INPUT"FILE";N$
350 PRINT:PRINT
360 PRINT TAB(4)
    "POSITION TAPE AT START OF STOCK"
370 PRINT TAB(4)
    "FILE, THEN PRESS ANY KEY."
380 GET A$:IF A$="" THEN 380:REM
    NO SPACE BETWEEN INVERTED COMMAS
390 PRINT CL$:PRINT:PRINT
400 OPEN 1,1,0,N$
410 FOR K=1 TO 10
420 INPUT# 1,D$(K)
430 INPUT# 1,N%(K,1)
440 INPUT# 1,N%(K,2)
450 INPUT# 1,N%(K,3)
460 NEXT:CLOSE 1
470 REM*****************************
480 PRINT CL$:PRINT:PRINT
490 PRINT TAB(8)CHR$(18)
    " STOP CASSETTE RECORDER "
500 PRINT:PRINT
510 PRINT TAB(6)
    "WHAT IS THE NAME OF THE"
520 PRINT TAB(6):INPUT
    "TRANSACTION FILE";N$
530 PRINT:PRINT
540 PRINT TAB(6)
    "POSITION TAPE AT START OF"
550 PRINT TAB(6)
    "TRANSACTION FILE, THEN PRESS"
560 PRINT TAB(6)"ANY KEY."
570 GET A$:IF A$="" THEN 570:REM
    NO SPACE BETWEEN INVERTED COMMAS
580 PRINT CL$:PRINT:PRINT
590 OPEN 1,1,0,N$
600 FOR K=1 TO 100
```

P23 Stock File Update and Report

```
610 INPUT# 1,T%(K,1)
620 INPUT# 1,T%(K,2)
630 INPUT# 1,T%(K,3)
640 NEXT:CLOSE 1
650 REM*****************************
660 PRINT CL$:PRINT:PRINT
670 PRINT TAB(8)CHR$(18)
    " STOP CASSETTE RECORDER "
680 PRINT:PRINT
690 PRINT TAB(11)"UPDATING COMMENCING"
700 FOR J=1 TO 100
710 K=T%(J,1)
720 IF T%(J,2)=1 THEN
    N%(K,1)=N%(K,1)-T%(J,3)
730 IF T%(J,2)=2 THEN
    N%(K,1)=N%(K,1)+T%(J,3)
740 PRINT".";
750 NEXT
760 PRINT:PRINT
770 PRINT TAB(12)"UPDATING COMPLETE"
780 REM*****************************
790 PRINT:PRINT
800 PRINT TAB(4)
    "WHAT IS THE NAME OF THE NEW STOCK"
810 PRINT TAB(4):INPUT"FILE";N$
820 PRINT CL$:PRINT:PRINT
830 PRINT TAB(4)
    "WIND TAPE TO WHERE YOU WISH TO"
840 PRINT TAB(4)
    "SAVE THE NEW STOCK FILE, THEN"
850 PRINT TAB(4)"PRESS ANY KEY."
860 REM*****************************
870 GET A$:IF A$="" THEN 870:REM
    NO SPACE BETWEEN INVERTED COMMAS
880 PRINT CL$:PRINT:PRINT TAB(4)
890 R$=CHR$(13):REM RETURN KEY
900 OPEN 1,1,1,N$
910 FOR K=1 TO 10
920 PRINT# 1,D$(K) R$ N%(K,1) R$ N%(K,2)
    R$ N%(K,3)
930 NEXT
940 CLOSE 1
950 REM*****************************
960 PRINT CL$:PRINT:PRINT
970 PRINT TAB(8)CHR$(18)
    " STOP CASSETTE RECORDER "
980 PRINT:PRINT
```

```
990 PRINT TAB(4)
    "REWIND THE TAPE TO THE START OF"
1000 PRINT TAB(4)
    "THE NEW STOCK FILE THEN PRESS"
1010 PRINT TAB(4)"ANY KEY."
1020 GET A$:IF A$="" THEN 1020:REM
    NO SPACE BETWEEN INVERTED COMMAS
1030 PRINT CL$:PRINT:PRINT
1040 REM***************************
1050 OPEN 1,1,0,N$
1060 FOR K=1 TO 10
1070 INPUT# 1,E$(K)
1080 INPUT# 1,J%(K,1)
1090 INPUT# 1,J%(K,2)
1100 INPUT# 1,J%(K,3)
1110 NEXT
1120 CLOSE 1
1130 REM***************************
1140 PRINT CL$:PRINT:PRINT
1150 PRINT TAB(8)CHR$(18)
    " STOP CASSETTE RECORDER "
1170 F=0
1180 FOR K=1 TO 10
1190 IF D$(K)<>E$(K) THEN F=1:K=10
1200 IF N%(K,1)<>J%(K,1) THEN F=1:K=10
1210 IF N%(K,2)<>J%(K,2) THEN F=1:K=10
1220 IF N%(K,3)<>J%(K,3) THEN F=1:K=10
1230 NEXT:PRINT:PRINT
1240 REM***************************
1250 IF F=0 THEN 1330:REM CHECK OK
1260 PRINT TAB(8)
    "VERIFICATION CHECK FAILED"
1270 PRINT:PRINT
1280 PRINT TAB(4)
    "REWIND TAPE TO THE START OF THE"
1290 PRINT TAB(4)
    "NEW STOCK FILE THEN PRESS ANY"
1300 PRINT TAB(4)"KEY."
1310 GOTO 870
1320 REM***************************
1330 PRINT TAB(8)
    "VERIFICATION CHECK PASSED"
1340 PRINT:PRINT
1350 PRINT TAB(4)
    "SELECT THE OUTPUT DEVICE FOR"
1360 PRINT TAB(4)
    "THE REORDER REPORT BY PRESSING:"
```

```
1370 PRINT
1380 PRINT TAB(10)CHR$(18)" KEY F1 "
     CHR$(146)" - SCREEN"
1390 PRINT
1400 PRINT TAB(10)CHR$(18)" KEY F3 "
     CHR$(146)" - PRINTER"
1410 GET A$:IF A$="" THEN 1410:REM
     NO SPACE BETWEEN INVERTED COMMAS
1420 IF ASC(A$)<133 OR ASC (A$)>134
     THEN 1410
1430 IF ASC(A$)=134 THEN 1760
1440 REM****************************
1450 FOR K=1 TO 10
1460 PRINT CL$:PRINT
1470 IF N%(K,1)>N%(K,2) THEN 1660
1480 PRINT TAB(8)CHR$(18)
     " ITEMS TO BE REORDERED "
1490 PRINT:PRINT
1500 PRINT TAB(14)"STOCK ITEM";K
1510 PRINT
1520 R%=(40-LEN(D$(K)))/2
1530 PRINT TAB(R%)D$(K)
1540 PRINT:PRINT
1550 PRINT TAB(10)"NUMBER IN STOCK";
     N%(K,1)
1560 PRINT
1570 PRINT TAB(10)" REORDER LEVEL ";
     N%(K,2)
1580 PRINT
1590 PRINT TAB(10)"REORDER QUANTITY";
     N%(K,3)
1600 PRINT:PRINT
1610 PRINT TAB(4)
     "NEGATIVE NUMBERS IN STOCK MEAN"
1620 PRINT TAB(4)
     "CUSTOMERS WAITING FOR GOODS."
1630 PRINT:PRINT
1640 PRINT TAB(4)CHR$(18)
     " PRESS ANY KEY FOR NEXT ITEM "
1650 GET A$:IF A$="" THEN 1650:REM
     NO SPACE BETWEEN INVERTED COMMAS
1660 NEXT
1670 PRINT CL$:PRINT:PRINT
1680 PRINT TAB(7)
     "NO FURTHER ITEMS ARE TO BE"
1690 PRINT TAB(7)"REORDERED."
1700 PRINT:PRINT
```

```
1710 PRINT TAB(12)"HAVE A NICE DAY."
1720 PRINT:PRINT
1730 PRINT TAB(17)CHR$(18)" BYE! "
1740 END
1750 REM****************************
1760 OPEN 3,4
1770 PRINT# 3,SPC(8)
     "ITEMS TO BE REORDERED"
1780 FOR K=1 TO 10
1790 PRINT# 3,:PRINT# 3,
1800 IF N%(K,1)>N%(K,2) THEN 1920
1810 PRINT# 3,SPC(14)"STOCK ITEM";K
1820 PRINT# 3,
1830 R%=(40-LEN(D$(K)))/2
1840 PRINT#3,SPC(R%)D$(K)
1850 PRINT# 3,
1860 PRINT# 3,SPC(10)"NUMBER IN STOCK";
     N%(K,1)
1870 PRINT# 3,SPC(10)" REORDER LEVEL ";
     N%(K,2)
1880 PRINT# 3,SPC(10)"REORDER QUANTITY";
     N%(K,3)
1900 PRINT# 3,
1910 PRINT# 3,
1920 NEXT
1930 PRINT# 3,
1940 PRINT# 3,
1950 PRINT# 3,
1960 PRINT# 3,SPC(4)
     "NEGATIVE NUMBERS IN STOCK MEAN"
1970 PRINT# 3,SPC(4)
     "CUSTOMERS WAITING FOR GOODS."
1980 PRINT# 3,
1990 PRINT# 3,
2000 PRINT# 3,SPC(12)"HAVE A NICE DAY."
2010 PRINT# 3,
2020 PRINT# 3,SPC(18)"BYE!"
2030 CLOSE 3
2040 END
2050 REM****************************
2060 REM****************************
```

P24 Tax Calculator

This program calculates the local or state tax on an item and tells you both the tax and the total cost.

The results of the calculation are rounded to the nearest cent.

If an amount ends in 10, 20, etc cents the last zero is not printed - e.g. a cost of $4.50 is printed 4.5. If this causes concern the solution is to change values from numbers to the equivalent string variables. The final zero may then be added if required. This is left as an exercise for the reader.

COMMANDS

Key in the program and RUN.

Enter data as required.

```
10 REM TAX CALCULATOR
20 REM **************
30 REM
100 PRINT CHR$(147):REM CLEAR SCREEN
110 POKE 53280,12:REM GRAY BORDER
120 POKE 53281,12:REM GRAY SCREEN
130 PRINT CHR$(31):REM BLUE INK
140 PRINT TAB(10)"$$$$$$$$$$$$$$$$$$"
150 PRINT TAB(10)"                  "
160 PRINT TAB(10)"   TAX CALCULATOR "
170 PRINT TAB(10)"                  "
180 PRINT TAB(10)"$$$$$$$$$$$$$$$$$$"
190 PRINT:PRINT
200 PRINT TAB(4)
    "THIS PROGRAM CAN BE USED TO"
210 PRINT TAB(4)
    "CALCULATE THE LOCAL OR STATE TAX"
220 PRINT TAB(4)
    "ON AN ITEM. IN THE UK IT CAN BE"
230 PRINT TAB(4)
    "USED TO HELP MAKE UP VAT RETURNS."
```

```
240 PRINT:PRINT
250 PRINT TAB(4)
    "WHAT IS THE CURRENT RATE (%)";
260 INPUT TAX
270 TAX=TAX/100
280 REM**************************
290 REM**************************
300 PRINT CHR$(147):REM CLEAR SCREEN
310 PRINT:PRINT:PRINT
320 DEF FNA(X)=INT(X*100+.5)/100
330 REM NUMBERS CORRECT TO 2 PLACES
        AFTER THE DECIMAL POINT
340 INPUT"COST OF ITEM =";CST
350 PRINT:PRINT
360 PRINT"TAX           =";FNA(CST*TAX)
370 PRINT:PRINT
380 PRINT"TOTAL COST    =";
    FNA(CST*(1+TAX))
390 PRINT:PRINT:PRINT
400 INPUT"ANOTHER RUN";Y$
410 IF ASC(Y$)=89 THEN 300
420 END
```

P25 True Rate of Interest

This program uses a simplistic approach to calculating the true rate of interest on a loan. It is assumed that repayments are on a monthly basis.

To calculate the true rate of interest we compute the amount of dollar-months that have been borrowed. (One dollar-month is equivalent to borrowing one dollar for one month, or fifty cents for two months.) We now calculate as a percentage the ratio of the total interest paid to the total number of dollar-months. We then multiply this number by twelve.

As no monetary units are entered, this program is not limited to dollars and will work for any currency.

COMMANDS

Key in the program and RUN.

Follow the instructions.

```
10 REM TRUE RATE OF INTEREST
20 REM ********************
30 REM
100 CL$=CHR$(147):REM TO CLEAR SCREEN
110 POKE 53280,9:REM BROWN BORDER
120 POKE 53281,1:REM WHITE SCREEN
130 PRINT CHR$(31):REM BLUE INK
140 PRINT CL$
150 PRINT:PRINT
160 PRINT TAB(9)"TRUE RATE OF INTEREST"
170 PRINT TAB(9)"====================="
180 PRINT:PRINT
190 PRINT TAB(4)
    "THIS PROGRAM COMPUTES THE TRUE"
200 PRINT TAB(4)
    "RATE OF INTEREST ON A LOAN"
210 PRINT TAB(4)
    "TRANSACTION. THE PROGRAM REQUIRES"
220 PRINT TAB(4)
    "THE AMOUNT BORROWED, THE ANNUAL"
```

```
230 PRINT TAB(4)
    "INTEREST RATE AND THE NUMBER OF"
240 PRINT TAB(4)
    "MONTHS OVER WHICH THE LOAN IS"
250 PRINT TAB(4)"TAKEN."
260 PRINT:PRINT:PRINT
270 PRINT TAB(7)CHR$(18)
    " PRESS ANY KEY TO CONTINUE "
280 GET A$:IF A$="" THEN 280:REM
    NO SPACE BETWEEN INVERTED COMMAS
300 REM******************************
310 PRINT CL$:PRINT:PRINT
320 PRINT TAB(4):INPUT
    "AMOUNT BORROWED";AMT
330 PRINT
340 PRINT TAB(4):INPUT
    "ANNUAL INTEREST RATE (%)";RT
350 PRINT
360 PRINT TAB(4):INPUT
    "NUMBER OF MONTHS";NM
370 PRINT:PRINT
380 IT=AMT*RT*NM/1200:REM TOTAL INTEREST
390 PB=(AMT+IT)/NM:REM PAYBACK PER MONTH
400 FOR J=0 TO NM-1
410 BR=BR+AMT-PB*J
420 NEXT
430 REM BR=TOTAL DOLLAR-MONTHS BORROWED
440 TRU=1200*IT/BR
450 TRU=INT(TRU*100+.5)/100
460 PRINT TAB(4)
    "TRUE RATE OF INTEREST IS";TRU;"%"
470 PRINT TAB(4)
    "================================"
480 PRINT:PRINT:PRINT
490 END
```

P26 Mailing List Creation

This program allows you to create a mailing list of up to fifty names and addresses and to save this information on cassette tape.

It could be extended to take more names and addresses and modified to use floppy disk storage.

COMMANDS

Key in the program and RUN.

Ensure you have a blank tape handy.

Follow the instructions.

```
10 REM MAILING LIST CREATION
20 REM ********************
30 REM
100 CL$=CHR$(147):REM TO CLEAR SCREEN
110 POKE 53280,9:REM BROWN BORDER
120 POKE 53281,1:REM WHITE SCREEN
130 PRINT CHR$(31):REM BLUE INK
140 PRINT CL$
150 PRINT:PRINT
160 PRINT TAB(9)"MAILING LIST CREATION"
170 PRINT TAB(9)"====================="
180 PRINT:PRINT
190 PRINT TAB(4)
    "THIS PROGRAM ALLOWS YOU TO TYPE"
200 PRINT TAB(4)
    "IN NAMES AND ADDRESSES AND TO"
210 PRINT TAB(4)
    "SAVE THESE ON TAPE AS A MAILING"
220 PRINT TAB(4)"LIST FILE."
230 PRINT
240 PRINT TAB(4)
    "YOU ARE ALLOWED 50 NAMES AND"
250 PRINT TAB(4)
    "ADDRESSES. EACH ADDRESS SHOULD BE"
```

```
260 PRINT TAB(4)
    "LIMITED TO FOUR LINES INCLUDING"
270 PRINT TAB(4)"THE POST CODE."
280 PRINT
290 PRINT TAB(4)
    "PLEASE ENTER DATA WHEN PROMPTED"
300 PRINT:PRINT
310 PRINT TAB(6)CHR$(18);
    " PRESS ANY KEY TO CONTINUE "
320 GET A$:IF A$="" THEN 320
330 REM NO SPACE BETWEEN INVERTED COMMAS
340 REM***************************
350 DIM NM$(49):DIM AD$(49,3):
    DIM AN$(49):DIM AA$(49,3)
360 FOR K=0 TO 49
370 PRINT CL$:PRINT:PRINT
380 FOR J=0 TO 3:AD$(K,J)="...":NEXT:
    REM PREVENT EMPTY STRINGS
390 PRINT TAB(6)CHR$(18)
    " ENTER END AS NAME TO FINISH "
400 PRINT
410 PRINT TAB(4):INPUT"NAME";NM$(K):IF
    NM$(K)="" THEN 410
420 IF NM$(K)="END" THEN K=49:GOTO 480
430 PRINT TAB(4)"ADDRESS:"
440 PRINT TAB(4):INPUT"LINE 1";AD$(K,0)
450 PRINT TAB(4):INPUT"LINE 2";AD$(K,1)
460 PRINT TAB(4):INPUT"LINE 3";AD$(K,2)
470 PRINT TAB(4):INPUT"POST CODE";
    AD$(K,3)
480 NEXT
490 REM***************************
500 PRINT CL$:PRINT:PRINT
510 PRINT TAB(4)
    "ENSURE THERE IS A TAPE IN THE"
520 PRINT TAB(4)
    "CASSETTE RECORDER READY FOR SAVING"
530 PRINT:PRINT
540 PRINT TAB(4)
    "WHAT IS THE NAME OF THE FILE"
550 PRINT TAB(4):INPUT N$
560 REM***************************
570 PRINT:PRINT TAB(4);:
    REM FILE SAVE STARTS HERE
580 OPEN 1,1,1,N$
590 R$=CHR$(13):REM RETURN KEY
600 FOR K=0 TO 49
```

P26 Mailing List Creation

```
610 PRINT# 1,NM$(K)
620 IF NM$(K)="END" THEN K=49:GOTO 640
630 FOR J=0 TO 3:PRINT# 1,AD$(K,J) R$:
    NEXT
640 NEXT:CLOSE 1
650 REM****************************
660 PRINT CL$
670 PRINT:PRINT
680 PRINT TAB(4)
    "REWIND CASSETTE RECORDER TO START"
690 PRINT TAB(4)"OF FILE"
700 PRINT:PRINT
710 PRINT TAB(4)
    "PRESS ANY KEY WHEN READY"
720 GET A$:IF A$="" THEN 720
730 REM NO SPACE BETWEEN INVERTED COMMAS
740 PRINT:PRINT
750 OPEN 1,1,0,N$
760 FOR K=0 TO 49
770 INPUT# 1,AN$(K)
780 IF AN$(K)="END" THEN K=49:GOTO 810
790 FOR J=0 TO 3:INPUT# 1,AA$(K,J)
800 NEXT
810 NEXT:CLOSE 1
820 PRINT CL$:PRINT:PRINT
830 FG=0:FOR K=0 TO 49
840 IF NM$(K)="END" THEN K=49:GOTO 880
850 IF NM$(K)<>AN$(K) THEN K=49:FG=1
860 FOR J=0 TO 3:IF AD$(K,J)<>AA$(K,J)
    THEN J=3:K=49:FG=1
870 NEXT
880 NEXT:IF FG=1 THEN 940
890 PRINT TAB(6)CHR$(18);
    " VERIFICATION CHECK PASSED "
900 PRINT:PRINT
910 PRINT TAB(6)"STOP CASSETTE RECORDER"
920 END
930 REM****************************
940 PRINT TAB(6)CHR$(18);
    " VERIFICATION CHECK FAILED "
950 PRINT:PRINT
960 PRINT TAB(4)
    "REWIND TAPE TO INITIAL POSITION."
970 PRINT:PRINT
980 PRINT TAB(4)
    "PRESS ANY KEY WHEN READY."
```

```
990 GET A$:IF A$="" THEN 990:
    REM NO SPACE
1000 GOTO 570
1010 REM***************************
1020 REM***************************
```

P27 Mailing List Maintenance

This program lets you amend a previously created mailing list and save the new list on cassette tape. It also lets you print the names and addresses on to labels.

The program could be extended to deal with more than fifty names and addresses and could be modified to use floppy disk storage. A useful additional feature would be a search facility which would allow you to specify that only names starting with (say) a particular letter would be printed out. Another useful feature would be the facility to display a telephone dialing code on the screen when a name is typed in.

If labels are to be printed a printer is required. As it stands the program will work with a Commodore MPS801 and most other printers. If your printer does not have automatic line feed on carriage return then change the printer control instructions to use a file number greater than 128.

COMMANDS

Key in the program and RUN.

Ensure you have your mailing list tape and a blank tape ready.

Adjust lines 4080, 4120 and 4140 if necessary to get the optimum print positioning on your labels.

```
10 REM MAILING LIST MAINTENANCE
20 REM ************************
30 REM
100 CL$=CHR$(147):REM TO CLEAR SCREEN
110 POKE 53280,9:REM BROWN BORDER
120 POKE 53281,1:REM WHITE SCREEN
130 PRINT CHR$(31):REM BLUE INK
140 PRINT CL$
150 PRINT:PRINT

160 PRINT TAB(8)
    "MAILING LIST MAINTENANCE"
```

```
170 PRINT TAB(8)
    "========================"
180 PRINT CHR$(31):REM BLUE INK
190 PRINT TAB(4)
    "THIS PROGRAM LETS YOU ADD NAMES"
200 PRINT TAB(4)
    "AND ADDRESSES TO, OR DELETE NAMES"
210 PRINT TAB(4)
    "AND ADDRESSES FROM A MAILING LIST"
220 PRINT TAB(4)
    "WHICH YOU HAVE PREVIOUSLY CREATED"
230 PRINT TAB(4)
    "AND SAVED ON CASSETTE TAPE."
240 PRINT
250 PRINT TAB(4)
    "IT ALSO LETS YOU PRINT THE LIST"
260 PRINT TAB(4)
    "ON TO ADDRESS LABELS."
270 PRINT
280 PRINT TAB(4)
    "POSITION THE TAPE AT THE START OF"
290 PRINT TAB(4)
    "THE REQUIRED MAILING LIST FILE,"
300 PRINT TAB(4)
    "THEN PRESS ANY KEY."
310 GET A$:IF A$="" THEN 310:REM
    NO SPACE BETWEEN INVERTED COMMAS
320 REM****************************
330 DIM NM$(49):DIM AD$(49,3):
    DIM AN$(49):DIM AA$(49,3)
340 PRINT CL$:PRINT:PRINT
350 PRINT TAB(4):INPUT
    "WHAT IS THE FILENAME";N$
360 PRINT:PRINT
370 OPEN 1,1,0,N$
380 FOR K=0 TO 49
390 INPUT# 1,NM$(K)
400 IF NM$(K)="END" THEN K=49:GOTO 430
410 FOR J=0 TO 3:INPUT# 1,AD$(K,J)
420 NEXT
430 NEXT:CLOSE 1
440 PRINT CL$:PRINT:PRINT
450 PRINT TAB(8)CHR$(18)
    " STOP CASSETTE RECORDER "
460 PRINT:PRINT
470 PRINT TAB(4)
    "SELECT THE OPERATION REQUIRED BY"
```

```
480 PRINT TAB(4)"PRESSING:"
490 PRINT
500 PRINT TAB(6)CHR$(18)" KEY F1 "
    CHR$(146)" - ADD ADDRESSES"
510 PRINT
520 PRINT TAB(6)CHR$(18)" KEY F3 "
    CHR$(146)" - REMOVE ADDRESSES"
530 PRINT
540 PRINT TAB(6)CHR$(18)" KEY F5 "
    CHR$(146)" - SAVE NEW MAIL LIST"
550 PRINT
560 PRINT TAB(6)CHR$(18)" KEY F7 "
    CHR$(146)" - PRINT LABELS"
570 PRINT:PRINT
580 PRINT TAB(6)CHR$(18)
    " ANY OTHER KEY ENDS PROGRAM "
590 GET A$:IF A$="" THEN 590:REM
    NO SPACE BETWEEN INVERTED COMMAS
600 IF ASC(A$)<133 OR ASC(A$)>136
    THEN END
610 SL=ASC(A$)-132
620 ON SL GOSUB 1000,2000,3000,4000
630 IF SL=4 THEN 440
640 PRINT CL$:GOTO 460
650 REM***************************
660 REM***************************
900 REM
910 REM         ***************
920 REM         *
930 REM         * SUBROUTINES
940 REM         *
950 REM         ***************
960 REM
970 REM***************************
980 REM***************************
1000 REM ADD AN ADDRESS
1010 T=50
1020 FOR K=0 TO 49:IF NM$(K)="END"
     THEN T=K:K=49
1030 NEXT
1040 PRINT CL$:PRINT:PRINT
1050 IF T=50 THEN PRINT TAB(11)
     "MAILING LIST FULL":GOTO 1270
1060 FOR K=T TO 49
1070 PRINT CL$:PRINT:PRINT
1080 PRINT TAB(8)CHR$(18)
     " ENTERING NEW INFORMATION "
```

```
1090 PRINT:PRINT:PRINT TAB(6)CHR$(18)
     " ENTER END AS NAME TO FINISH "
1100 PRINT:PRINT:NM$(K)=""
1110 PRINT TAB(4):INPUT"NAME";NM$(K):
     IF NM$(K)="" THEN 1110
1120 IF NM$(K)="END" THEN K=49:
     GOTO 1180
1130 PRINT TAB(4)"ADDRESS:"
1140 AD$(K,0)="...":PRINT TAB(4):INPUT
     "LINE 1";AD$(K,0)
1150 AD$(K,1)="...":PRINT TAB(4):INPUT
     "LINE 2";AD$(K,1)
1160 AD$(K,2)="...":PRINT TAB(4):INPUT
     "LINE 3";AD$(K,2)
1170 AD$(K,3)="...":PRINT TAB(4):INPUT
     "POST CODE";AD$(K,3)
1180 NEXT
1190 REM***************************
1200 PRINT CL$:PRINT:PRINT
1210 PRINT TAB(6)
     "THE NEW INFORMATION HAS BEEN"
1220 PRINT TAB(6)
     "ADDED TO THE MAILING LIST."
1230 PRINT
1240 PRINT TAB(6)
     "REMEMBER YOU STILL HAVE TO"
1250 PRINT TAB(6)
     "SAVE THE NEW LIST IF YOU"
1260 PRINT TAB(6)
     "HAVE FINISHED UPDATING IT."
1270 PRINT:PRINT
1280 PRINT TAB(6)CHR$(18)
     " PRESS ANY KEY FOR MAIN MENU "
1290 GET B$:IF B$="" THEN 1290:REM
     NO SPACE BETWEEN INVERTED COMMAS
1300 GET B$:IF B$<>"" THEN 1300:REM
     NO SPACE BETWEEN INVERTED COMMAS
1310 REM FLUSH KEYBOARD BUFFER
1320 RETURN
1330 REM***************************
1340 REM***************************
2000 REM REMOVE ADDRESS
2010 PRINT CL$:PRINT:PRINT
2020 PRINT TAB(9)CHR$(18)
     " DELETING INFORMATION "
2030 PRINT:PRINT
```

P27 Mailing List Maintenance

```
2040 PRINT TAB(4)
     "PLEASE ENTER THE EXACT NAME"
2050 PRINT TAB(4)
     "CORRESPONDING TO THE ENTRY YOU"
2060 PRINT TAB(4)
     "WISH TO DELETE. IF THERE ARE TWO"
2070 PRINT TAB(4)
     "ADDRESSES CORRESPONDING TO THE"
2080 PRINT TAB(4)
     "SAME NAME THE FIRST OF THESE"
2090 PRINT TAB(4)"WILL BE DELETED."
2100 PRINT:PRINT:PRINT TAB(4):INPUT
     "NAME";NA$
2110 T=50:R=50
2120 FOR K=0 TO 49
2130 IF NM$(K)=NA$ AND R=50 THEN R=K
2140 IF NM$(K)="END" THEN T=K:K=49
2150 NEXT
2160 PRINT CL$:PRINT:PRINT
2170 IF R=50 THEN PRINT TAB(13)
     "NAME NOT FOUND":GOTO 2260
2180 PRINT TAB(16)"UPDATING":PRINT
2190 FOR K=R TO T-2
2200 NM$(K)=NM$(K+1)
2210 FOR J=0 TO 3:AD$(K,J)=AD$(K+1,J)
2220 NEXT
2230 PRINT".";
2240 NEXT
2250 NM$(T-1)="END"
2260 PRINT:PRINT
2270 Y$="N":PRINT TAB(9):INPUT
     "ANOTHER DELETION (Y/N)";Y$
2280 IF ASC(Y$)=89 THEN 2010
2290 REM*************************
2300 PRINT CL$:PRINT:PRINT
2310 PRINT TAB(6)
     "THE REQUIRED DELETIONS HAVE"
2320 PRINT TAB(6)"BEEN MADE."
2330 PRINT
2340 PRINT TAB(6)
     "REMEMBER YOU STILL HAVE TO"
2350 PRINT TAB(6)
     "SAVE THE NEW LIST IF YOU"
2360 PRINT TAB(6)
     "HAVE FINISHED UPDATING IT."
2370 PRINT:PRINT
```

```
2380 PRINT TAB(6)CHR$(18)
     " PRESS ANY KEY FOR MAIN MENU "
2390 GET B$:IF B$="" THEN 2390:REM
     NO SPACE BETWEEN INVERTED COMMAS
2400 GET B$:IF B$<>"" THEN 2400:REM
     NO SPACE BETWEEN INVERTED COMMAS
2410 REM FLUSH KEYBOARD BUFFER
2420 RETURN
2430 REM***************************
2440 REM***************************
3000 REM SAVE NEW MAILING LIST
3010 PRINT CL$:PRINT:PRINT
3020 PRINT TAB(4)
     "POSITION THE CASSETTE TAPE TO"
3030 PRINT TAB(4)
     "WHERE YOU WISH TO SAVE THE NEW"
3040 PRINT TAB(4)"FILE."
3050 PRINT:PRINT
3060 PRINT TAB(4):INPUT
     "WHAT IS THE FILENAME";N$
3070 REM***************************
3080 PRINT:PRINT TAB(4);:
     REM FILE SAVE STARTS HERE
3090 OPEN 1,1,1,N$
3100 R$=CHR$(13):REM RETURN KEY
3110 FOR K=0 TO 49
3120 PRINT# 1,NM$(K)
3130 IF NM$(K)="END" THEN K=49:
     GOTO 3150
3140 FOR J=0 TO 3:PRINT# 1,AD$(K,J):NEXT
3150 NEXT:CLOSE 1
3160 REM***************************
3170 PRINT CL$
3180 PRINT:PRINT
3190 PRINT TAB(4)
     "REWIND CASSETTE RECORDER TO START"
3200 PRINT TAB(4)
     "OF FILE, THEN PRESS ANY KEY."
3210 PRINT:PRINT
3230 GET A$:IF A$="" THEN 3230
3240 REM NO SPACE BETWEEN COMMAS
3250 PRINT:PRINT
3260 OPEN 1,1,0,N$
3270 FOR K=0 TO 49
3280 INPUT# 1,AN$(K)
3290 IF AN$(K)="END" THEN K=49:
     GOTO 3320
```

```
3300 FOR J=0 TO 3:INPUT# 1,AA$(K,J)
3310 NEXT
3320 NEXT:CLOSE 1:F=0
3330 PRINT CL$:PRINT:PRINT
3340 FOR K=0 TO 49
3350 IF NM$(K)="END" THEN K=49:
     GOTO 3390
3360 IF NM$(K)<>AN$(K) THEN K=49:F=1
3370 FOR J=0 TO 3:IF AD$(K,J)<>AA$(K,J)
     THEN J=3:K=49:F=1
3380 NEXT
3390 NEXT:IF F=0 THEN 3500:REM CHECK OK
3400 REM**************************
3410 REM CHECK FAILED
3420 PRINT TAB(6)CHR$(18);
     " VERIFICATION CHECK FAILED "
3430 PRINT:PRINT
3440 PRINT TAB(4)
     "REWIND TAPE TO INITIAL POSITION."
3450 PRINT:PRINT
3460 PRINT TAB(4)
     "PRESS ANY KEY WHEN READY."
3470 GET A$:IF A$="" THEN 3470:
     REM NO SPACE
3480 PRINT:PRINT:GOTO 3080:
     REM SAVE FILE AGAIN
3490 REM**************************
3500 REM CHECK OK
3510 PRINT TAB(6)CHR$(18);
     " VERIFICATION CHECK PASSED "
3520 PRINT
3530 PRINT
3540 PRINT TAB(9)
     "STOP CASSETTE RECORDER"
3550 PRINT:PRINT
3560 PRINT TAB(5)CHR$(18)
     " PRESS ANY KEY FOR MAIN MENU "
3570 GET B$:IF B$="" THEN 3570:REM
     NO SPACE BETWEEN INVERTED COMMAS
3580 GET B$:IF B$<>"" THEN 3580:REM
     NO SPACE BETWEEN INVERTED COMMAS
3590 REM FLUSH KEYBOARD BUFFER
3600 RETURN
3610 REM**************************
3620 REM**************************
4000 REM PRINT LABELS
4010 PRINT CL$:PRINT:PRINT
```

```
4020 PRINT TAB(7)
     "ENSURE LABELS ARE CORRECTLY"
4030 PRINT TAB(7)
     "ALIGNED AND PRINTER IS ON."
4040 PRINT:PRINT
4050 PRINT TAB(7)CHR$(18)
     " PRESS ANY KEY WHEN READY "
4060 GET A$:IF A$="" THEN 4060:REM
     NO SPACE BETWEEN INVERTED COMMAS
4070 OPEN 3,4
4080 FOR K=0 TO 3:PRINT# 3,:NEXT
4090 REM ADJUST LINE 4080 TO POSITION
     PRINT ON LABELS
4100 FOR K=0 TO 49
4110 IF NM$(K)="END" THEN K=49:
     GOTO 4150
4120 SP=10:PRINT# 3,SPC(SP)NM$(K):REM
     ADJUST SP TO GET CORRECT MARGIN
4130 FOR J=0 TO 3:PRINT# 3,SPC(SP)
     AD$(K,J):NEXT
4140 FOR J=0 TO 3:PRINT# 3,:NEXT:REM
     ADJUST TO KEEP LABELS ALIGNED
4150 NEXT
4160 CLOSE 3
4170 PRINT:PRINT
4180 PRINT TAB(13)"PRINT COMPLETE"
4190 PRINT:PRINT
4200 PRINT TAB(6)CHR$(18)
     " PRESS ANY KEY FOR MAIN MENU "
4210 GET B$:IF B$="" THEN 4210:REM
     NO SPACE BETWEEN INVERTED COMMAS
4220 GET B$:IF B$<>"" THEN 4220:REM
     NO SPACE BETWEEN INVERTED COMMAS
4230 REM FLUSH KEYBOARD BUFFER
4240 RETURN
4250 REM****************************
4260 REM****************************
```

Point of Sale System

This is our example of a suite of programs which should give you an idea of how to develop a more commercial set of programs. The programs as presented are disk based, since this is the only feasible way for a commercial set of programs to work. However if you only have a tape based system you can still with care use these programs. You will have to make the following changes:

Where you see a command of the form

```
LOAD "filename",8
```

replace it with the set of commands

```
        PRINT "WIND TAPE TO POSITION xx"
100 GET A$: IF A$="" THEN GOTO 100
        LOAD "filename".
```

Position xx is where the file is held on the cassette.

Let's get back to our suite of programs. These programs are designed to turn the Commodore-64 into a point of sale machine. The suite consists of five programs.

1. PRICELIST MENU : This is the main menu of the system. This program controls which subsidiary program is called in. All programs return to this program when finished.

2. MAINTENANCE: This program allows the user to maintain pricing information.

3. POS: This is the point of sale program and is used to produce the price that the customer pays

4. PRINT: This is the main report program in the system.

5. FDUMP: This program can be used to dump the contents of any file to either the screen or the printer. It can be useful outside this system.

P28   Price List — Main Menu Program

This is the main control program of the system.

COMMANDS

Please ensure that the whole system is loaded before running this program.

Key in program.
Save the program to your backing storage device.
Type RUN.
Select from the menu.

(Note: make amendments if you are using tape.)

```
10 REM PRICE LIST SUITE
20 REM PROGRAM - MAIN MENU
30 POKE53280,0:POKE53281,0
40 PRINT "[CS RON ]                    50 PRINT "[RON ]
             PRICE LIST MENU                [ROF ]";
60 PRINT "[RON ]                       70 PRINT:PRINT
80 PRINT "[RON ]    1.  CHANGE PRICE LIST90 PRINT
100 PRINT "[RON ]   2.  USE CBM-64 AS POS TERMINAL
    [ROF ]"
110 PRINT
120 PRINT "[RON ]   3.  PRINT OUT PRICE LIST
    [ROF ]"
125 PRINT "[RON ]   4.  DUMP A DISK FILE TO SCREEN
    [ROF ]";
126 PRINT "[RON ]            OR PRINTER         130 PRINT "[RON ]
    5.  QUIT THE PROGRAM140 PRINT "[CD CD ]SELECT NUMBER
FOR FUNCTION FROM MENU"
150 GET A$:IF A$<>"" THEN GOTO 150
160 GET A$:IF A$="" THEN GOTO 160
170 A=VAL(A$)
```

P28 Price List Menu

```
190 IF A<>1 AND A<>2 AND A<>3 AND A<>4 AND A<>5 THEN
    GOTO 150
200 PRINT A
210 IF A=1 THEN PRINT "ABOUT TO LOAD PRICE LIST
    MAINTENANCE"
220 IF A=2 THEN PRINT "ABOUT TO USE CBM AS POS"
230 IF A=3 THEN PRINT "ABOUT TO LOAD PRINT PROGRAM"
240 IF A=4 THEN PRINT "ABOUT TO LOAD DUMP PROGRAM"
245 IF A=5 THEN PRINT "ABOUT TO QUIT PROGRAM"
250 PRINT "OK? ENTER Y OR N"
260 GET A$:IF A$<>"" THEN GOTO 260
270 GET A$:IF A$="" THEN GOTO 270
280 IF A$="N" THEN RUN
290 IF A=1 THEN LOAD "MAINT",8
300 IF A=2 THEN LOAD "POS",8
310 IF A=3 THEN LOAD "PRINT",8
320 IF A=4 THEN LOAD"FDUMP",8
```

P29   MAINT –
Price List Maintenance Program

This program can be used to:

    Enter a new price list or
    Change the values on a price list.

It allows the user to keep his price lists up to date.

COMMANDS

Key in the program and save to disk or tape.
Call the program from the main menu.
Follow instructions.

```
10 REM PRICE LIST SUITE
20 REM PROGRAM - MAINTENANCE OF PRICE LIST
30 POKE53280,0:POKE53281,0
40 PRINT "[CS CD CD RON ]
        [ROF ]";
50 PRINT "[RON ]          PRICE LIST MENU
[ROF ]";
60 PRINT "[RON ]
[ROF ]"
70 PRINT:PRINT:PRINT
80 PRINT "[RON ]    1. ENTER A NEW PRICE LIST
[ROF ]"
90 PRINT
100 PRINT "[RON ]    2. CHANGE THE VALUES ON A PRICE LIST[ROF ]"
110 PRINT
120 PRINT "[RON ]    3. GO BACK TO MAIN MENU
[ROF ]"
130 PRINT
140 PRINT "ENTER NUMBER CORRESPONDING TO FUNCTION"
150 GET A$:IF A$="" THEN GOTO 150
160 A=VAL(A$)
170 IF A<>1 AND A<>2 AND A<>3 THEN GOTO 150
180 IF A=1 THEN GOSUB 1000
190 IF A=2 THEN GOSUB 2000
200 IF A=3 THEN LOAD "PRICELIST",8
210 GOTO 10
990 REM ROUTINE TO SET UP NEW PRICE LIST
```

P29 Price List Maintenance

```
1000 PRINT "[CS RON ]            NEW PRICE LIST
     [ROF ]"
1010 PRINT:PRINT:PRINT
1020 PRINT "WHAT IS THE NAME OF THE PRICE LIST":INPUT N$
1030 PRINT "THE FORMAT OF THE PRICE LIST IS AS"
1040 PRINT "FOLLOWS:"
1050 PRINT
1060 PRINT "SUPPLIER NUMBER,DESCRIPTION,PRICE"
1070 PRINT
1080 PRINT "THE LIST SHOULD BE IN ALPHABETIC ORDER"
1090 PRINT "BASED ON THE DESCRIPTION"
1100 PRINT
1110 PRINT "ENTER 0 FOR LAST SUPPLIER NUMBER"
1120 PRINT
1130 OPEN 2,8,2,"0:"+N$+",S,W":T$=""
1140 REM LOOP BACK POINT
1150 INPUT "SUPPLIER NUMBER (0 FOR LAST)";S
1160 INPUT "DESCRIPTION";D$
1170 INPUT "PRICE $";P
1180 IF NOT(D$>T$) THEN PRINT "WRONG ORDER":GOTO 1150
1190 T$=D$
1200 PRINT
1210 PRINT#2,S
1220 PRINT#2,D$
1230 PRINT#2,P
1240 IF S<>0 THEN GOTO 1150
1250 CLOSE 2
1260 RETURN
1990 REM ROUTINE TO CHANGE PRICE LIST
2000 PRINT "[CS RON ]           CHANGE PRICE LIST
     [ROF ]"
2010 PRINT:PRINT:PRINT
2020 PRINT "WHAT IS THE NAME OF THE OLD PRICE
LIST":INPUT OP$
2030 PRINT "WHAT IS THE NAME OF THE NEW PRICE
LIST":INPUT NP$
2040 OPEN 2,8,2,"0:"+OP$+",S,R"
2050 DIM S(100),D$(100),P(100):REM UP TO 100 ITEMS ON
PRICE LIST
2060 REM READ IN THE OLD PRICE LIST
2070 I=0
2080 PRINT "READING IN DATA.";
2090 I=I+1 : REM LOOP BACK POINT
2100 PRINT ".";
2110 INPUT#2,S(I)
2120 INPUT#2,D$(I)
2130 INPUT#2,P(I)
```

```
2140 IF S(I)<>0 AND I<100 THEN GOTO 2090
2150 PRINT
2160 PRINT "THE PRICE LIST HAS NOW BEEN READ IN"
2170 PRINT "PRESS ANY KEY TO CONTINUE"
2180 GET A$:IF A$="" THEN GOTO 2180
2190 PRINT "[CS ]"
2200 FOR J=1 TO I
2210 PRINT "[CS ]DO YOU WISH TO CHANGE THIS ITEM (Y/N)"
2220 PRINT:PRINT:PRINT
2230 PRINT "SUPPLIER NUMBER ";S(J)
2240 PRINT "DESCRIPTION ";D$(J)
2250 PRINT "PRICE ";P(J)
2260 GET A$:IF A$="" THEN GOTO 2260
2270 IF A$="N" THEN GOTO 2540
2280 PRINT:PRINT "ENTER NEW DETAILS"
2290 PRINT "[CU CU CU CU CU CU ]"
2300 PRINT CHR$(28);"SUPPLIER NUMBER   ";
2310 S$=""
2320 GET A$:IF A$="" THEN GOTO 2320
2330 PRINT A$;
2340 IF ASC(A$)=13 THEN 2370
2350 S$=S$+A$
2360 GOTO 2320
2370 S(J)=VAL(S$)
2380 PRINT "DESCRIPTION ";
2390 D$=""
2400 GET A$:IF A$="" THEN GOTO 2400
2410 PRINT A$;
2420 IF ASC(A$)=13 THEN 2450
2430 D$=D$+A$
2440 GOTO 2400
2450 D$(J)=D$
2460 PRINT "PRICE    ";
2470 P$=""
2480 GET A$:IF A$="" THEN GOTO 2480
2490 PRINT A$;
2500 IF ASC(A$)=13 THEN 2530
2510 P$=P$+A$
2520 GOTO 2480
2530 P(J)=VAL(P$)
2535 PRINT CHR$(5);
2540 NEXT J
2550 OPEN 4,8,4,"0:"+NP$+",S,W"
2560 FOR J=1 TO I
2570 PRINT#4,S(I)
2580 PRINT#4,D$(I)
2590 PRINT#4,P(I)
```

```
2600 NEXT J
2610 CLOSE2
2620 CLOSE4
2630 RETURN
```

P30　POS – Point of Sale Program

This program is used as the point of sale utility in the system. In order to be able to use the program a price list has to be set up before hand.

The program uses the binary search method of finding an item in the price list.

COMMANDS

Key in program and save to disk.
Ensure that a price list exists on the disk.
Call the program from the main menu.
Follow instructions.

```
10 REM PRICE LIST SUITE
20 REM PROGRAM - POINT OF SALE PROGRAM
30 POKE53280,0:POKE53281,0
40 PRINT "[CS ]GOOD MORNING - WELCOME TO THE CBM-64"
50 PRINT "POINT OF SALE PROGRAM."
60 PRINT
70 PRINT"BEFORE STARTING WE HAVE SET UP SOME"
80 PRINT "INITIAL DATA."
90 PRINT
100 INPUT "WHAT IS TODAY'S DATE";DT$
110 INPUT "WHAT IS THE PRICE LIST";PL$
120 INPUT "WHAT IS THE STORE NAME";S$
130 PRINT
140 PRINT "PLEASE ENSURE THAT THE CORRECT PAPER"
150 PRINT "IS IN THE PRINTER, AND THAT IT IS LINED"
160 PRINT "UP CORRECTLY."
170 PRINT
180 PRINT"PLEASE ENSURE THAT YOU HAVE A CLEAN"
190 PRINT "NEW'ED DISK TO STORE YOUR DAILY RECORD"
200 PRINT "ON."
210 PRINT
220 PRINT"IF ALL THESE ACTIONS HAVE BEEN CARRIED"
230 PRINT "OUT. THEN PRESS ANY KEY."
240 GET A$:IF A$="" THEN GOTO 240
250 PRINT "[CS ]THE DATA ENTERED TODAY WILL BE HELD ON"
260 PRINT "DISK WITH THE NAME "DT$
270 PRINT "[CD ]TO USE THE PROGRAM ENTER THE DESCRIPTION";
280 PRINT "OF THE ITEM, AND THE QUANTITY SOLD"
```

```
290 PRINT "[CD ]TO OBTAIN A TOTAL ENTER 'T'"
300 PRINT "A TOTAL SLIP WILL THEN BE PRINTED"
310 PRINT "[CD ]YOU WILL THEN ENTER AMOUNT TENDERED"
320 PRINT "AND THE PROGRAM WILL INFORM YOU OF THE"
330 PRINT "AMOUNT OF CHANGE TO BE RETURNED"
340 PRINT "[CD ]ENTER 'EOD' WHEN THE DAY'S WORK IS DONE"
350 PRINT "[CD ]IF EVERYTHING IS OK THEN PRESS ANY KEY"
360 GET A$:IF A$="" THEN GOTO 360
370 OPEN 2,8,2,"0:"+PL$+",S,R"
380 DIM N(100),D$(100),P(100)
390 I=0
400 I=I+1
410 INPUT#2,N(I)
420 INPUT#2,D$(I)
430 INPUT#2,P(I)
440 IF N(I)<>0 THEN GOTO 400
450 I=I-1
460 CLOSE2
470 PRINT "PRICE LIST NOW IN MEMORY"
480 PRINT "PUT IN NEW DATA DISK, THEN PRESS ANY KEY"
485 OPEN2,8,2,"0:"+DT$+",S,W"
490 GET A$:IF A$="" THEN GOTO 490
500 OPEN1,4:REM OPEN PRINTER
505 REM LOOP BACK POINT
510 PRINT "[CS RON ]          CBM-64  POS PROGRAM
    [ROF ]"
520 T=0:A$=" ":REM FOR NEW CUSTOMER
530 PRINT "[CH CD CD CD CD CD CD ]" :D$="":REM FOR NEXT
ITEM
534 PRINT "                                        "
535 PRINT "[CU ]DESCRIPTION    "+A$+"[CL CL ]";
540 INPUT D$:D$=A$+D$
550 IF D$="T" THEN GOTO 650
560 IF D$="EOD" THEN GOTO 820
570 GOSUB 1000: REM SEARCH PRICE LIST
575 IF F=1 THEN GOTO 635
576 PRINT "
":PRINT"[CU ]";
580 INPUT "QUANTITY";Q
585 PRINT "
":PRINT"[CU ]";
590 PRINT "PRICE ";P
595 PRINT "
":PRINT"[CU ]";
600 PRINT "COST[]";P*Q
610 PRINT#1,D$,Q,P*Q
620 T=T+P*Q
```

```
630 PRINT#2,D$:PRINT#2,Q:PRINT#2,P:PRINT#2,P*Q
635 GET A$:IF A$="" THEN GOTO 635
640 GOTO 530
650 REM TOTAL PRINTING
660 PRINT#1,""
670 PRINT#1,"TOTAL IS ";T
680 PRINT#1,""
690 PRINT#1,"THANK YOU FOR SHOPPING AT "S$
700 PRINT#1,"DATE IS "DT$
710 PRINT#2,T
720 PRINT "[CD CD CD CD CD CD CD CD ]TOTAL IS "T
730 PRINT "ENTER AMOUNT TENDERED"
740 INPUT A
750 IF A<T THEN GOTO 730
760 PRINT "CHANGE IS "A-T
770 GT=GT+T
780 PRINT "PRESS ANY KEY FOR NEXT CUSTOMER"
790 GET A$:IF A$="" THEN GOTO 790
800 GOTO 510
810 REM END OF DAY ROUTINE
820 PRINT "[CS ]"
830 PRINT "TOTAL SALES WERE "GT
840 CLOSE 2
850 PRINT "PLACE MAIN PROGRAM DISK IN DRIVE"
860 PRINT "PRESS ANY KEY WHEN READY"
870 GET A$:IF A$="" THEN GOTO 870
880 LOAD"PRICELIST",8
890 END
950 REM BINARY SEARCH ALGORITHM
960 REM DESCRIPTION IN D$
970 REM DESCRIPTIONS IN D$(I)
980 REM PRICE IN P(I)
990 REM LIST IS ALPHABETICAL
1000 N=I:F=0:D$(0)=" "
1010 M=INT(N/2)
1020 L=M
1025 IF LEFT$(D$,1)=" "THEN D$=MID$(D$,2):GOTO 1025
1030 IF D$=D$(M) THEN P=P(M):RETURN
1040 IF D$<D$(M) THEN L=INT(L/2):M=M-1
1050 IF D$>D$(M) THEN L=INT(L/2):M=M+1
1060 IF M>N THEN L=INT(L/2):M=M-1
1070 IF M>N THEN GOTO 1060
1080 IF L=0 THEN L=2
1090 IF D$<D$(M+1) AND D$>D$(M) THEN PRINT "NOT IN LIST":F=1:RETURN
1100 IF M=1 AND D$<D$(M) THEN PRINT "NOT IN LIST":F=1:RETURN
```

```
1110 GOTO 1030
1120 F=1:RETURN
```

P31 PRINT – Price List Print Program

This is the main report program of the system. It allows the user to produce a nicely laid out report of the prices in his store.

COMMANDS

Key in program and save to disk or tape.
Call the program from the main menu.
Follow instructions.

```
10 REM PRICE LIST SUITE
20 REM PROGRAM - PRICE LIST PRINT PROGRAM
30 POKE53280,0:POKE53281,0
40 PRINT "[CS CD CD RON ]
        [ROF ]";
50 PRINT "[RON ]              PRINTER OPTIONS
[ROF ]";
60 PRINT "[RON ]
[ROF ]"
70 PRINT:PRINT:PRINT
80 PRINT "[RON ]    1.  PRINT LIST TO SCREEN
[ROF ]"
90 PRINT
100 PRINT "[RON ]   2.  PRINT LIST TO PRINTER
[ROF ]"
110 PRINT
120 PRINT "[RON ]   3.  PRINT LIST TO BOTH
[ROF ]"
130 PRINT
140 PRINT "[RON ]   4.  GO BACK TO MAIN MENU
[ROF ]"
150 PRINT
160 PRINT "ENTER NUMBER CORRESPONDING TO FUNCTION"
170 GET A$:IF A$="" THEN GOTO 170
180 A=VAL(A$)
190 IF A<>1 AND A<>2 AND A<>3 AND A<>4 THEN GOTO 150
200 IF A=4 THEN LOAD "PRICELIST",8
210 PRINT "[CS ]"
220 PRINT "WHAT IS THE NAME OF THE PRICE LIST":INPUT N$
230 OPEN2,8,2,"0:"+N$+",S,R"
240 I=0
250 IF A=2 THEN GOTO 300
```

P31 Price List Print

```
260 PRINT "[CS RON ]                PRICE LIST
    [ROF]"
270 PRINT
280 PRINT "NUMBER","DESCRIPTION","PRICE
290 IF A=1 THEN GOTO 330
300 OPEN 1,4
310 PRINT#1,"                 PRICE LIST"
320 PRINT#1,"NUMBER","DESCRIPTION","PRICE"
330 I=I+1
340 INPUT#2,N
350 INPUT#2,D$
360 INPUT#2,P
365 IF N=0 THEN GOTO 470
370 IF A=1 OR A=3 THEN PRINT N,D$,P
380 IF A=2 OR A=3 THEN PRINT#1,N,D$,P
390 IF A=2 THEN GOTO 330
400 IF 20*INT(I/20)<>I THEN GOTO 330
410 PRINT "PRESS ANY KEY FOR NEXT PAGE"
420 GET A$:IF A$="" THEN GOTO 420
430 PRINT "[CS RON ]                PRICE LIST
    [ROF]"
440 PRINT
450 PRINT "NUMBER","DESCRIPTION","PRICE
460 GOTO 330
470 CLOSE 1
480 CLOSE2
490 PRINT:PRINT
500 PRINT "PRESS ANY KEY TO RETURN TO MENU"
510 GET A$:IF A$="" THEN GOTO 510
520 GOTO 10
```

P32 FDUMP — File Dump Utility

This program can be used to dump a disk file to either the screen or printer. It is very useful to check that a data file has been set up correctly.

However, we have found it useful on other occasions as well. If you have a disk then the routine will find a useful place in your library.

The program can be amended to examine tape files as well.

COMMANDS

Key in program and save to disk or tape.
Call the program via MENU program.
Follow instructions.

```
10 REM PRICE LIST SUITE
20 REM PROGRAM - FILE DUMP UTILITY
30 POKE53280,0:POKE53281,0
40 PRINT "[CS RON ]
   [ROF ]";
50 PRINT "[RON ]            FILE DUMP UTILITY
   [ROF ]";
60 PRINT "[RON ]
   [ROF ]"
70 PRINT:PRINT
80 PRINT "THIS PROGRAM CAN BE USED TO OBTAIN A"
90 PRINT "DUMP OF A DISK FILE TO SCREEN OR PRINTER";
100 PRINT "THE OPTIONS AVAILABLE ARE:"
110 PRINT:PRINT
120 PRINT "1. DUMP A FILE TO SCREEN"
130 PRINT "2. DUMP A FILE TO PRINTER"
140 PRINT "3. RETURN TO MAIN MENU"
150 PRINT
160 PRINT "ENTER NUMBER CORRESPONDING TO CHOICE":INPUT A
170 IF A<>1 AND A<>2 AND A<>3 THEN GOTO    160
180 IF A=3 THEN LOAD"PRICELIST",8
190 PRINT "ENTER THE NAME OF THE FILE TO BE "
200 INPUT "DUMPED";A$
210 OPEN 5,8,5,"0:"+A$+",S,R"
215 IF A=1 THEN OPEN1,4
220 GET#5,A$
230 IF ST<>0 THEN PRINT:PRINT"SYSTEM STATUS IS "ST:
```

```
    GOTO 260
240 IF A=1 THEN PRINT A$;
245 IF A=2 THEN PRINT#1,A$;
250 GOTO 220
260 IF A=2 THEN PRINT#1:CLOSE 1
270 CLOSE 5
280 PRINT "PRESS ANY KEY TO RETURN TO MENU"
290 GET A$:IF A$="" THEN GOTO 290
300 GOTO 10
310 END
```

P33 Monthly Accounts

In our households, one of the tasks which has to be done is the monthly budget. It seemed to us that this was an ideal use for the CBM-64.

In this program we again make use of the alternative character set of the CBM-64, all words presented are in both upper and lower case. Thus when entering the program we first tell you to press the Commodore and shift keys together.

Once the program is running, it prompts the user to enter all their outgoings and income. The program ends with a report onto paper or screen of the monthly budget.

COMMANDS

Press the Commodore and shift keys together.
Key in the program and type RUN.
Follow instructions.

```
10 rem program - monthly accounts
20 print "[cs cd cd cd cd cd cd cd cd cd cd cd cr cr cr cr cr cr cr cr cr cr ]";
30 print "[ron ]monthly accounts[rof ]"
40 a=ti
50 if ti<a+150 then 50
55 print chr$(14):poke 53280,12:poke 53281,15
60 print "[cs cd cd cd cd cd ]"
70 print " This program helps you to budget your"
80 print " monthly outgoings and incomings."
90 print " The program prompts you to enter your"
100 print " financial dealings and produces a"
110 print " balance sheet for the next month."
120 print "[cd cd ]"
130 print " If you want to use a printer then "
140 print " ensure that it is connected up now."
150 print "[cd cd ] Press any key to continue";
160 get a$:if a$="" then 160
170 print "[cs ]";
```

P33 Monthly Accounts

```
180 print "[ron ]          Regular Outgoings
    [rof ]";
190 print
200 print "Enter mortgage repayments. $";
290 input m
300 input "Enter rent payments. $";re
310 input "Enter property taxes. $";pt
320 input "Enter electricity payments. $";el
330 input "Enter gas payments. $";gs
340 cr=0
350 rem take in all credit card repayments
360 print "[cd ron ]Credit Card Repayments[rof cd ]"
370 input "Enter credit repayment. 0 for last";c
380 cr=cr+c
390 if c<>0 then goto 370
400 print "[cd ron ]Enter any other regular
    payments.[rof cd ]"
410 input "Enter total. $";ot
420 rg=m+re+pt+el+gs+cr+ot:rem regular payments
430 print "[cs ]";
440 print "[ron ]       Other Outgoings This Month
    [rof ]"
450 print "Use estimates if actual amounts are not"
460 print "known.[cd cd ]"
470 print "Enter total of all outstanding bills."
480 input "$";ob:rem old bills
490 input "Grocery bill. $";g
500 input "Butcher's bill. $";b
510 input "Entertainment allowance. $";en
520 print "[cs ]";
530 bt=g+b+en:rem bills this month
540 print "[ron ]       Other bills due this month
    [rof ]"
550 print "[cd ]Enter other bills - use 0 to finish[cd
    ]"
560 input "Amount of bill. $";bl
570 bs=bs+bl
580 if bl<>0 then goto 560
590 bt=bt+bs
600 tt=rg+ob+bt:rem total outgoings
610 print "[cd cd ]Total outgoings = $";tt
620 print "[cd cd ]Press any key to continue"
625 get a$:if a$="" then 625
630 print "[cs ]";
640 print "[ron ]          Monthly Income
    [rof ]"
650 input "[cd ]Enter your monthly net income. $";i1
```

```
660 print "[cd ]Enter your spouse's monthly net income"
670 input "$";i2
680 input "[cd ]Enter any other net income. $";i3
690 i=i1+i2+i3
700 ba=i-tt:rem balance
710 print "[cd cd ]Total income is $";i
720 print "[cd cd ]Press any key to continue"
730 get a$:if a$="" then 730
740 print "[cs cd cd cd cd cd ]"
750 print " Do you want the report to be printed"
760 print " on the screen or onto the printer?"
770 print
780 print "         1.   Screen"
790 print "         2.   Printer"
800 print
810 input " Enter 1 or 2 ";r
820 if r<>1 and r<>2 then print "[cu ]
    [cu ]":goto 810
830 if r=2 then open 1,4,7:cmd 1
840 print "[cs ]";
850 print "[ron ]              MONTHLY BUDGET
    [rof ]"
860 print
870 print "[ron ]COMMENT          OUT       IN       [rof
]"
880 print "Regular"
890 print "amounts";spc(18-len(str$(rg)));rg
900 print "[cd ]Bills this"
910 print "month  ";spc(18-len(str$(bt)));bt
920 print "[cd ]Outstanding "
930 print "bills from"
940 print"last month";spc(15-len(str$(ob)));ob
950 print
960 print "[ron ]Total Out[rof ]";
    spc(16-len(str$(tt)));tt
970 print
980 print "[ron ]Total Income[rof ]";
    spc(23-len(str$(i)));i
990 print
1000 if ba<0 then print "[ron ]Debit Balance[rof ]";
     spc(22-len(str$(ba)));ba:goto 1010
1010 print "[ron ]Credit Balance[rof ]";
     spc(11-len(str$(ba)));ba
1020 get a$:if a$="" then goto 1020
1030 if r=2 then close 1
1040 end
1050 print chr$(142)
```

P34 Conversion

This is a general purpose conversion utility, which we have implemented with eighteen different conversion factors. It is fairly straightforward to choose other units to be converted by changing the data statements at the end of the program.

Eighteen conversion factors were chosen to make the main menu fit the screen.

Once the conversion has been chosen, you have to decide which way the conversion has to proceed. For example, centimeters to inches or inches to centimeters.

COMMANDS

Key in the program and type RUN.
Select from menu.

```
10 REM PROGRAM - CONVERSIONS UTILITY
20 PRINT "[CS CD CD CD CD CD CD CD CD CD ]"
30 PRINT "          CONVERSIONS UTILITY"
40 A=TI
50 IF TI<A+150 THEN GOTO 50
60 PRINT "[CS ]"
70 PRINT " THIS PROGRAM IS USED AS A GENERAL"
80 PRINT " PURPOSE CONVERSION UTILITY. THE DATA"
90 PRINT " FOR THE CONVERSIONS ARE HELD WITHIN"
100 PRINT " THE PROGRAM."
110 PRINT "[CD ]PRESS ANY KEY TO CONTINUE"
120 DIM C$(18,2),D(18)
130 GET A$:IF A$="" THEN GOTO 130
140 PRINT "[CS RON ]          CONVERSIONS
    [ROF ]"
150 RESTORE
160 FOR I=1 TO 18
170 READ C$(I,1),C$(I,2)
180 PRINT I SPC(6-LEN(STR$(I)));C$(I,1);" TO ";C$(I,2)
190 NEXT I
200 PRINT
210 PRINT "CHOOSE ITEM BY ENTERING THE REQUIRED"
220 INPUT "NUMBER";C
```

```
230 FOR I=1 TO 18:READ D(I):NEXT I
240 PRINT "[CS ]"
250 PRINT "[RON ]          OPTIONS AVAILABLE
    [ROF ]"
260 PRINT:PRINT
270 PRINT "1. ";C$(C,1);" TO ";C$(C,2)
280 PRINT "2. ";C$(C,2);" TO ";C$(C,1)
290 PRINT
300 PRINT "CHOOSE OPTION BY ENTERING APPROPRIATE "
310 INPUT "NUMBER";CH
320 IF CH=2 THEN D(C)=1/D(C):T$=C$(C,1):
    C$(C,1)=C$(C,2):C$(C,2)=T$
330 REM IF ALTERNATIVE OPTION REQUIRED
340 REM THEN INVERT FACTOR AND SWAP ITEMS
350 PRINT:PRINT
360 PRINT "ENTER VALUE OF "C$(C,1);
370 INPUT A
380 B=A*D(C)
390 PRINT:PRINT
400 PRINT A;" ";C$(C,1);" = ";B;" ";C$(C,2)
410 PRINT:PRINT
420 PRINT "PRESS ANY KEY TO CONTINUE"
430 GET A$:IF A$="" THEN 430
440 GOTO   140
450 END
1000 DATA INCHES, CM, FEET, METERS, YARDS, METERS,
          MILES, KM
1010 DATA TEASPOONS, CC, TABLESPOONS, CC, CUPS,
          LITRES, PINTS
1020 DATA LITRES, QUARTS, LITRES, GALLONS, LITRES,
          OZ, GRAMS
1030 DATA POUNDS, KILOGRAMS, TONS, KILOGRAMS,
          MILES PER HOUR, METERS PER SEC
1040 DATA SQUARE YARDS, SQUARE METERS, YEARS, SECONDS
1050 DATA ATMOSPHERES, CM HG, ACRES, HECTARES
1060 REM CONVERSION DATA
1070 DATA 2.540, .3048,   .9144, 1.609, 4.929,
          14.788, .2366
1080 DATA .4732, .7463, 3.785, 28.3495, .4536,
          907.2, .447, .8361, 31536000
1090 DATA 76, .4047
```

P35 Birthday List

This program uses one of the SORT routines developed elswhere in the book, the so-called Bubble Sort.

The Birthday List program is used to store all those birthdays that you have to remember. The program sorts the birthdays into date order, and then prints out all birthdays left in the current year. All birthdays are stored in data statements.

COMMANDS

Key in the program and type RUN.
Follow instructions.
When you can folllow the operation of the program, amend the data statements.

```
10 REM PROGRAM - BIRTHDAY LIST
20 PRINT "[CS ]            BIRTHDAYS[CD CD ]"
30 PRINT "THE BIRTHDAYS HELD IN THIS PROGRAM ARE"
40 PRINT"HELD IN THE FORM OF DATA STATEMENTS"
50 PRINT "STARTING AT LINE 2000."
60 PRINT
70 PRINT "THE PROGRAM CAN BE USED TO HOLD UP TO "
80 PRINT "100 BIRTHDAYS, BUT OF COURSE THIS COULD"
90 PRINT "BE AMENDED IF YOU SO WISH."
100 PRINT "THE FORMAT OF THE DATA IS AS FOLLOWS:"
110 PRINT
120 PRINT "DATA   NAME,MMDD"
130 PRINT
140 PRINT "WHERE MM IS THE MONTH NUMBER AND DD IS"
150 PRINT "THE DAY NUMBER"
160 PRINT
170 PRINT "MAKE THE LAST TWO ELEMENTS OF THE DATA"
180 PRINT "BE   EOF,0"
190 PRINT
200 PRINT "PRESS ANY KEY TO CONTINUE"
210 GET A$:IF A$="" THEN GOTO 210
```

```
215 PRINT "[CS CD CD CD ]"
220 DIM N$(100),D(100)
230 REM READ IN DATA
340 I=0
350 I=I+1
360 READ N$(I),D(I)
370 IF N$(I)<>"EOF" THEN GOTO 350
380 I=I-1
390 GOSUB 1000
395 REM USEFUL GET DATE ROUTINE
400 PRINT "WHAT IS TODAY'S DATE (MM/DD)
    [CL CL CL CL CL CL ]";:D$=""
410 GET A$:IF A$="" THEN 410
420 PRINT A$;:D$=D$+A$
430 GET A$:IF A$="" THEN 430
440 PRINT A$;:D$=D$+A$
450 PRINT "/";
460 GET A$:IF A$="" THEN 460
470 PRINT A$;:D$=D$+A$
480 GET A$:IF A$="" THEN 480
490 PRINT A$;:D$=D$+A$
500 FOR Z=1 TO 4
510 V=ASC(MID$(D$,Z,1))
520 IF V<48 OR V>57 THEN Z=4:T=1
530 NEXT Z
540 IF T=1 THEN PRINT:T=0:D$="":GOTO 400
550 D=VAL(D$)
560 PRINT "[CS ]"
570 PRINT : PRINT : PRINT
580 PRINT "THE BIRTHDAYS LEFT THIS YEAR ARE:"
585 PRINT : PRINT : PRINT
590 MT$="JANFEBMARAPRMAYJUNJULAUGSEPOCTNOVDEC"
600 FOR J=1 TO I
610 IF D(J)<D THEN NEXT J
620 DAY=D(J)-100*INT(D(J)/100)
630 MO=INT(D(J)/100)-1
640 PRINT N$(J);"'S BIRTHDAY IS ";DAY;
    " ";MID$(MT$,3*MO+1,3)
650 NEXT J
660 END
990 REM SORT ROUTINE
1000 FOR X=1 TO I-1
1010 FOR Y=X+1 TO I
1020 IF D(Y)<D(X) THEN GOSUB 1100
1030 NEXT Y
1040 NEXT X
1050 RETURN
```

P35 Birthday List

```
1090 REM SWAP ROUTINE
1100 T=D(Y):T$=N$(Y)
1110 D(Y)=D(X):N$(Y)=N$(X)
1120 D(X)=T:N$(X)=T$
1130 RETURN
1990 REM BIRTHDAYS
2000 DATA JIM SMITH,1130,BILL SMYTHE,0812,
     LIZ GRAHAM,0303
2010 DATA JOHN GORDON,0419,JOHN FERGUSON,0407,
     TERESA GORDON,1222,EOF,0
```

P36 Calendar

This program can be used to print out the calendar for any month in the twentieth century.

COMMANDS

Key in the program and type RUN.
Enter month and year when requested.

```
10 REM PROGRAM - CALENDAR
20 PRINT "[CS CD CD CD ]THIS PROGRAM CAN BE USED TO PRINT THE "
30 PRINT "CALENDAR FOR ANY MONTH IN THE TWENTIETH"
40 PRINT "CENTURY."
50 DIM C(7,6)
60 RESTORE
65 PRINT "[CD CD ]"
70 INPUT "WHICH MONTH DO YOU REQUIRE";M$
80 INPUT "WHICH YEAR DO YOU REQUIRE";Y
90 PRINT "CALCULATING - PLEASE WAIT"
100 D$="MONTUEWEDTHUFRISATSUN"
110 REM GET NUMBER OF DAYS IN MONTH
120 M=0
130 READ Q$,F,D
140 M=M+1
150 IF M=13 THEN PRINT "INVALID MONTH":GOTO 60
160 IF LEFT$(M$,3)<>LEFT$(Q$,3) THEN GOTO 130
170 IF Y>1900 THEN Y=Y-1900
180 L=INT(Y/4)
190 OF=Y+L
200 IF Y-INT(Y/4)*4=0 AND M<3 THEN OF=OF-1
210 IF Y-INT(Y/4)*4=0 AND M=2 THEN D=29
220 OF=OF-INT(OF/7)*7
230 F=F+OF
240 F=F-INT(F/7)*7
250 IF F=0 THEN F=7
260 FOR I=1 TO F-1
270 C(I,1)=0
280 NEXT I
290 DY=1
300 FOR I=F TO 7
310 C(I,1)=DY
320 DY=DY+1
330 NEXT I
```

P36 Calendar

```
340 FOR J=2 TO 6
350 FOR I=1 TO 7
360 C(I,J)=DY
370 DY=DY+1
380 IF DY>D THEN I=7:J=6
390 NEXT I
400 NEXT J
410 PRINT "[CS ]"
420 PRINT "[CD CD CD CR CR CR CR CR CR CR CR CR CR CR CR
CR CR ]";M$;"    ";Y+1900;"[CD CD ]"
430 FOR I=1 TO 7
440 PRINT "       ";MID$(D$,(I-1)*3+1,3)
450 NEXT I
460 PRINT "[CH CD CD CD CD CD CD CD CR CR CR CR CR CR CR
CR CR ]";
470 FOR J=1 TO 6
480 FOR I=1 TO 7
485 C$=STR$(C(I,J)):IF LEN(C$)=2 THEN C$=" "+C$
490 IF C(I,J)<>0 THEN PRINT C$;"[CD CL CL CL ]";
495 IF C(I,J)=0 THEN PRINT"    ";"[CD CL CL CL ]";
500 NEXT I
510 PRINT "[CU CU CU CU CU CU CU CR CR CR ]";
520 NEXT J
530 GET A$:IF A$="" THEN 530
540 DATA JANUARY,1,31, FEBRUARY,4,28, MARCH,4,31,
        APRIL,7,30, MAY,2,31, JUNE,5,30
550 DATA JULY,7,31, AUGUST,3,31, SEPTEMBER,6,30,
        OCTOBER,1,31
560 DATA NOVEMBER,4,30, DECEMBER,6,31
570 DATA ,,
```

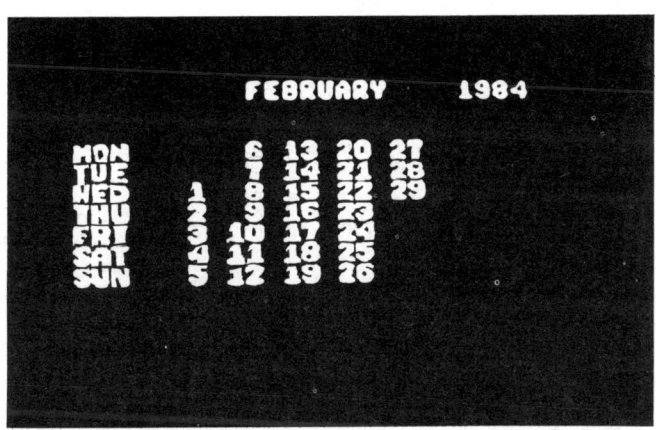

P37 Telephone List

This program allows the user to select a telephone number from a list held as data statements.

You do not have to enter the full name to select the number. As long as the string entered is part of one of the names, then the telephone number is displayed.

COMMANDS

Key in the program and type RUN.
Follow instructions.

```
10 REM PROGRAM - TELEPHONE LIST
20 PRINT "[CS ]"
30 PRINT
40 PRINT "THIS PROGRAM IS USED AS A PERSONAL "
50 PRINT "TELEPHONE DIRECTORY."
60 PRINT
70 PRINT "THE DATA ARE HELD IN THE LINES FROM 1000"
80 PRINT "THE PROGRAM CAN HOLD A DATABASE OF UP TO";
90 PRINT "100 NAMES AND TELEPHONE NUMBERS. THIS"
100 PRINT "CAN OF COURSE BE AMENDED BY THE USER."
110 PRINT
120 PRINT "THE PROGRAM WILL SEARCH THROUGH THE"
130 PRINT "DATABASE LOOKING FOR A MATCH AGAINST"
140 PRINT "A NAME INPUT TO THE COMPUTER."
150 PRINT
160 PRINT "A PARTIAL MATCH WILL ALSO GIVE NUMBER."
170 PRINT "FOR EXAMPLE, IF YOU INPUT 'BILL', THEN"
180 PRINT "A MATCH WILL BE FOUND FOR BILL SMITH "
190 PRINT "AND BILL JONES"
200 PRINT
210 PRINT "PRESS ANY KEY TO CONTINUE"
220 GET A$:IF A$="" THEN GOTO 220
230 DIM N$(100,2)
240 I=0
250 I=I+1
260 READ N$(I,1),N$(I,2)
270 IF N$(I,1)<>"EOF" THEN GOTO 250
280 I=I-1
290 C=0
300 PRINT "[CS ]"
```

P37 Telephone List

```
305 PRINT "WHOSE NUMBER DO YOU REQUIRE"
310 INPUT N$
320 LA=LEN(N$):F=0
330 FOR J=1 TO I
340 LB=LEN(N$(J,1))
350 IF LA>LB THEN NEXT J
360 FOR K=1 TO LB-LA
370 IF N$=MID$(N$(J,1),K,LA) THEN F=1
380 NEXT K
390 IF F=1 THEN PRINT N$(J,1);"'S NUMBER IS ";
    N$(J,2):F=0:C=C+1
400 NEXT J
410 IF C=0 THEN PRINT "WE HAVE NO NUMBER FOR ";N$
420 PRINT "ANOTHER NUMBER (Y/N)"
430 GET A$:IF A$="" THEN GOTO 430
440 IF A$="Y" THEN GOTO 290
450 END
1000 DATA BILL SMITH,1235,BILL JONES,45678
1010 DATA ALICE GRAHAM,0101 256 3456
1020 DATA JOHN GORDON,03552 49400
1030 DATA EOF,0
```

P38 Investments

This program calculates how much income can be generated from capital if the interest earned by that capital is known.

The user is presented with the choice of increasing his or her income at the expense of reducing capital.

COMMANDS

Key in program and type RUN.

```
10 REM PROGRAM - INVESTMENTS
20 PRINT "[CS ]"
30 PRINT "THIS PROGRAM ALLOWS YOU TO PLAN YOUR "
40 PRINT "FUTURE INVESTMENTS, GIVEN THAT YOU WISH"
50 PRINT "YOUR INVESTMENTS TO SUPPLY A REGULAR"
60 PRINT "INCOME."
70 PRINT
80 PRINT "PRESS ANY KEY TO CONTINUE"
90 GET A$:IF A$="" THEN GOTO 90
100 PRINT
110 INPUT "MONTHLY INCOME REQUIRED $";I
120 PRINT "ENTER CURRENT ANNUAL INTEREST RATE (%)"
130 INPUT R
140 R=R/100
150 IN=I*12/R
160 PRINT "AN INVESTMENT OF $";INT(IN*100)/100
170 PRINT "WILL PROVIDE A MONTHLY INCOME OF $";I
180 PRINT
190 PRINT "NOTE THAT NO CAPITAL HAS BEEN USED"
200 PRINT
210 PRINT "IF YOU WISH TO USE UP YOUR CAPITAL."
220 PRINT "HOW MANY YEARS DO YOU WISH AN INCOME"
230 PRINT "FOR? ENTER NUMBER OF YEARS."
240 INPUT YR
250 R=R/12
260 T=(1+R)^(12*YRS)
270 IN=I*(T-1)/R/T
280 PRINT
290 PRINT "AN INVESTMENT OF $";INT(IN*100)/100
```

```
300 PRINT "WILL PROVIDE AN INCOME OF $";I
310 PRINT "FOR ";YR;" YEARS"
320 END
```

P39 Loan Repayment Schedule

We use this program to try to dissuade ourselves from buying something using a loan from a finance house.

It can be quite illuminating to have a note of the full schedule of repayments for a loan and to see how slowly the amount owed drops.

If the interest rate changes during the period of a loan, then simply RUN the program again as if you had taken out a new loan, with a reduced amount borrowed.

The program allows you to choose either a screen or a printer output. If you have a printer which does not have automatic line feed on carriage return, then use a file number greater than 128 for the printer control instructions. As it stands the program will work with the Commodore MPS801 and with most other printers.

COMMANDS

Key in the program and RUN.

Follow the instructions.

```
10 REM LOAN REYPAYMENT SCHEDULE
20 REM ************************
30 REM
100 CL$=CHR$(147):REM TO CLEAR SCREEN
120 POKE 53280,0:REM BLACK BORDER
130 POKE 53281,0:REM BLACK SCREEN
140 PRINT CHR$(159):REM CYAN INK
150 PRINT CL$:PRINT
160 PRINT TAB(8)
    "LOAN REPAYMENT SCHEDULE"
170 PRINT TAB(8)
    "$$$$$$$$$$$$$$$$$$$$$$$"
180 PRINT:PRINT
190 PRINT TAB(4)
    "THIS PROGRAM CAN BE USED TO PLAN"
```

P39 Loan Repayment Schedule

```
200 PRINT TAB(4)
    "THE REPAYMENTS SCHEDULE FOR A"
210 PRINT TAB(4)
    "LOAN. THE LOAN IS PAID BACK AT A"
220 PRINT TAB(4)
    "FIXED MONTHLY RATE. THE INTEREST"
230 PRINT TAB(4)
    "IS ALSO FIXED. THE PROGRAM"
240 PRINT TAB(4)
    "PRODUCES A REPAYMENT TABLE."
250 PRINT
260 PRINT TAB(4)
    "IF YOU WISH TO USE A PRINTER,"
270 PRINT TAB(4)
    "ENSURE ONE IS CONNECTED NOW. THE"
280 PRINT TAB(4)
    "PROGRAM ASSUMES THE PRINTER IS"
290 PRINT TAB(4)"DEVICE NUMBER 4."
300 PRINT:PRINT
310 PRINT TAB(6)CHR$(18)
    " PRESS ANY KEY TO CONTINUE "
320 GET A$:IF A$="" THEN 320:REM
    NO SPACE BETWEEN INVERTED COMMAS
330 REM*****************************
340 PRINT CL$:PRINT:INPUT
    "WHAT IS THE AMOUNT OF THE LOAN";AM
350 PRINT
360 INPUT
    "WHAT IS THE INTEREST/MONTH (%)";IT
370 PRINT
380 PRINT
    "WHAT IS THE NUMBER (1-12) OF THE"
390 INPUT
    "FIRST REPAYMENT MONTH";MN
400 PRINT
410 INPUT
    "WHAT IS THE MONTHLY REPAYMENT";RP
420 PRINT
430 INPUT"WHAT YEAR IS IT";YR
440 REM NO TRAPS ON ENTRIES. SILLY
    ENTRIES WILL GIVE SILLY RESULTS.
450 REM*****************************
460 PRINT CL$:PRINT:PRINT:PRINT:PRINT
470 PRINT TAB(4)
    "SELECT YOUR OUTPUT DEVICE BY"
480 PRINT TAB(4)"PRESSING:"
490 PRINT
```

```
500 PRINT TAB(10)CHR$(18)" KEY 1 "
    CHR$(146)" - SCREEN"
510 PRINT
520 PRINT TAB(10)CHR$(18)" KEY 2 "
    CHR$(146)" - PRINTER"
530 GET A$:IF A$="" THEN 530:REM
    NO SPACE BETWEEN INVERTED COMMAS
540 IF A$<>"1" AND A$<>"2" THEN 530
550 DV=VAL(A$)
560 REM*****************************
570 PRINT CL$
580 ON DV GOSUB 1000,2000:REM HEADINGS
590 PD=0:REM AMOUNT PAID BACK
600 REM*****************************
610 REM CALCULATION
620 MN=MN+1
630 IF MN=13 THEN YR=YR+1:MN=1
640 AM=AM*(1+IT/100)
650 AM=AM-RP
660 PD=PD+RP
670 IF AM<0 THEN
    PD=PD+INT(100*AM+.5)/100:AM=0
680 ON DV GOSUB 3000,4000:
    REM PRINT RESULTS
690 IF AM>0 THEN 610
700 IF DV=2 THEN CLOSE 3
710 END
720 REM*****************************
730 REM*****************************
900 REM
910 REM          ***************
920 REM          *
930 REM          * SUBROUTINES
940 REM          *
950 REM          ***************
960 REM
1000 REM SCREEN HEADING
1010 PRINT TAB(3)
     "YEAR","MONTH","AMOUNT","AMOUNT"
1020 PRINT TAB(21)"PAID"," OWED"
1030 PRINT TAB(3)
     "----","-----","------","------"
1040 RETURN
1050 REM*****************************
1060 REM*****************************
2000 REM PRINTER HEADING
2010 OPEN 3,4
```

P39 Loan Repayment Schedule

```
2020 PRINT#3,TAB(3)
     "YEAR","MONTH","AMOUNT","AMOUNT"
2030 PRINT#3,TAB(33)"PAID","  OWED"
2040 PRINT#3,TAB(3)
     "----","-----","------","------"
2050 RETURN
2060 REM****************************
2070 REM****************************
3000 REM SCREEN RESULTS
3010 PRINT TAB(2)
     YR,MN,PD,INT(AM*100+.5)/100
3020 RETURN
3030 REM****************************
3040 REM****************************
4000 REM PRINTER RESULTS
4010 PRINT#3,TAB(2)
     YR,MN,PD,INT(AM*100+.5)/100
4020 RETURN
4030 REM****************************
4040 REM****************************
```

YEAR	MONTH	AMOUNT PAID	AMOUNT OWED
1984	7	200	4875
1984	8	400	4748.13
1984	9	600	4619.35
1984	10	800	4488.64
1984	11	1000	4355.97
1985	12	1200	4221.31
1985	1	1400	4084.63
1985	2	1600	3945.9
1985	3	1800	3805.08
1985	4	2000	3662.16
1985	5	2200	3517.09
1985	6	2400	3369.85
1985	7	2600	3220.4
1985	8	2800	3068.7
1985	9	3000	2914.73
1985	10	3200	2758.45
1985	11	3400	2599.83
1986	12	3600	2438.83
1986	1	3800	2275.41
1986	2	4000	2109.54
1986	3	4200	1941.18
1986	4	4400	1770.3
1986	5	4600	1596.86
1986	6	4800	1420.81
1986	7	5000	1242.12
1986	8	5200	1060.75
1986	9	5400	876.67
1986	10	5600	689.82
1986	11	5800	500.16
1987	12	6000	307.66
1987	1	6200	112.28
1987	2	6313.96	0

P40 Monitor

This program allows you to poke about in the micro's memory. You can examine or change portions of memory, you can also save and load portions of memory to tape.

This is where micros can become fun. You can use this program to change your machine, but bear in mind that it is possible to damage your equipment if you poke about at random.

Therefore consult a Commodore-64 manual while messing about in the system.

We have used this program to find out many things about the computer.

COMMANDS

Key in the program and type RUN.
Follow instructions.

```
100 REM PROGRAM - MONITOR
110 PRINT"[CS ]"
120 PRINT"[CD CD CD CR CR CR CR CR CR CR CR CR CR CR CR CR CR RON ]MONITOR[ROF]"
130 PRINT"[CD CD ]THIS PROGRAM IS USED TO ALLOW YOU TO:"
140 PRINT"[CD CD CR CR CR ]1. INPUT A MACHINE CODE PROGRAM"
150 PRINT"[CR CR CR ]2. EXAMINE A PORTION OF MEMORY"
160 PRINT"[CR CR CR ]3. SAVE A BLOCK OF RAM MEMORY"
170 PRINT"[CR CR CR ]4. LOAD A BLOCK OF RAM MEMORY"
180 PRINT"[CR CR CR ]5. END THIS SESSION"
190 PRINT"[CD CD CD ]PRESS THE APPROPRIATE NUMBER"
200 GET R$:IF R$="" THEN 200
210 IF R$="5" THEN END
220 ON VAL(R$) GOSUB 1000,2000,3000,4000
230 IF VAL(R$)<1 OR VAL(R$)>5 THEN GOTO 100
240 GOTO 100
999 REM ROUTINE TO INPUT A SERIES OF BYTES
1000 PRINT"[CS ]"
1010 PRINT"THIS ROUTINE ALLOWS YOU TO INPUT A"
1020 PRINT"SERIES OF BYTES IN EITHER HEX OR DECIMAL"
1030 PRINT"[CD CD CD ]INPUT 'D' FOR DECIMAL"
1040 PRINT"INPUT 'H' FOR HEXADECIMAL"
```

```
1050 GET R$:IF R$="" OR (R$<>"D" AND R$<>"H") THEN 1050
1060 IF R$="D" THEN GOSUB 1300
1070 IF R$="H" THEN GOSUB 1600
1080 RETURN
1299 REM DECIMAL INPUT SUBROUTINE
1300 PRINT"[CS ]"
1310 PRINT"WHAT IS THE STARTING ADDRESS OF BYTES"
1320 INPUT S
1330 PRINT "ENTER BYTES USE . TO FINISH"
1340 PRINT S;" ";PEEK(S);" ";
1350 INPUT B$
1360 IF B$="." THEN RETURN
1370 POKE S,VAL(B$)
1380 S=S+1
1390 GOTO 1340
1599 REM HEX INPUT SUBROUTINE
1600 PRINT "[CS ]"
1610 PRINT"WHAT IS THE STARTING ADDRESS OF BYTES"
1620 INPUT S$
1630 PRINT "ENTER BYTES USE . TO FINISH"
1640 H$=S$
1650 GOSUB 5000:S=DC
1660 PRINT H$;" ";PEEK(S);" ";
1670 INPUT B$
1680 IF B$="." THEN RETURN
1690 H$=B$
1700 GOSUB 5000
1710 POKE S,DC
1720 S=S+1
1730 D$=MID$(STR$(S),2):GOSUB 6000
1740 GOTO 1650
1999 REM ROUTINE TO EXAMINE A SERIES OF BYTES
2000 PRINT"[CS ]"
2010 PRINT"THIS ROUTINE ALLOWS YOU TO EXAMINE"
2020 PRINT"A SERIES OF BYTES IN BOTH HEX AND"
2030 PRINT"DECIMAL"
2040 PRINT"WHAT IS THE STARTING ADDRESS OF BYTES"
2050 INPUT "IN DECIMAL ";S
2060 PRINT "PRESS SPACE FOR MORE RETURN TO FINISH"
2065 PRINT"ADDRESS","DEC","HEX","ASC"
2070 B=PEEK(S)
2080 D$=MID$(STR$(B),2):GOSUB 6000
2090 PRINT S,B,H$,CHR$(B)
2100 GET A$:IF A$="" THEN 2100
2110 IF ASC(A$)=13 THEN 2140
2120 S=S+1
2130 GOTO 2070
```

```
2140 PRINT"PRESS ANY KEY TO RETURN TO MAIN MENU"
2150 GET A$:IF A$="" THEN 2150
2160 RETURN
2999 REM ROUTINE TO SAVE A BLOCK OF RAM MEMORY
3000 PRINT "[CS ]"
3010 INPUT "ENTER START ADDRESS OF BLOCK";S
3020 INPUT "ENTER FINISH ADDRESS OF BLOCK";F
3030 L=F-S:IF L<0 THEN 3000
3040 INPUT "ENTER FILE NAME";F$
3050 OPEN 1,1,2,F$
3060 PRINT#1,S
3070 PRINT#1,F
3080 FOR I=1 TO L+1
3090 B=PEEK(S+I-1)
3100 PRINT#1,B
3110 NEXT I
3120 CLOSE 1
3130 PRINT "BLOCK WRITTEN TO TAPE"
3140 PRINT"[CD CD ]PRESS ANY KEY TO RETURN TO MAIN MENU"
3150 GET A$:IF A$="" THEN 3150
3160 RETURN
3999 REM ROUTINE TO LOAD A BLOCK OF RAM MEMORY
4000 PRINT "[CS ]"
4010 INPUT "ENTER FILE NAME";F$
4020 OPEN 1,1,0,F$
4030 INPUT#1,S
4040 INPUT#1,F
4050 L=F-S
4060 FOR I=1 TO L+1
4070 INPUT#1,B
4080 POKE S+I-1,B
4090 NEXT I
4100 PRINT "BLOCK WRITTEN TO RAM"
4110 PRINT"[CD CD ]PRESS ANY KEY TO RETURN TO MAIN MENU"
4120 GET A$:IF A$="" THEN 4120
4130 RETURN
4990 REM SUBROUTINE TO CONVERT HEX TO DECIMAL
4991 REM HEX NUMBER ENTERED AS H$
4992 REM DECIMAL NUMBER RETURNED AS DC
4993 REM LOCAL VARIABLES: N,ER,HX,D
5000 DC=0
5010 FOR N=1 TO LEN(H$)
5020 ER=1
5030 HX=ASC(MID$(H$,N,1))
5040 IF HX>47 AND HX<58 THEN HX=HX-48:ERR=0
5050 IF HX>64 AND HX<71 THEN HX=HX-55:ERR=0
5060 IF ER=1 THEN PRINT"INVALID HEX":RETURN
```

P40 Monitor

```
5070 D=HX*16^(LEN(H$)-N)
5080 DC=DC+D
5090 NEXT N
5100 RETURN
5990 REM SUBROUTINE TO CONVERT DECIMAL TO HEX
5991 REM DECIMAL ENTERED AS D$
5992 REM HEX RETURNED AS H$
5993 REM LOCAL VARIABLES: N,D,DC,C
6000 FOR N=1 TO LEN(D$)
6010 C=ASC(MID$(D$,N,1))
6020 IF C<48 OR C>57 THEN PRINT "INVALID DECIMAL":RETURN
6030 NEXT N
6040 DC=VAL(D$)
6050 H$=""
6060 D=16*(DC/16-INT(DC/16))
6070 IF DC<16 THEN D=DC
6080 DC=INT(DC/16)
6090 D=D+48
6100 IF D>57 THEN D=D+7
6110 H$=CHR$(D)+H$
6120 IF DC>0 THEN GOTO 6060
6130 RETURN
```

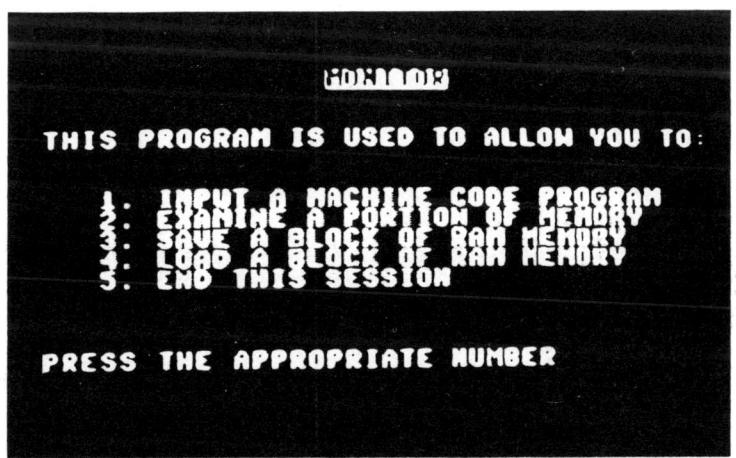

P41 Renumber

This is a very useful routine to have available when developing programs. The program can be renumbered by simply calling this routine.

The program will renumber both GOTOs and GOSUBs, but will not renumber an IF...THEN line number if the GOTO is not present.

The routine deletes itself after the renumber has been completed.

A short sample program is shown in the code.

COMMANDS

Key in routine and save to tape.
Load the program before writing your code.
When code has been fully developed then call the subroutine.

```
100 GOTO300
200 GOSUB400
300 GOTO600
400 REMSUB
500 RETURN
600 END
9999 REM RENUMBER PROGRAM
10000 REM PLACE THIS ROUTINE AT THE END
10001 REM OF YOUR PROGRAM THEN GOTO 10000
10002 BE=10:IN=10:REM STARTING LINE NUMBER AND INCREMENT
10003 DIM TB(200,2):I=1:REM TABLE OF LINE NOS OLD AND
      NEW
10004 LI=BE:TB(I,1)=LI:REM LINE NUMBER
10005 PT=2049:REM POINTER TO MEMORY
10006 LO=PEEK(PT):HI=PEEK(PT+1)
10007 AD=LO+HI*256:REM STARTING ADDRESS OF NEXT LINE
10008 LO=PEEK(PT+2):HI=PEEK(PT+3)
10009 NU=LO+HI*256:TB(I,2)=NU:REM VALUE OF CURRENT LINE
      NUMBER
10010 IF NU=9999 THEN 10016
10011 HI=INT(LI/256):LO=LI-HI*256:REM NEW LINE NUMBER
10012 POKE (PT+2),LO:POKE (PT+3),HI
10013 PT=AD:LI=LI+IN
```

P41 Renumber

```
10014 I=I+1:TB(I,1)=LI
10015 GOTO 10006
10016 REM NOW WE RENUMBER THE GOTOS AND GOSUBS
10017 PT=2049
10018 LO=PEEK(PT):HI=PEEK(PT+1)
10019 AD=LO+HI*256
10020 LO=PEEK(PT+2):HI=PEEK(PT+3)
10021 NU=LO+HI*256
10022 IF NU=9999 THEN 20000
10023 PT=PT+4
10024 IF PEEK(PT)=137 OR PEEK(PT)=141 GOTO 10027
10025 IF PEEK(PT)=0 THEN PT=PT+1:GOTO 10018
10026 PT=PT+1:GOTO 10024
10027 D$="":K=0
10028 PT=PT+1
10029 IF PEEK(PT)<48 OR PEEK(PT)>57 GOTO 10028
10030 K=K+1:D$=D$+CHR$(PEEK(PT)):PT=PT+1
10031 IF PEEK(PT)>47 AND PEEK(PT)<58 GOTO 10030
10032 D=VAL(D$)
10033 FOR J=1 TO I
10034 IF TB(J,2)=D THEN D=TB(J,1):J=I
10035 NEXT J
10036 D$=STR$(D)
10037 IF LEN(D$)<K THEN D$=" "+D$:GOTO 10037
10038 FOR J=1 TO K
10039 POKE (PT-K-1+J),(ASC(MID$(D$,J,1)))
10040 NEXT J
10041 IF PEEK(PT)=ASC(",") THEN GOTO10027
10042 GOTO 10024
20000 POKE PT,0:POKE (PT+1),0:REM PUT IN END OF PROGRAM MARKER
```

P42 Delete

This program can be used in program development to allow you to delete portions of a program when you no longer require them. Typically, you would use extra lines of code when debugging a program, and after the program had been debugged, you would delete your debug lines.

The routine is appended to your program when you are at the development stage. When you execute the routine, it deletes your section of code and then removes itself. Thus in the present state of the routine you can only use it once.

The program makes use of some of the special memory locations in the CBM-64 to carry out the delete.

COMMANDS

Key in this program and save to tape.
When about to develop a new program, load this routine first, then enter your code.
If you wish to delete a section of program then type GOTO 60000.

```
10 REM SAMPLE LINE
20 REM SAMPLE LINE
30 REM SAMPLE LINE
40 REM SAMPLE LINE
50 REM SAMPLE LINE
60 REM SAMPLE LINE
60000 REM DELETE ROUTINE
60010 REM APPEND THIS ROUTINE TO YOUR
60020 REM PROGRAM WHILE DEVELOPING CODE
60030 REM THE ROUTINE DELETES ITSELF
60040 REM AFTER IT HAS BEEN USED
60050 PRINT "ENTER RANGE OF DELETE"
60060 INPUT"STARTING LINE NUMBER";S
60070 INPUT "FINISHING LINE NUMBER";F
60080 PT=2049
60090 AD=PEEK(PT)+PEEK(PT+1)*256
60100 NO=PEEK(PT+2)+PEEK(PT+3)*256
60110 IF NO<S THEN PT=AD:GOTO 60090
```

```
60120 FRS=PT:REM FRS IS STARTING ADDRESS OF LINE TO BE
DELETED
60130 PT=AD
60140 AD=PEEK(PT)+PEEK(PT+1)*256
60150 NO=PEEK(PT+2)+PEEK(PT+3)*256
60160 IF NO<F AND NO>0 THEN PT=AD:GOTO 60140
60170 LAS=PT:REM LAS=STARTING ADDRESS OF LAST LINE TO BE
DELETED
60180 REM AD = STARING ADDRESS OF REST OF PROGRAM
60190 BL=AD-FRS:REM BL=LENGTH OF BLOCK TO BE DELETED
60200 PT=AD
60210 AD=PEEK(PT)+PEEK(PT+1)*256
60220 NO=PEEK(PT+2)+PEEK(PT+3)*256
60230 IF NO=60000 THEN GOTO 60360
60240 NAD=AD-BL
60250 POKE(PT-BL),(NAD-INT(NAD/256)*256)
60260 POKE(PT-BL+1),INT(NAD/256)
60270 POKE(PT-BL+2),PEEK(PT+2)
60280 POKE(PT-BL+3),PEEK(PT+3)
60290 REM NOW THE REST OF THE LINE
60300 I=4
60310 BT=PEEK(PT+I)
60320 IF BT=0 THEN POKE(PT-BL+I),0:GOTO 60200
60330 POKE(PT-BL+I),BT
60340 I=I+1
60350 GOTO 60310
60360 REM POKE TO END PROGRAM
60370 POKE (PT-BL),0:POKE(PT-BL+1),0
60380 REM TIDY UP BASIC POINTERS
60390 BL=BL+1482:REM BLOCK LENGTH INCREASED BY ROUTINE
LENGTH
60410 VL=PEEK(47)+PEEK(48)*256-BL
60420 POKE(47),(VL-INT(VL/256)*256)
60430 POKE(48),INT(VL/256)
60440 VL=PEEK(49)+PEEK(50)*256-BL
60450 POKE(49),(VL-INT(VL/256)*256)
60460 POKE(50),INT(VL/256)
60470 VL=PEEK(45)+PEEK(46)*256-BL+84
60480 POKE(49152),(VL-INT(VL/256)*256)
60490 POKE(49153),INT(VL/256)
60500 POKE45,PEEK(49152)
60510 POKE46,PEEK(49153)
60520 END
```

P43 Tidy

This is the only program in the book that cannot be easily adapted for use with a cassette.

This program tidied up our outputs for the purposes of printing this book.

You might find it useful when you send your listings to magazines, or whatever.

The program takes the CBM-64 cursor control characters and writes them out in a printable form.

COMMANDS

Key in program and type RUN.
Follow instructions.

```
10 REM PROGRAM GRAPHICS TIDY
20 PRINT "[CS ]"
30 PRINT "[CD CD ]THIS PROGRAM IS USED TO TIDY UP PRINTER"
40 PRINT "OUTPUT FOR OUR LISTINGS. WE HAVE USED"
50 PRINT "THE FOLLOWING CONVENTION FOR PRINTING"
60 PRINT "GRAPHICS."
70 PRINT "[CD CD CR ]1. ALL GRAPHICS ARE ENCLOSED BETWEEN [ ]";
120 PRINT "[CR ]2. THE CURSOR CONTROL KEYS ARE SHOWN"
130 PRINT "[CR CR CR CR ]AS CL,CR,CU AND CD FOR LEFT"
140 PRINT "[CR CR CR CR ]RIGHT, UP AND DOWN"
150 PRINT "[CR ]3. CLEAR IS SHOWN AS C-S, HOME AS C-H"
155 PRINT "[CR ]4. REVERSE ON AND OFF ARE SHOWN"
156 PRINT "[CR CR CR CR ]AS RON AND ROF"
160 PRINT "[CD CD ]WHAT IS THE NAME OF THE SEQUENTIAL"
170 PRINT "PROGRAM FILE";
180 INPUT F$
190 INPUT"ENTER OUTPUT FILE NAME";FO$
200 PRINT "PROCESSING";
210 OPEN 6,8,6,"0:"+F$+",S,R"
220 OPEN 5,8,5,"0:"+FO$+",S,W"
230 OPEN 15,8,15
```

P43 Tidy

```
240 GOSUB 1000
245 Z=0:REM FLAG TO SAY WE ARE IN GRAPHICS
250 REM THE FOLLOWING LOOP IS THE TIDY LOOP
260 GET#6,A$
265 IF ST<>0 THEN 500
270 A=ASC(A$+CHR$(0))
280 IF A>31 AND A<95 THEN GOTO 400
285 IF A=13 THEN GOTO 400
290 IF Z=0 THEN PRINT#5,"[";:Z=1
300 IF A=17 THEN PRINT#5,"CD ";
310 IF A=19 THEN PRINT#5,"CH ";
320 IF A=29 THEN PRINT#5,"CR ";
330 IF A=145 THEN PRINT#5,"CU ";
340 IF A=157 THEN PRINT#5,"CL ";
350 IF A=147 THEN PRINT#5,"CS ";
351 IF A=18 THEN PRINT#5,"RON ";
352 IF A=146 THEN PRINT#5,"ROF ";
360 GOTO 420
400 IF Z=1 THEN PRINT#5,"]";:Z=0
410 PRINT#5,A$;
420 PRINT ".";
430 GOTO 260
500 CLOSE 6
510 CLOSE 5
520 PRINT:PRINT "JOB FINISHED"
530 PRINT "STATUS = "ST
540 END
1000 REM CHECK SUCCESSFUL OPEN
1010 INPUT#15,A$,B$,C$,D$
1020 IF VAL(A$)>0 THEN PRINT "DISC FAULT":
     PRINT A$,B$,C$,D$:STOP
1030 RETURN
```

Graphics Programs

The following programs are used to exhibit the high resolution graphics capability of the Commodore-64.

We have included programs to show shading, movement, rotations, perspective, etc. There are of course many graphics text books available to you. Our programs take a rather simple approach to graphics, but we believe that this approach is best for the first time graphics user.

The BASIC provided with the Commodore-64 is not the best around for using graphics, and it could be better to use a more up to date BASIC, such as SIMON'S BASIC.

However, we wish to allow everyone who has access to a Commodore-64 to be able to develop graphics routines.

We have, therefore taken two approaches to graphics.

1. We show how to access the graphics routines fully from BASIC.
2. We include a machine code graphics patch, which gives the user a higher level approach to graphics using SYS commands.

P44   Hi-res Screen Utility

This program gives both a BASIC and a machine code routine for putting the computer into high resolution bit map mode and clearing the high resolution screen. The BASIC program is shorter and easier to understand. The machine code program, as you will discover, is much faster.

It is interesting that, provided you RUN this program once, the machine code routine will remain in memory until you power the machine down or until you load the part of memory in which it is held with something else. You can therefore clear BASIC memory with the NEW command and use the instruction SYS 49152 in your own graphics programs.

COMMANDS

Key in the program and RUN.

Select the BASIC routine first. See how slow it is.

Press RUN/STOP and RESTORE simultaneously.

RUN the program again, this time selecting the machine code routine.

Press RUN/STOP and RESTORE simultaneously.

```
10 REM HI-RES SCREEN UTILITY
20 REM ********************
30 REM
100 POKE 53280,2:REM RED BORDER
110 POKE 53281,3:REM CYAN SCREEN
120 PRINT CHR$(147):REM CLEAR SCREEN
130 PRINT:PRINT
140 PRINT TAB(9)CHR$(149)CHR$(18)
    "_____"
150 PRINT TAB(9)CHR$(149)CHR$(18)
    " HI-RES SCREEN UTILITY "
160 PRINT TAB(9)CHR$(149)CHR$(18)
    "_____"
170 PRINT CHR$(31):REM BLUE INK
```

```
180 PRINT TAB(6)
    "THIS PROGRAM DEMONSTRATES TWO"
190 PRINT TAB(6)
    "METHODS OF PUTTING THE MACHINE"
200 PRINT TAB(6)
    "INTO HIGH RESOLUTION GRAPHICS"
210 PRINT TAB(6)
    "MODE AND CLEARING THE HIGH"
220 PRINT TAB(6)"RESOLUTION SCREEN."
230 PRINT
240 PRINT TAB(6)
    "IT THUS LETS YOU COMPARE THE"
250 PRINT TAB(6)
    "SPEEDS OF SUBROUTINES IN BASIC"
260 PRINT TAB(6)
    "AND IN MACHINE CODE WHICH"
270 PRINT TAB(6)
    "PERFORM THE SAME FUNCTION."
280 PRINT:PRINT
290 FOR N=49152 TO 49221:READ A:
    POKE N,A:NEXT:REM MACINE CODE POKE
300 PRINT TAB(6)CHR$(18)
    " PRESS ANY KEY TO CONTINUE "
310 GET A$:IF A$="" THEN 310:REM
    NO SPACE BETWEEN INVERTED COMMAS
320 REM****************************
330 PRINT CHR$(147):PRINT:PRINT
340 PRINT TAB(6)
    "PRESS KEY 1 OR 2 AS INDICATED"
350 PRINT TAB(6)"BELOW."
360 PRINT
370 PRINT TAB(8)CHR$(18)" KEY 1 "
    CHR$(146)" - MACHINE CODE"
380 PRINT
390 PRINT TAB(8)CHR$(18)" KEY 2 "
    CHR$(146)" - BASIC"
400 PRINT:PRINT
410 PRINT TAB(6)
    "ONCE THE HIGH RESOLUTION SCREEN"
420 PRINT TAB(6)
    "HAS BEEN CLEARED, PRESS THE"
430 PRINT TAB(6)
    "RESTORE AND RUN/STOP KEYS"
440 PRINT TAB(6)
    "SIMULTANEOUSLY TO GET BACK"
450 PRINT TAB(6)
    "TO STANDARD CHARACTER MODE."
```

P44 Hi-res Screen Utility

```
460 REM*****************************
470 GET A$:IF A$="" THEN 470:REM
    NO SPACE BETWEEN INVERTED COMMAS
480 IF ASC(A$)<49 OR ASC(A$)>50
    THEN 470
490 A=VAL(A$)
500 ON A GOSUB 1000,1500
510 REM*****************************
520 GOTO 520
530 END
540 REM*****************************
550 REM*****************************
900 REM
910 REM             ***************
920 REM             *
930 REM             * SUBROUTINES
940 REM             *
950 REM             ***************
960 REM
1000 REM MACHINE CODE ROUTINE
1010 SYS 49152
1020 RETURN
1030 REM*****************************
1040 REM*****************************
1500 REM BASIC SUBROUTINE
1510 POKE 53272,PEEK(53272) OR 8:
     REM BIT MAP AT 8192
1520 POKE 53265,PEEK(53265) OR 32:
     REM SWITCH ON BIT MAP MODE
1530 FOR N=8192 TO 16191: POKE N,0:NEXT:
     REM CLEAR BIT MAP
1540 FOR N=1024 TO 2023: POKE N,1:NEXT:
     REM WHITE SCREEN, BLACK INK
1550 RETURN
1560 REM*****************************
1570 REM*****************************
1700 REM
1710 REM             ********
1720 REM             *
1730 REM             * DATA
1740 REM             *
1750 REM             ********
1760 REM
2000 REM DATA FOR M/C CODE ROUTINE
2010 DATA 169,8:REM          LDA# 8
2020 DATA 13,24,208:REM      ORA 53272
2030 DATA 141,24,208:REM     STA 53272
```

```
2040 DATA 169,32:REM         LDA# 32
2050 DATA 13,17,208:REM      ORA 53265
2060 DATA 141,17,208:REM     STA 53265
2070 DATA 169,0:REM          LDA# 00
2080 DATA 133,2:REM          STA 02
2090 DATA 169,32:REM         LDA# 32
2100 DATA 133,3:REM          STA 03
2110 DATA 160,0:REM          LDY# 00
2120 DATA 169,0:REM       L1:LDA# 00
2130 DATA 145,2:REM       L2:STA(02),Y
2140 DATA 200:REM            INY
2150 DATA 208,251:REM        BNE L2
2160 DATA 230,3:REM          INC 03
2170 DATA 169,64:REM         LDA# 64
2180 DATA 197,3:REM          CMP 03
2190 DATA 208,241:REM        BNE L1
2200 DATA 169,4:REM          LDA# 4
2210 DATA 133,3:REM          STA 03
2220 DATA 169,1:REM       L3:LDA# 01
     WHITE SCREEN, BLACK INK
2230 DATA 145,2:REM       L4:STA(02),Y
2240 DATA 200:REM            INY
2250 DATA 208,251:REM        BNE L4
2260 DATA 230,3:REM          INC 03
2270 DATA 169,7:REM          LDA# 7
2280 DATA 197,3:REM          CMP 03
2290 DATA 208,241:REM        BNE L3
2300 DATA 169,1:REM          LDA# 01
2310 DATA 145,2:REM       L5:STA(02),Y
2320 DATA 200:REM            INY
2330 DATA 192,232:REM        CPY# 232
2340 DATA 208,249:REM        BNE L5
2350 DATA 96:REM             RTS
2360 REM*****************************
2370 REM*****************************
```

P45 Text on Graphics Screen

This is a demonstration program to show how to print messages on your graphic displays.

The program works by copying the pattern for the letters stored in ROM onto the graphics area of memory.

To show the technique, we have included some sample graphics and text on the graphics screen.

COMMANDS

Key in program and type RUN.

```
10 REM TEXT ON GRAPHICS SCREEN
20 REM ***********************
30 REM
100 POKE 53280,2:REM RED BORDER
110 POKE 53281,3:REM CYAN SCREEN
120 PRINT CHR$(147):REM CLEAR SCREEN
130 PRINT:PRINT
140 PRINT TAB(9)CHR$(149)CHR$(18)
    "----------------------"
150 PRINT TAB(9)CHR$(149)CHR$(18)
    " TEXT ON GRAPHICS SCREEN"
160 PRINT TAB(9)CHR$(149)CHR$(18)
    "----------------------"
170 PRINT CHR$(31):REM BLUE INK
180 PRINT TAB(6)
    "THIS PROGRAM DEMONSTRATES THE"
190 PRINT TAB(6)
    "METHOD OF PUTTING TEXT ON THE"
200 PRINT TAB(6)
    "HIGH RESOLUTION GRAPHICS MODE"
210 PRINT:PRINT
220 FOR N=49152 TO 49221:READ A:
    POKE N,A:NEXT:REM MACHINE CODE POKE
230 PRINT TAB(6)CHR$(18)
    " PRESS ANY KEY TO CONTINUE "
240 GET A$:IF A$="" THEN 240
```

```
250 PRINT CHR$(147):PRINT:PRINT
260 PRINT TAB(6)
    "ENTER STRING TO BE PLACED ON"
270 PRINT TAB(6)
    "GRAPHICS SCREEN"
280 PRINT TAB(6);:INPUT S1$
290 PRINT "[CD CD ]"TAB(6);:
        INPUT "ROW NUMBER";R1
300 PRINT "[CD CD ]"TAB(6);:
        INPUT "CHARACTER NUMBER";C1
310 PRINT "[CD CD ]"TAB(6)
    "THE PROGRAM WORKS BY COPYING "
320 PRINT TAB(6)
    "BLOCKS OF CHARACTER ROM"
330 PRINT TAB(6)
    "[CD CD ]PRESS ANY KEY TO SEE RESULT"
340 GET A$:IF A$="" THEN GOTO 340
350 SYS 49152:GOSUB 3000:
    REM DRAW GRAPHIC
360 POKE56334,PEEK(56334)AND254
370 POKE1,PEEK(1)AND251
380 S$="COSINE CURVE"
390 R=2
400 C=4
410 GOSUB 4000
420 S$=S1$
430 R=R1
440 C=C1
450 GOSUB 4000
460 GOSUB 5000
470 S$="SINE CURVE"
480 R=25:C=4
490 GOSUB 4000
500 POKE1,PEEK(1)OR4
510 POKE56334,PEEK(56334)OR1
520 GET A$:IF A$="" THEN GOTO 500
530 POKE 53265,PEEK(53265)AND 223
540 END
1900 REM MACHINE CODE ROUTINE
1910 REM SCREEN LOCATED AT 49152
1920 REM BIT MAP AT 8192
1930 REM
1940 REM              ********
1950 REM              *      *
1960 REM              * DATA *
1970 REM              *      *
1980 REM              ********
```

P45 Text on Graphics Screen

```
1990 REM
2000 REM DATA FOR M/C CODE ROUTINE
2010 DATA 169,8:REM          LDA# 8
2020 DATA 13,24,208:REM      ORA 53272
2030 DATA 141,24,208:REM     STA 53272
2040 DATA 169,32:REM         LDA# 32
2050 DATA 13,17,208:REM      ORA 53265
2060 DATA 141,17,208:REM     STA 53265
2070 DATA 169,0:REM          LDA# 00
2080 DATA 133,2:REM          STA 02
2090 DATA 169,32:REM         LDA# 32
2100 DATA 133,3:REM          STA 03
2110 DATA 160,0:REM          LDY# 00
2120 DATA 169,0:REM       L1:LDA# 00
2130 DATA 145,2:REM       L2:STA(02),Y
2140 DATA 200:REM            INY
2150 DATA 208,251:REM        BNE L2
2160 DATA 230,3:REM          INC 03
2170 DATA 169,64:REM         LDA# 64
2180 DATA 197,3:REM          CMP 03
2190 DATA 208,241:REM        BNE L1
2200 DATA 169,4:REM          LDA# 4
2210 DATA 133,3:REM          STA 03
2220 DATA 169,1:REM       L3:LDA# 01
     WHITE SCREEN, BLACK INK
2230 DATA 145,2:REM       L4:STA(02),Y
2240 DATA 200:REM            INY
2250 DATA 208,251:REM        BNE L4
2260 DATA 230,3:REM          INC 03
2270 DATA 169,7:REM          LDA# 7
2280 DATA 197,3:REM          CMP 03
2290 DATA 208,241:REM        BNE L3
2300 DATA 169,1:REM          LDA# 01
2310 DATA 145,2:REM       L5:STA(02),Y
2320 DATA 200:REM            INY
2330 DATA 192,232:REM        CPY# 232
2340 DATA 208,249:REM        BNE L5
2350 DATA 96:REM             RTS
2360 REM****************************
2370 REM****************************
2980 REM SAMPLE PIECE OF GRAPHIC
2990 REM COSINE CURVE
3000 FOR X=0TO319 STEP .5
3010 Y=INT(90+80*COS(X/10))
3020 BY=8192+(INT(Y/8))*320 +
        8*INT(X/8)+(Y AND 7)
3030 BI=7-(XAND7)
```

```
3040 POKEBY,PEEK(BY)OR(2^BI)
3050 NEXT X
3060 RETURN
3980 REM SUBROUTINE TO PRINT STRING S$
3990 REM AT ROW R AND CHARACTER C
4000 GM=8192+(R-1)*320 +(C-1)*8
4010 FOR I=1 TO LEN(S$)
4020 K=ASC(MID$(S$,I,1))
4030 REM CONVERT FROM ASCII TO SCREEN
        CODE
4040 IF K>63 AND K<91 THEN K=K-64
4050 K=K*8+53248
4060 FOR J=0 TO 7
4070 BT=PEEK(K+J)
4080 POKE(GM+J),BT
4090 NEXT J
4100 GM=GM+8
4110 NEXT I
4120 RETURN
4980 REM SAMPLE PIECE OF GRAPHIC
4990 REM SINE CURVE
5000 FOR X=0TO319 STEP .5
5010 Y=INT(90+80*SIN(X/10))
5020 BY=8192+(INT(Y/8))*320 +
        8*INT(X/8)+(Y AND 7)
5030 BI=7-(XAND7)
5040 POKEBY,PEEK(BY)OR(2^BI)
5050 NEXT X
5060 RETURN
```

P46 Worm

This is a high resolution graphics program written entirely in BASIC with no calls to machine code subroutines. Its purpose is to demonstrate that you are not debarred from using high resolution graphics if you do not wish to become involved with machine code.

Pixels are inked in at the front of a squiggly shape and deleted behind it. As a result a little worm slithers across the screen.

The actual movement is fairly smooth for a BASIC program and is not ridiculously slow. The main disadvantage is the very slow screen clear which precedes the drawing of the worm. The program would be greatly improved if the machine code routine given in the hi-res utility program replaced the BASIC screen clear routine.

COMMANDS

Key in the program and RUN.

Stop the program by pressing the RUN/STOP and RESTORE keys simultaneously.

```
10 REM WORM
20 REM ****
30 REM
100 POKE 53265,PEEK(53265) OR 32:
    REM HI-RES BIT MAP MODE
110 B=8192:POKE 53272,PEEK(53272)OR 8:
    REM BIT MAP STARTS AT 8192
120 FOR N=0 TO 7999:POKE B+N,0:NEXT:
    REM CLEAR HI-RES SCREEN
130 FOR K=1024 TO 2023:POKE K,1:NEXT:
    REM WHITE HIRES SCREEN, BLACK INK
140 REM****************************
150 FOR N=0 TO 359:X=N:IF X>319 THEN
    X=319
160 R=N-40:IF R<0 THEN R=0
170 Y=INT(90+10*SIN(X/4))
```

```
180 CH=INT(X/8):RO=INT(Y/8):LN=Y AND 7
190 BY=B+RO*320+CH*8+LN:
    REM IDENTIFY BYTE TO BE CHANGED
200 BI=7-(X AND 7):REM BIT WITHIN THAT
    BYTE
210 POKE BY,PEEK(BY) OR (2^BI):
    REM DRAW WORM
220 REM*****************************
230 W=INT(90+10*SIN(R/4))
240 CA=INT(R/8):RA=INT(W/8):LA=W AND 7
250 BA=B+RA*320+CA*8+LA:
    REM IDENTIFY BYTE TO BE RESTORED
260 AA=7-(R AND 7):REM BIT WITHIN THAT
    BYTE
270 POKE BA,PEEK(BA) AND (255-2^AA):
    REM DELETE WORM
280 NEXT
290 GOTO 150
```

P47 Colors

This program is used to exhibit the colors available on the Commodore-64. The program first of all asks for your name in order to have some text to print out. The text is then printed using all the colors available.

COMMANDS

Key in the program and type RUN.
Follow instructions

```
10 REM PROGRAM - COLORS
20 PRINT"[CS ]"
30 PRINT:PRINT:PRINT:PRINT:PRINT
40 PRINT:PRINT:PRINT:PRINT:PRINT
50 PRINT "                COLORS"
60 L=TI:REM REMEMBER TIME VALUE
70 IF TI<L+150 THEN GOTO 70:REM 3 SEC DELAY
80 PRINT "[CS CD CD CD CD CD ]"
90 PRINT "THIS PROGRAM IS USED TO EXHIBIT THE."
100 PRINT "COLORS AVAILABLE ON THE COMMODORE 64"
110 PRINT "THE PROGRAM FIRST OF ALL ACCEPTS IN"
120 PRINT "YOUR NAME, AND THEN PRINTS YOUR NAME"
130 PRINT "IN THE VARIOUS COLORS AVAILABLE ON THE"
140 PRINT "COMMODORE 64."
150 PRINT
160 PRINT "TO SEE ANOTHER COLOR, PRESS ANY KEY"
170 PRINT "PRESS ANY KEY TO START"
180 GET A$:IF A$="" THEN 180
190 PRINT "[CS ]"
200 PRINT"[CD CD CD CD CD CD CD CD ]"
210 INPUT"       WHAT IS YOUR NAME";N$
220 N=LEN(N$)
230 IF N>40 THEN PRINT "NAME IS TOO LONG, PLEASE SHORTEN":GOTO 170
235 PRINT"[CS ]"
240 S=1504:K=55776
250 FOR I=1 TO N
260 POKE(S+(40-N)/2+I-1),(ASC(MID$(N$,I,1))-64)
270 NEXT I
280 C=0
290 C=C+1:IF C=16 THEN C=0
300 FOR I=1 TO N
310 POKE(K+(40-N)/2+I-1),C
```

```
320 NEXT I
330 PRINT "[CH CD CD ]PRESS ANY KEY, FOR NEW COLOR"
340 PRINT "[CH CD CD CD ]M FOR MULTICOLOR"
350 GET A$:IF A$="" THEN 340
360 IF A$<>"M" THEN 290
370 REM NOW WE SHOW MULTICOLOR MODE
380 POKE 53270,PEEK(53270) OR 16
390 REM SET THE COLORS
400 PRINT "[CH CD CD ]PRESS ANY KEY, FOR NEW COLOR"
410 PRINT "[CH CD CD CD ]S FOR SINGLE COLOR"
420 D=0
430 D=D+1:IFD=14 THEN D=0
440 POKE52381,D
450 POKE52382,D+1
460 POKE52383,D+2
470 GET A$:IF A$="" THEN 470
480 IF A$<>"S" THEN 430
490 REM MULTICOLOR OFF
500 POKE 53270,PEEK(53270) AND 239
510 GOTO 235
```

P48 Graphics Utility

This program is based on MINIGRAPH by Paul Schatz and can be found in Tim Onosko's book "Commodore 64: getting the most from it", which is published by Prentice/Hall International.

The program loads a set of machine code subroutines into memory locations 36883 to 37681. Using these routines we can reduce our own programs dramatically.

Once the routines have been installed, we can do the following.

Bit map is enabled by issuing the command SYS 50195.
Bit map is disabled with SYS 50198.
Bit map is cleared with SYS 50207.
Colors displayed on the bit map are set with SYS 50210, F, B.
F and B are the Foreground and Background numbers, and have values between 0 and 15.
A point is plotted on the bit map with SYS 50201, X, Y, M.
X and Y are the horizontal and vertical positions of the point. The horizontal position can be from 0 to 319 and the vertical position can be from 0 to 199. The upper left hand corner is 0, 0. The last variable M, sets the plotting mode. If M=1 the foreground color is used. If M=2 the background color is used. If M=3 then the color of the point is flipped.
A line is drawn with the command SYS 50204, X, Y, M.
X and Y are the coordinates of the end point of the line; the color of the line is determined by M, as before.

The program has some error correcting features to help you to enter the data correctly.

This program must be run before any of our graphics programs can be run.

COMMANDS

Key in the program and save to tape.
Type RUN.

Repeat until you have no errors.
Note that the program clears itself from memory when it has been run. Remember to SAVE.

```
10 REM PROGRAM - GRAPHICS
20 REM BASED ON MINIGRAPH BY PAUL SCHATZ
30 REM PROGRAM LOADS SOME GRAPHICS PRIMITIVES
40 REM INTO RAM FOR USE BY GRAPHICS PROGRAMS
50 I=50194:L=190:K=17:PRINT"[CS CD CD CD CD CD CD CD ]"
60 PRINT"[CS CD CD CD CD CD CD ]"
70 PRINT "          LOADING GRAPHICS"
80 A=0:L=L+10
90 PRINT"[ ]";
100 FOR J=1 TO K
110 READ BY
120 I=I+1:POKE I, BY:A=A+BY
130 NEXT J
140 READ SM
150 IF SM<>A THEN PRINT "DATA ERROR IN LINE"L:STOP
160 IF I=50959 THEN K=16:GOTO 80
170 IF I<>50975 THEN GOTO 80
180 PRINT"   GRAPHICS LOADED"
190 NEW
200 DATA 76, 244, 198, 76, 7, 199, 76, 37, 196, 76, 114,
        197, 76, 30, 197, 76, 66, 1941
210 DATA 197, 169, 0, 141, 4, 196, 32, 253, 174, 32, 235,
        183, 224, 200, 144, 3, 76, 2263
220 DATA 26, 199, 142, 3, 196, 166, 20, 165, 21, 240, 8,
        201, 1, 208, 240, 224, 64, 2124
230 DATA 176, 236, 141, 2, 196, 142, 1, 196, 32, 253, 174,
        32, 158, 183, 224, 3, 176, 2325
240 DATA 220, 142, 0, 196, 173, 0, 196, 240, 27, 74, 144,
        12, 32, 174, 196, 32, 135, 1993
250 DATA 196, 29, 158, 196, 145, 251, 96, 32, 174, 196, 32,
        135, 196, 61, 166, 196, 145, 2404
260 DATA 251, 96, 32, 174, 196, 32, 135, 196, 93, 158, 196,
        145, 251, 96, 173, 1, 196, 2421
270 DATA 41, 7, 170, 120, 160, 52, 132, 1, 160, 0, 177, 251
        160, 55, 132, 1, 88, 1707
280 DATA 160, 0, 96, 128, 64, 32, 16, 8, 4, 2, 1, 127, 191,
        223, 239, 247, 251, 1789
290 DATA 253, 254, 169, 0, 133, 251, 169, 224, 133, 252,
        173, 1, 196, 41, 248, 24, 101, 2622
```

P48 Graphics Utility

```
300 DATA 251, 133, 251, 173, 2, 196, 101, 252, 133, 252,
         173, 3, 196, 72, 41, 7, 24, 2260
310 DATA 101, 251, 133, 251, 144, 2, 230, 252, 104, 74, 74,
         74, 10, 170, 189, 236, 196, 2491
320 DATA 24, 101, 251, 133, 251, 189, 237, 196, 101, 252,
         133, 252, 96, 0, 0, 64, 1, 2281
330 DATA 128, 2, 192, 3, 0, 5, 64, 6, 128, 7, 192, 8, 0, 10,
         64, 11, 128, 948
340 DATA 12, 192, 13, 0, 15, 64, 16, 128, 17, 192, 18, 0, 20,
         64, 21, 128, 22, 922
350 DATA 192, 23, 0, 25, 64, 26, 128, 27, 192, 28, 0, 30,
         162, 32, 169, 224, 133, 1455
360 DATA 252, 169, 0, 133, 251, 168, 145, 251, 200, 208,
         251, 230, 252, 202, 208, 246, 96, 3262
370 DATA 32, 253, 174, 32, 158, 183, 224, 16, 144, 3, 76,
         26, 199, 96, 169, 192, 133, 2110
380 DATA 252, 169, 0, 133, 251, 32, 52, 197, 138, 10, 10,
         10, 10, 141, 9, 196, 32, 1642
390 DATA 52, 197, 138, 13, 9, 196, 162, 2, 160, 0, 145, 251,
         200, 208, 251, 230, 252, 2466
400 DATA 202, 16, 246, 145, 251, 200, 192, 232, 144, 249,
         96, 169, 0, 141, 8, 196, 141, 2628
410 DATA 10, 196, 32, 253, 174, 32, 235, 183, 224, 200, 144,
         3, 76, 26, 199, 142, 7, 2136
420 DATA 196, 166, 20, 165, 21, 240, 8, 201, 1, 208, 240,
         224, 64, 176, 236, 141, 6, 2313
430 DATA 196, 142, 5, 196, 32, 253, 174, 32, 158, 183, 201,
         3, 176, 220, 142, 0, 196, 2309
440 DATA 173, 5, 196, 56, 237, 1, 196, 141, 12, 196, 173, 6,
         196, 237, 2, 196, 141, 2164
450 DATA 13, 196, 16, 20, 206, 10, 196, 56, 169, 0, 237, 12,
         196, 141, 12, 196, 169, 1845
460 DATA 0, 237, 13, 196, 141, 13, 196, 169, 0, 141, 11, 196,
         173, 7, 196, 56, 237, 1982
470 DATA 3, 196, 141, 14, 196, 173, 8, 196, 237, 4, 196, 141,
         15, 196, 16, 20, 206, 1958
480 DATA 11, 196, 56, 169, 0, 237, 14, 196, 141, 14, 196,
         169, 0, 237, 15, 196, 141, 1988
490 DATA 15, 196, 169, 0, 141, 18, 196, 173, 14, 196, 56,
         237, 12, 196, 173, 15, 196, 2003
500 DATA 237, 13, 196, 144, 27, 174, 14, 196, 173, 12, 196,
         141, 14, 196, 142, 12, 196, 2083
510 DATA 174, 15, 196, 173, 13, 196, 141, 15, 196, 142, 13,
         196, 206, 18, 196, 173, 12, 2075
520 DATA 196, 141, 16, 196, 173, 13, 196, 141, 17, 196, 32,
         91, 196, 173, 18, 196, 208, 2199
```

```
530 DATA 18, 173, 1, 196, 205, 5, 196, 208, 27, 173, 2, 196,
         205, 6, 196, 208, 19, 2034
540 DATA 240, 16, 173, 3, 196, 205, 7, 196, 208, 9, 173, 4,
         196, 205, 8, 196, 208, 2243
550 DATA 1, 96, 173, 18, 196, 208, 6, 32, 192, 198, 76, 118,
         198, 32, 218, 198, 32, 1992
560 DATA 152, 198, 32, 152, 198, 16, 20, 173, 18, 196, 208,
         6, 32, 218, 198, 76, 140, 2033
570 DATA 198, 32, 192, 198, 32, 172, 198, 32, 172, 198, 32,
         91, 196, 76, 64, 198, 173, 2254
580 DATA 16, 196, 56, 237, 14, 196, 141, 16, 196, 173, 17,
         196, 237, 15, 196, 141, 17, 2060
590 DATA 196, 96, 173, 16, 196, 24, 109, 12, 196, 141, 16,
         196, 173, 17, 196, 109, 13, 1879
600 DATA 196, 141, 17, 196, 96, 173, 10, 196, 208, 9, 238, 1,
         196, 208, 3, 238, 2, 2128
610 DATA 196, 96, 173, 1, 196, 208, 3, 206, 2, 196, 206, 1,
         196, 96, 173, 11, 196, 2156
620 DATA 208, 9, 238, 3, 196, 208, 3, 238, 4, 196, 96, 173,
         3, 196, 208, 3, 206, 2188
630 DATA 4, 196, 206, 3, 196, 96, 173, 0, 221, 41, 252, 141,
         0, 221, 169, 59, 141, 2119
640 DATA 17, 208, 169, 8, 141, 24, 208, 96, 173, 0, 221, 9,
         3, 141, 0, 221, 169, 1808
650 DATA 27, 141, 17, 208, 169, 21, 141, 24, 208, 96, 32, 7,
         199, 76, 72, 178, 1616
```

P49 Shading

This program uses the plot routine of the graphics package to draw a line by placing a series of dots along it. The density of the dots gives a measure of the illumination of the line.

The points on the line are calculated by using the formula:

$$Y=M*X+C.$$

This formula leads to the following rules for calculating M and C.

$$M=(Y2-Y1)/(X2-X1)$$
$$C=Y2-M*X2$$

where X1,Y1 and X2,Y2 are two points on the line. These rules fall down when the line is vertical and the program has a small adjustment when this situation arises.

COMMANDS

Load in the graphics module and RUN.
Key in the program and type RUN.
Follow instructions.

```
10 REM PROGRAM -SHADING
20 PRINT"[CS ]"
30 PRINT"[CD CD CD CD CD CD CD CD ]"
40 PRINT "                SHADING"
50 A=TI
60 IF TI<A+150 THEN 60
70 PRINT "[CS ]"
80 PRINT"THIS PROGRAM USES THE PLOT COMMAND"
90 PRINT "TO SHOW THE EFFECT OF 'SHADING' A LINE"
100 PRINT "THE EFFECT OF SHADING IS ACHIEVED BY "
110 PRINT "PLACING A SERIES OF DOTS ALONG THE "
120 PRINT "LINE, THE NUMBER OF DOTS CORRESPONDING"
130 PRINT "TO THE ILLUMINATION OF THE LINE."
140 PRINT "THE ILLUMINATION CONSTANT LIES BETWEEN"
150 PRINT ".05 AND .9"
160 PRINT
170 INPUT "ENTER FIRST POINT X1,Y1";X1,Y1
```

```
180 IF X1<0 OR X1>319 OR Y1<0 OR Y1>199 THEN PRINT
    "INVALID": GOTO 170
190 INPUT "ENTER SECOND POINT X2,Y2";X2,Y2
200 IF X2<0 OR X2>319 OR Y2<0 OR Y2>199 THEN PRINT
    "INVALID": GOTO 190
210 INPUT "ENTER ILLUMINATION CONSTANT";I
220 IF I<.05 OR I>.9 THEN PRINT "INVALID":GOTO 210
230 SYS 50207:REM CLEAR BIT MAP
240 SYS 50195:REM TURN ON BIT MAP
250 SYS 50210,0,1:REM SELECT COLORS
260 GOSUB 1000
270 GET A$:IF A$="" THEN GOTO 250
280 SYS 50198:REM TURN OFF BIT MAP
290 END
985 REM SHADE LINE SUBROUTINE
990 REM LINE IS DRAWN FROM X1,Y1 TO X2,Y2
995 REM WITH ILLUMINATION CONSTANT I
1000 IF X2=X1 THEN GOTO 1120
1010 M=(Y2-Y1)/(X2-X1)
1020 C=Y1-M*X1
1030 D=SQR((X1-X2)^2+(Y2-Y1)^2)
1040 N=D*I
1050 DX=(X2-X1)/N
1060 FOR K=1 TO N
1070 J=INT(X1+K*DX)
1080 L=INT(M*J+C)
1090 SYS 50201,J,L,1
1100 NEXT K
1110 RETURN
1120 REM TAKE CARE OF VERTICAL LINES
1130 D=ABS(Y2-Y1)
1140 N=D*I
1150 IF Y2<Y1 THEN Y2=T:Y2=Y1:Y1=T
1160 DY=(Y2-Y1)/N
1170 FOR K=1 TO N
1180 J=INT(Y1+K*DY)
1190 L=INT(X1)
1200 SYS 50201,L,J,1
1210 NEXT K
1220 RETURN
```

P50 **Translation**

To translate, or to move a line, we must compute the new end points of the line and then draw it.

If we can move a single line, then we have the capability of moving line drawings about the screen.

To move a line we must know the end points of the original line, and the distance to be moved in both the X and Y directions.

The program uses the shading routine developed earlier to redraw the line.

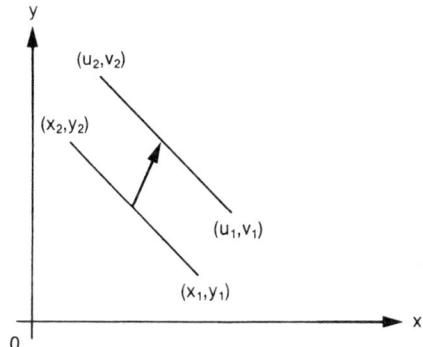

COMMANDS

Load in the graphics routine and RUN.
Key in the program and type RUN.
Follow instructions.

```
10 REM PROGRAM -TRANSLATION
20 PRINT"[CS ]"
30 PRINT"[CD CD CD CD CD CD CD CD ]"
40 PRINT "              TRANSLATION"
50 A=TI
60 IF TI<A+150 THEN 60
70 PRINT "[CS ]"
80 PRINT"THIS PROGRAM INTRODUCES A SIMPLE ROUTINE"
90 PRINT "FOR CHANGING THE POSITION OF A LINE. IF"
100 PRINT "YOU HAVE A ROUTINE FOR MOVING SINGLE"
110 PRINT "LINES THEN YOU CAN MOVE COMPLETE LINE"
```

```
120 PRINT "DRAWINGS ABOUT THE SCREEN AT YOUR OWN"
130 PRINT "CONVENIENCE.[CD CD CD ]"
140 PRINT "TO MOVE A LINE WE MUST KNOW ITS ORIGINAL";
150 PRINT"POSITION AND THE DISTANCE TO BE MOVED."
160 PRINT "IN BOTH THE X AND Y DIRECTIONS."
170 INPUT "ENTER FIRST POINT X1,Y1";X1,Y1
180 IF X1<0 OR X1>319 OR Y1<0 OR Y1>199 THEN PRINT
    "INVALID": GOTO 170
190 INPUT "ENTER SECOND POINT X2,Y2";X2,Y2
200 IF X2<0 OR X2>319 OR Y2<0 OR Y2>199 THEN PRINT
    "INVALID": GOTO 190
210 INPUT "ENTER ILLUMINATION CONSTANT";I
220 IF I<.05 OR I>.9 THEN PRINT "INVALID":GOTO 210
230 INPUT "ENTER X MOVEMENT";K1
240 INPUT "ENTER Y MOVEMENT";K2
250 SYS 50207:REM CLEAR BIT MAP
260 SYS 50195:REM TURN ON BIT MAP
270 SYS 50210,0,1:REM SELECT COLORS
280 GOSUB 1000
285 PRINT CHR$(7)
290 GOSUB 2000
300 GET A$:IF A$="" THEN GOTO 300
310 SYS 50198:REM TURN OFF BIT MAP
320 END
985 REM SHADE LINE SUBROUTINE
990 REM LINE IS DRAWN FROM X1,Y1 TO X2,Y2
995 REM WITH ILLUMINATION CONSTANT I
1000 IF X2=X1 THEN GOTO 1120
1010 M=(Y2-Y1)/(X2-X1)
1020 C=Y1-M*X1
1030 D=SQR((X1-X2)^2+(Y2-Y1)^2)
1040 N=D*I
1050 DX=(X2-X1)/N
1060 FOR K=1 TO N
1070 J=INT(X1+K*DX)
1080 L=INT(M*J+C)
1090 SYS 50201,J,L,1
1100 NEXT K
1110 RETURN
1120 REM TAKE CARE OF VERTICAL LINES
1130 D=ABS(Y2-Y1)
1140 N=D*I
1150 IF Y2<Y1 THEN Y2=T:Y2=Y1:Y1=T
1160 DY=(Y2-Y1)/N
1170 FOR K=1 TO N
1180 J=INT(Y1+K*DY)
1190 L=INT(X1)
```

P50 Translation

```
1200 SYS 50201,L,J,1
1210 NEXT K
1220 RETURN
1230 END
1960 REM TRANSLATION SUBROUTINE
1970 REM LINE FROM X1,Y1 TO X2,Y2 IS
1980 REM MOVED K1 IN X-DIRECTION
1990 REM AND K2 IN THE Y-DIRECTION
2000 X1=X1+K1:Y1=Y1+K2
2010 X2=X2+K1:Y2=Y2+K2
2020 GOSUB 1000
2030 RETURN
```

P51 Parallelogram

Using the routines developed in the previous programs we can shade a parallelogram.

The parallelogram is drawn by taking a vector (a straight line) and moving it to a new position, drawing many intermediate lines between the starting and finishing vectors. As before we use the shading routine to mimic illumination.

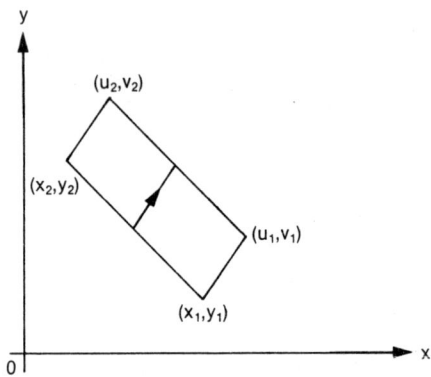

COMMANDS

Load in the graphics module and RUN.
Key in the program and type RUN.
Follow instructions.

```
10 REM PROGRAM -PARALLELOGRAM
20 PRINT"[CS ]"
30 PRINT"[CD CD CD CD CD CD CD CD ]"
40 PRINT "                PARALLELOGRAM"
50 A=TI
60 IF TI<A+150 THEN 60
70 PRINT "[CS ]"
80 PRINT"THIS PROGRAM USES THE ROUTINES DEVELOPED";
90 PRINT "IN THE PREVIOUS PROGRAMS TO SHADE A"
100 PRINT "PARALLELOGRAM. AS POINTED OUT IN THE "
110 PRINT "DESCRIPTION, WE CAN NOW SPECIFY"
120 PRINT "ILLUMINATION IN TWO DIRECTIONS TO "
130 PRINT "PRODUCE VARIABLE SHADING.[CD CD ]"
140 PRINT "TO DRAW THE PARALLELOGRAM WE NEED TO KNOW"
150 PRINT"THE GENERATING VECTOR POSITION AND THE"
```

P51 Parallelogram

```
155 PRINT "DISTANCE TO BE MOVED IN BOTH THE X AND"
160 PRINT "Y DIRECTIONS."
170 INPUT "ENTER FIRST POINT X1,Y1";X1,Y1
180 IF X1<0 OR X1>319 OR Y1<0 OR Y1>199 THEN PRINT
    "INVALID":GOTO 170
190 INPUT "ENTER SECOND POINT X2,Y2";X2,Y2
200 IF X2<0 OR X2>319 OR Y2<0 OR Y2>199 THEN PRINT
    "INVALID":GOTO 190
210 INPUT "ENTER X-ILLUMINATION CONSTANT";I1
220 IF I1<.05 OR I1>.9 THEN PRINT "INVALID":GOTO 210
230 INPUT "ENTER Y-ILLUMINATION CONSTANT";I2
240 IF I2<.05 OR I2>.9 THEN PRINT "INVALID":GOTO 230
250 INPUT "ENTER X MOVEMENT";R1
260 INPUT "ENTER Y MOVEMENT";R2
270 SYS 50207:REM CLEAR BIT MAP
280 SYS 50195:REM TURN ON BIT MAP
290 SYS 50210,0,1:REM SELECT COLORS
300 GOSUB 3000
310 GET A$:IF A$="" THEN GOTO 310
320 SYS 50198:REM TURN OFF BIT MAP
330 END
985 REM SHADE LINE SUBROUTINE
990 REM LINE IS DRAWN FROM X1,Y1 TO X2,Y2
995 REM WITH ILLUMINATION CONSTANT I
1000 IF X2=X1 THEN GOTO 1120
1010 M=(Y2-Y1)/(X2-X1)
1020 C=Y1-M*X1
1030 D=SQR((X1-X2)^2+(Y2-Y1)^2)
1040 N=D*I
1050 DX=(X2-X1)/N
1060 FOR K=1 TO N
1070 J=INT(X1+K*DX)
1080 L=INT(M*J+C)
1090 SYS 50201,J,L,1
1100 NEXT K
1110 RETURN
1120 REM TAKE CARE OF VERTICAL LINES
1130 D=ABS(Y2-Y1)
1140 N=D*I
1150 IF Y2<Y1 THEN Y2=T:Y2=Y1:Y1=T
1160 DY=(Y2-Y1)/N
1170 FOR K=1 TO N
1180 J=INT(Y1+K*DY)
1190 L=INT(X1)
1200 SYS 50201,L,J,1
1210 NEXT K
1220 RETURN
```

```
1230 END
1960 REM TRANSLATION SUBROUTINE
1970 REM LINE FROM X1,Y1 TO X2,Y2 IS
1980 REM MOVED K1 IN X-DIRECTION
1990 REM AND K2 IN THE Y-DIRECTION
2000 X1=X1+K1:Y1=Y1+K2
2010 X2=X2+K1:Y2=Y2+K2
2020 GOSUB 1000
2030 RETURN
2960 REM PARALLELOGRAM SHADING ROUTINE
2970 REM GENERATING VECTOR IS X1,Y1 TO X2,Y2
2980 REM ILLUMINATION CONSTANTS I1,I2
2990 REM X MOVEMENT R1 ; Y MOVEMENT R2
3000 I=I1
3100 GOSUB 1000:REM DRAW VECTOR
3110 LN=SQR(R1*R1+R2*R2)
3120 M=LN*I2
3130 D1R=R1/M
3140 D2R=R2/M
3150 FOR P=1 TO M
3160 K1=D1R
3170 K2=D2R
3180 I=I1
3190 GOSUB 2000
3200 NEXT P
3210 RETURN
```

P52 Shape Grabber

When dealing with line drawings one only needs to know the end points of each line and the method of drawing the lines. The end points of the lines can be held in a two dimensional array, and there are various methods of drawing in the lines. In this program the array is set up in such a way that the lines are drawn in order.

COMMANDS

Load in the graphics module and RUN.
Key in the program and RUN.
Follow instructions.

```
10 REM PROGRAM - SHAPE GRABBER
20 PRINT "[CS CD CD CD CD CD CD CD CD CD ]"
30 PRINT "            SHAPE GRABBER"
40 A=TI
50 IF TI<A+150 THEN GOTO 50
60 PRINT "[CS ]"
70 PRINT "THIS PROGRAM IS USED TO DRAW SHAPES"
80 PRINT "IN HI-RES GRAPHICS. THE SHAPE IS"
90 PRINT "RECORDED AS AN ARRAY OF POINTS, WHICH"
100 PRINT "WHEN JOINED TOGETHER FORM A LINE DRAWING";
110 PRINT "[CD ]NOTE THAT THE ORDER IN WHICH THE POINTS"
120 PRINT"ARE DRAWN IS IMPORTANT"
130 PRINT "[CD ]PRESS ANY KEY TO CONTINUE"
140 GET A$:IF A$="" THEN GOTO 140
150 SYS 50207:REM CLEAR BIT MAP
160 SYS 50210,0,1:REM COLOR BIT MAP
170 PRINT "[CS ]    SHAPE DRAWING ROUTINE"
180 PRINT "[CD CD ]ENTER NUMBER OF POINTS IN SHAPE"
190 INPUT N
200 DIM S(2,N)
210 PRINT "ENTER THE COORDINATES OF THE POINTS"
220 PRINT "IN THE SHAPE"
230 FOR I=1 TO N
240 PRINT "POINT ";I;" X,Y";
250 INPUT S(1,I),S(2,I)
260 NEXT I
```

```
270 PRINT "[CS ]THE POINTS ARE:"
280 L=1
290 FOR I=1 TO N
300 PRINT S(1,I),S(2,I)
310 L=L+1
320 IF L<20 THEN GOTO 360
330 PRINT "PRESS ANY KEY TO CONTINUE"
340 GET A$:IF A$="" THEN GOTO 340
350 L=0
360 NEXT I
370 PRINT "PRESS ANY KEY TO SEE DRAWING"
380 PRINT "ANOTHER KEY TO RELEASE DRAWING"
390 GET A$:IF A$="" THEN GOTO 390
400 SYS 50207:REM CLEAR BIT MAP
410 SYS 50210,1,0:REM COLOR BIT MAP
420 SYS 50195:REM TURN ON BIT MAP
430 X=INT(S(1,1)):Y=INT(S(2,1))
440 SYS 50201,X,Y,1
450 FOR I=2 TO N
460 X=INT(S(1,I)):Y=INT(S(2,I))
470 SYS 50204,X,Y,1
480 NEXT I
490 X=INT(S(1,1)):Y=INT(S(2,1))
500 SYS 50204,X,Y,1
510 GET A$:IF A$="" THEN GOTO 510
520 SYS 50198
530 END
```

P53 Rotation

This program uses the shape grabbing routine to get a user defined shape. The shape is then rotated through an angle of PI/2 radians, the screen is cleared and the new view is shown.

The program shows the advantage of using arrays to process shapes. The rotation problem is reduced to that of matrix (array) multiplication.

COMMANDS

Load in graphics module and RUN.
Key in the program and RUN.
Enter coordinates of shape when prompted.
Press any key to rotate figure.

```
10 REM PROGRAM - ROTATION
20 PRINT "[CS CD CD CD CD CD CD CD CD CD ]"
30 PRINT "            ROTATION"
40 A=TI
50 IF TI<A+150 THEN GOTO 50
60 PRINT "[CS ]"
70 PRINT "THIS PROGRAM FIRST OF ALL ALLOWS THE"
80 PRINT "USER TO ENTER A SHAPE, THE SHAPE IS"
90 PRINT "THEN ROTATED ABOUT THE ORIGIN THROUGH"
100 PRINT "90 DEGREES. THE ROTATION CAN BE REPEATED";
120 PRINT "[CD ]PRESS ANY KEY TO CONTINUE"
130 GET A$:IF A$="" THEN GOTO 130
140 SYS 50207:REM CLEAR BIT MAP
150 SYS 50210,1,0:REM COLOR BIT MAP
160 GOSUB 2000:REM GET SHAPE AND TURN ON BIT MAP
170 DIM NS(2,N)
180 GOSUB 1000:REM DRAW SHAPE
190 REM LOOP BACK POSITION
200 GOSUB 3000:REM COMPUTE NEW SHAPE
210 FOR I=1 TO N
220 S(1,I)=NS(1,I):S(2,I)=NS(2,I)
230 NEXT I
240 GOSUB 1000:REM DRAW NEW SHAPE
250 GOTO 200
260 END
999 REM SHAPE DRAWING ROUTINE
```

```
1000 GET A$:IF A$="" THEN GOTO 1000
1010 SYS 50207:REM CLEAR BIT MAP
1020 X=INT(S(1,1)+159):Y=INT(S(2,1)+100)
1030 SYS 50201,X,Y,1
1040 FOR I=2 TO N
1050 X=INT(S(1,I)+159):Y=INT(S(2,I)+100)
1060 SYS 50204,X,Y,1
1070 NEXT I
1080 X=INT(S(1,1)+159):Y=INT(S(2,1)+100)
1090 SYS 50204,X,Y,1
1100 RETURN
1999 REM SHAPE GRABBING ROUTINE
2000 PRINT "[CS ]    SHAPE GRABBING ROUTINE"
2010 PRINT "[CD CD ]ENTER NUMBER OF POINTS IN SHAPE"
2020 INPUT N
2030 DIM S(2,N)
2040 PRINT "ENTER THE COORDINATES OF THE POINTS"
2050 PRINT "IN THE SHAPE"
2060 FOR I=1 TO N
2070 PRINT "POINT ";I;" X,Y";
2080 INPUT S(1,I),S(2,I)
2090 NEXT I
2100 PRINT "[CS ]THE POINTS ARE:"
2110 L=1
2120 FOR I=1 TO N
2130 PRINT S(1,I),S(2,I)
2140 L=L+1
2150 IF L<20 THEN GOTO 2190
2160 PRINT "PRESS ANY KEY TO CONTINUE"
2170 GET A$:IF A$="" THEN GOTO 2170
2180 L=0
2190 NEXT I
2200 PRINT "PRESS ANY KEY TO SEE DRAWING"
2210 PRINT "ANY OTHER KEY TO ROTATE"
2220 GET A$:IF A$="" THEN 2220
2230 SYS 50195
2240 RETURN
2997 REM ROTATION SUBROUTINE
2998 REM OLD SHAPE HELD IN S(2,N)
2999 REM NEW SHAPE HELD IN NS(2,N)
3000 FOR I=1 TO N
3010 NS(1,I)=-S(2,I)
3020 NS(2,I)=S(1,I)
3030 NEXT I
3040 RETURN
```

P54 Transformations

This program uses the shape grabbing routine to allow the user to enter a line drawing, and this is then displayed on the screen.

The user can then use the program to perform various transformations on his line drawing.

The program informs the user of the options available.

COMMANDS

Load in graphics module and RUN.
Key in program and RUN.
Follow instructions.

```
10 REM PROGRAM - TRANSFORMATIONS
20 PRINT "[CS CD CD CD CD CD CD CD CD CD ]"
30 PRINT "        TRANSFORMATIONS"
40 A=TI
50 IF TI<A+150 THEN GOTO 50
60 PRINT "[CS ]"
70 PRINT "THIS PROGRAM FIRST OF ALL ALLOWS THE"
80 PRINT "USER TO ENTER A SHAPE, THE USER THEN"
90 PRINT "CHOOSES WHICH TRANSFORMATION TO PUT THE"
100 PRINT "SHAPE THROUGH. THE CHOICES ARE :"
101 PRINT "[CD CD ]I-IDENTITY     R-REFLECTION IN Y=X"
102 PRINT "H-HAL TURN    X-REFLECTION IN X-AXIS"
103 PRINT "Q-QUARTER     Y-REFLECTION IN Y-AXIS"
104 PRINT "  TURN        B-BACK QUARTER TURN"
120 PRINT "[CD ]PRESS ANY KEY TO CONTINUE"
130 GET A$:IF A$="" THEN GOTO 130
140 SYS 50207:REM CLEAR BIT MAP
150 SYS 50210,1,0:REM COLOR BIT MAP
160 GOSUB 2000:REM GET SHAPE AND TURN ON BIT MAP
170 DIM NS(2,N),T(2,2)
180 GOSUB 1000:REM DRAW SHAPE
190 REM LOOP BACK POSITION
191 GET A$:IF A$="" THEN GOTO 191
192 IF A$="I" THEN T(1,1)=1:T(1,2)=0:T(2,1)=0:T(2,2)=1
193 IF A$="R" THEN T(1,1)=0:T(1,2)=1:T(2,1)=1:T(2,2)=0
194 IF A$="H" THEN T(1,1)=-1:T(1,2)=0:T(2,1)=0:T(2,2)=-1
```

```
195 IF A$="X" THEN T(1,1)=1:T(1,2)=0:T(2,1)=0:T(2,2)=-1
196 IF A$="Q" THEN T(1,1)=0:T(1,2)=-1:T(2,1)=1:T(2,2)=0
197 IF A$="Y" THEN T(1,1)=-1:T(1,2)=0:T(2,1)=0:T(2,2)=1
198 IF A$="B" THEN T(1,1)=0:T(1,2)=1:T(2,1)=-1:T(2,2)=0
199 A=A$<>"I"ANDA$<>"R"ANDA$<>"H"ANDA$<>"X"
    ANDA$<>"Q"ANDA$<>"Y"ANDA$<>"B"
200 IF A THEN 190
209 GOSUB 3000:REM COMPUTE NEW SHAPE
210 FOR I=1 TO N
220 S(1,I)=NS(1,I):S(2,I)=NS(2,I)
230 NEXT I
240 GOSUB 1000:REM DRAW NEW SHAPE
250 GOTO 200
260 END
999 REM SHAPE DRAWING ROUTINE
1000 GET A$:IF A$="" THEN GOTO 1000
1010 SYS 50207:REM CLEAR BIT MAP
1020 X=INT(S(1,1)+159):Y=INT(S(2,1)+100)
1030 SYS 50201,X,Y,1
1040 FOR I=2 TO N
1050 X=INT(S(1,I)+159):Y=INT(S(2,I)+100)
1060 SYS 50204,X,Y,1
1070 NEXT I
1080 X=INT(S(1,1)+159):Y=INT(S(2,1)+100)
1090 SYS 50204,X,Y,1
1100 RETURN
1999 REM SHAPE GRABBING ROUTINE
2000 PRINT "[CS ]    SHAPE GRABBING ROUTINE"
2010 PRINT "[CD CD ]ENTER NUMBER OF POINTS IN SHAPE"
2020 INPUT N
2030 DIM S(2,N)
2040 PRINT "ENTER THE COORDINATES OF THE POINTS"
2050 PRINT "IN THE SHAPE"
2060 FOR I=1 TO N
2070 PRINT "POINT ";I;" X,Y";
2080 INPUT S(1,I),S(2,I)
2090 NEXT I
2100 PRINT "[CS ]THE POINTS ARE:"
2110 L=1
2120 FOR I=1 TO N
2130 PRINT S(1,I),S(2,I)
2140 L=L+1
2150 IF L<20 THEN GOTO 2190
2160 PRINT "PRESS ANY KEY TO CONTINUE"
2170 GET A$:IF A$="" THEN GOTO 2170
2180 L=0
2190 NEXT I
```

P54 Transformations

```
2200 PRINT "PRESS ANY KEY TO SEE DRAWING"
2210 PRINT "ANY OTHER KEY TO ROTATE
2220 GET A$:IF A$="" THEN 2220
2230 SYS 50195
2240 RETURN
2997 REM ROTATION SUBROUTINE
2998 REM OLD SHAPE HELD IN S(2,N)
2999 REM NEW SHAPE HELD IN NS(2,N)
3000 FOR I=1 TO N
3010 NS(1,I)=T(1,1)*S(1,I)+T(1,2)*S(2,I)
3020 NS(2,I)=T(2,1)*S(1,I)+T(2,2)*S(2,I)
3030 NEXT I
3040 RETURN
```

P55 General Transformation

This program allows the user to enter a shape and then to rotate it round the origin.

The programs switches to and from the hires screen, to display graphics and text when required.

COMMANDS

Load in the graphics module and RUN.
Key in the program and RUN.
Follow instructions.

```
10 REM PROGRAM - GENERAL TRANSFORMATION
20 PRINT "[CS CD CD CD CD CD CD CD CD CD ]"
30 PRINT "        GENERAL TRANSFORMATION"
40 A=TI
50 IF TI<A+150 THEN GOTO 50
60 PRINT "[CS ]"
70 PRINT "THIS PROGRAM FIRST OF ALL ALLOWS THE"
80 PRINT "USER TO ENTER A SHAPE, THE USER THEN"
90 PRINT "ENTERS THE ANGLE OF ROTATION OF THE"
100 PRINT "TRANSFORMATION TO BE EXECUTED."
110 PRINT "THE USER THEN HAS THE OPPORTUNITY OF"
120 PRINT "[CD CD RON ]R[ROF ]EPEATING THE ROTATION OR [RON ]Q[ROF ]UITTING"
130 PRINT "[CD CD ]THE USER PRESSES THE APPROPRIATE KEY"
140 PRINT "AS REQUIRED."
150 PRINT "[CD ]PRESS ANY KEY TO CONTINUE"
160 GET A$:IF A$="" THEN GOTO 160
170 SYS 50207:REM CLEAR BIT MAP
180 SYS 50210,1,0:REM COLOR BIT MAP
190 GOSUB 2000:REM GET SHAPE AND TURN ON BIT MAP
200 DIM NS(2,N),T(2,2)
210 GOSUB 1000:REM DRAW SHAPE
220 REM LOOP BACK POSITION
230 GET A$:IF A$="" THEN GOTO 230
240 IF A$="Q" THEN GOTO 320
250 IF A$<>"R" THEN GOTO 220
260 GOSUB 3000:REM COMPUTE NEW SHAPE
270 FOR I=1 TO N
```

P55 General Transformation

```
280 S(1,I)=NS(1,I):S(2,I)=NS(2,I)
290 NEXT I
300 GOSUB 1000:REM DRAW NEW SHAPE
310 GOTO 220
320 SYS 50198
330 END
999 REM SHAPE DRAWING ROUTINE
1000 REM SHAPE HELD IN ARRAY S(2,N)
1010 SYS 50207:REM CLEAR BIT MAP
1020 X=INT(S(1,1)+159):Y=INT(S(2,1)+100)
1030 SYS 50201,X,Y,1
1040 FOR I=2 TO N
1050 X=INT(S(1,I)+159):Y=INT(S(2,I)+100)
1060 SYS 50204,X,Y,1
1070 NEXT I
1080 X=INT(S(1,1)+159):Y=INT(S(2,1)+100)
1090 SYS 50204,X,Y,1
1100 RETURN
1999 REM SHAPE GRABBING ROUTINE
2000 PRINT "[CS ]   SHAPE GRABBING ROUTINE"
2010 PRINT "[CD CD ]ENTER NUMBER OF POINTS IN SHAPE"
2020 INPUT N
2030 DIM S(2,N)
2040 PRINT "ENTER THE COORDINATES OF THE POINTS"
2050 PRINT "IN THE SHAPE"
2060 FOR I=1 TO N
2070 PRINT "POINT ";I;" X,Y";
2080 INPUT S(1,I),S(2,I)
2090 NEXT I
2100 PRINT "[CS ]THE POINTS ARE:"
2110 L=1
2120 FOR I=1 TO N
2130 PRINT S(1,I),S(2,I)
2140 L=L+1
2150 IF L<20 THEN GOTO 2190
2160 PRINT "PRESS ANY KEY TO CONTINUE"
2170 GET A$:IF A$="" THEN GOTO 2170
2180 L=0
2190 NEXT I
2200 PRINT "ENTER ROTATION ANGLE (RADIANS)"
2210 INPUT TH
2220 PRINT "PRESS ANY KEY TO SEE DRAWING"
2230 GET A$:IF A$="" THEN 2230
2240 SYS 50195
2250 RETURN
2996 REM ROTATION SUBROUTINE
2997 REM OLD SHAPE HELD IN S(2,N)
```

```
2998 REM NEW SHAPE HELD IN NS(2,N)
2999 REM ANGLE OF ROTATION TH
3000 S=SIN(TH):C=COS(TH)
3010 FOR I=1 TO N
3020 NS(1,I)=C*S(1,I)-S*S(2,I)
3030 NS(2,I)=S*S(1,I)+C*S(2,I)
3040 NEXT I
3050 RETURN
```

P56 3D Rotation

The object of this program is to rotate a two dimensional shape in the plane of the screen.

The shape chosen is a regular polygon. (Note that in the limit the polygon becomes a circle.)

The polygon is centred at the point X0,Y0,Z0 and has NS sides.

The program uses the ideas of the rotation program presented earlier.

COMMANDS

Load in the graphics module and RUN.
Key in the program and type RUN.
Follow instructions.

```
10 REM PROGRAM - 3D ROTATION
20 PRINT "[CS CD CD CD CD CD CD CD CD CD ]"
30 PRINT "          3D ROTATION"
40 PRINT "          ABOUT X-AXIS"
50 A=TI
60 IF TI<A+150 THEN GOTO 60
70 PRINT "[CS ]"
80 PRINT "THE OBJECT OF THIS PROGRAM IS TO FORM"
90 PRINT "A THREE DIMENSIONAL SHAPE BY ROTATING"
100 PRINT "A TWO DIMENSIONAL OBJECT ON THE PLANE"
110 PRINT "OF THE SCREEN. THE COORDINATES OF THE"
120 PRINT "SHAPE ARE HELD IN THE ARRAY S(3,50)."
130 PRINT "NOTE THAT THE TWO DIMENSIONAL SHAPE"
140 PRINT "HAS A MAXIMUM OF 50 SIDES. THE SHAPE"
150 PRINT "IS A POLYGON, AND A POLYGON WITH 50"
160 PRINT "SIDES IS ALMOST A CIRCLE, SO IN THE"
170 PRINT "LIMIT WE WILL FORM A SPHERE."
180 PRINT "[CD CD CD ]THE POLYGON IS CENTERED ON THE
    SCREEN"
190 PRINT "AND ROTATED ABOUT AN AXIS HORIZONTALLY"
200 PRINT "IN THE CENTER OF THE SCREEN"
210 PRINT "[CD CD ]PRESS ANY KEY TO CONTINUE"
220 GET A$:IF A$="" THEN GOTO 220
```

```
230 PRINT "[CS CD CD CD CD CD ]"
240 DIM S(3,50),NS(3,50),C(3,3)
250 INPUT "ENTER POLYGON RADIUS";R
260 INPUT "ENTER NUMBER OF SIDES";N
270 INPUT "ENTER Y-AXIS ROTATION (DEGS)";B
280 B=B*[]/180
290 SYS 50207:REM CLEAR BIT MAP
300 SYS 50210,1,0:REM COLOR BIT MAP
310 TH=B
320 GOSUB 1000:REM ROTATION-X MATRIX CALCULATION
330 GOSUB 2000:REM SHAPE ROUTINE
340 SYS 50195:REM TURN ON BIT MAP
350 GOSUB 3000:REM DRAW SHAPE
360 FOR TH=B TO 2*[] STEP B
370 GOSUB 4000:REM CALCULATE NEW VIEW
380 GOSUB 3000:REM DRAW SHAPE
390 NEXT TH
400 END
990 REM X-ROTATION MATRIX
1000 C(1,1)=1
1010 C(1,2)=0
1020 C(1,3)=0
1030 C(2,1)=0
1040 C(2,2)=COS(TH)
1050 C(2,3)=SIN(TH)
1060 C(3,1)=0
1070 C(3,2)=-SIN(TH)
1080 C(3,3)=COS(TH)
1090 RETURN
1990 REM SHAPE SUBROUTINE
2000 DA=2*[]/N
2010 A=-DA
2020 FOR I=1 TO N
2030 A=A+DA
2040 S(1,I)=R*COS(A)
2050 S(2,I)=R*SIN(A)
2060 S(3,I)=0
2070 NEXT I
2080 RETURN
2990 REM DRAW SHAPE ROUTINE
3000 X=INT(S(1,1)+160):Y=INT(S(2,1)+100)
3010 SYS 50201,X,Y,1
3020 FOR I=2 TO N
3030 X=INT(S(1,I)+160):Y=INT(S(2,I)+100)
3040 SYS 50204,X,Y,1
3050 NEXT I
3060 X=INT(S(1,1)+160):Y=INT(S(2,1)+100)
```

P56 3D Rotation

```
3070 SYS 50204,X,Y,1
3080 RETURN
3990 REM NEW VIEW CALCULATION
4000 FOR I=1 TO N
4010 NS(1,I)=S(1,I)*C(1,1)+S(2,I)*C(2,1)+S(3,I)*C(3,1)
4020 NS(2,I)=S(1,I)*C(1,2)+S(2,I)*C(2,2)+S(3,I)*C(3,2)
4030 NS(3,I)=S(1,I)*C(1,3)+S(2,I)*C(2,3)+S(3,I)*C(3,3)
4040 NEXT I
4050 FOR J=1 TO N
4060 FOR K=1 TO 3
4070 S(K,J)=NS(K,J)
4080 NEXT K
4090 NEXT J
4100 RETURN
```

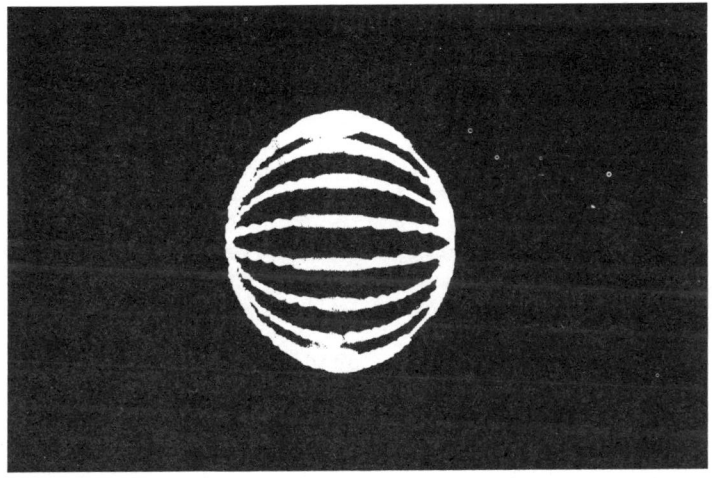

P57 Perspective

Most people will remember from school days about perspective. The method usually remembered is to locate a vanishing point, and all parallel lines should converge to that point. We use a slight variation on this idea in this program.

In this routine we imagine that we have a fixed view point, the point (0,0,0), say, and we calculate the projection of the three dimensional object on an image plane, Z=K, say. We will then have a two dimensional representation of the three dimensional object which will be in perspective.

Normally, we do not wish to view from the point (0,0,0) and with an image plane at Z=K. We will normally have an arbitrary view point (VX,VY,VZ) and use the plane Z=0 as the image plane.

The algorithm to find the coordinates of an image point is then:

1. Rewrite the coordinates of the point with respect to the view point.
2. Calculate the coordinates of the projection in the plane Z=-VZ.
3. Rewrite the coordinates with respect to the old coordinates.
4. Draw the shape with the new coordinates.

This program uses the above routine to implement a perspective algorithm.

COMMANDS

Load in graphics module and RUN.
Key in program and type RUN.
Follow instructions.

```
10 REM PROGRAM - PERSPECTIVE
20 PRINT "[CS CD CD CD CD CD CD CD CD CD CD CD ]"
30 PRINT "                PERSPECTIVE"
40 A=TI
50 IF TI<A+150 THEN GOTO 50
```

P57 Perspective

```
60 PRINT "[CS CD ]"
70 PRINT "THIS PROGRAM FIRST OF ALL SHOWS A FIGURE";
80 PRINT "WITHOUT CONSIDERING PERSPECTIVE, THEN"
90 PRINT "AFTER THE USER PRESSES ANY KEY, THE "
100 PRINT "FIGURE IN PERSPECTIVE."
110 PRINT "[CD ]THE FIGURE CHOSEN IS A LINE DRAWING"
120 PRINT "OF A HOUSE. THE FRAME OF REFERENCE IS"
130 PRINT "CENTRED ON THE HOUSE"
140 PRINT "[CD CD ]PRESS ANY KEY TO CONTINUE"
150 GET A$:IF A$="" THEN GOTO 150
160 PRINT "[CS ]"
170 DIM H(10,3),S(10,3),P(10,3)
180 FOR I=1 TO 10
190 FOR J=1 TO 3
200 READ H(I,J):S(I,J)=H(I,J)
210 NEXT J
220 NEXT I
230 REM DATA FOR HOUSE
240 DATA 0,0,-100,50,0,-100,50,-40,-100,25,-50
250 DATA -100,0,-40,-100,0,0,-25,50 ,0,-25,50
260 DATA -40,-25,25,-50 ,-25,0,-40,-25
270 REM END OF DATA
280 SYS 50207:REM CLEAR BIT MAP
290 SYS 50210,1,0:REM COLOR BIT MAP
300 GOSUB 1000:REM CLEAR MAP AND DRAW HOUSE
310 REM LOOP BACK POINT
320 GET A$:IF A$="" THEN GOTO 320
330 SYS 50198:REM BIT MAP OFF
340 INPUT "VIEW POINT (X,Y,Z)";VX,VY,VZ
345 IF VZ=-100 THEN PRINT "CANNOT SEE SHAPE FROM INSIDE
    WALL":GOTO 340
350 REM PERSPECTIVE ROUTINE
360 FOR I=1 TO 10
370 PX=S(I,1)-VX
380 PY=S(I,2)-VY
390 PZ=S(I,3)-VZ
400 R=-VZ/PZ
410 QX=R*PX+VX
420 QY=R*PY+VY
430 P(I,1)=QX
440 P(I,2)=QY
450 P(I,3)=0
460 NEXT I
470 FOR I=1 TO 10
480 FOR J=1 TO 3
490 H(I,J)=P(I,J)
500 NEXT J
```

```
510 NEXT I
520 GOSUB 1000:REM CLEAR BIT MAP AND DRAW HOUSE
530 GOTO 310
990 REM CLEAR BIT MAP AND DRAW HOUSE
1000 SYS 50207
1010 SYS 50195
1020 K=1:GOSUB 2000
1030 SYS 50201,X,Y,1
1040 FOR J=2 TO 5
1050 K=J:GOSUB 2000
1060 SYS 50204,X,Y,1
1070 NEXT J
1080 K=1:GOSUB 2000
1090 SYS 50204,X,Y,1
1100 REM NEXT THE BACK OF THE HOUSE
1110 K=6:GOSUB 2000
1120 SYS 50201,X,Y,1
1130 FOR J=7 TO 10
1140 K=J:GOSUB 2000
1150 SYS 50204,X,Y,1
1160 NEXT J
1170 K=6:GOSUB 2000
1180 SYS 50204,X,Y,1
1190 REM NEXT JOIN THE BACK TO FRONT
1200 K=6:GOSUB 2000
1210 SYS 50201,X,Y,1
1220 K=1:GOSUB 2000
1230 SYS 50204,X,Y,1
1240 K=10:GOSUB 2000
1250 SYS 50201,X,Y,1
1260 K=5:GOSUB 2000
1270 SYS 50204,X,Y,1
1280 K=9:GOSUB 2000
1290 SYS 50201,X,Y,1
1300 K=4:GOSUB 2000
1310 SYS 50204,X,Y,1
1320 K=8:GOSUB 2000
1330 SYS 50201,X,Y,1
1340 K=3:GOSUB 2000
1350 SYS 50204,X,Y,1
1360 K=7:GOSUB 2000
1370 SYS 50201,X,Y,1
1380 K=2:GOSUB 2000
1390 SYS 50204,X,Y,1
1400 RETURN
1990 REM CLIPPING ROUTINE
2000 X=INT(H(K,1)+160)
```

P57 Perspective

```
2010 IF X>319 THEN X=319
2020 IF X<0 THEN X=0
2030 Y=INT(H(K,2)+100)
2040 IF Y>199 THEN Y=199
2050 IF Y<0 THEN Y=0
2060 RETURN
```

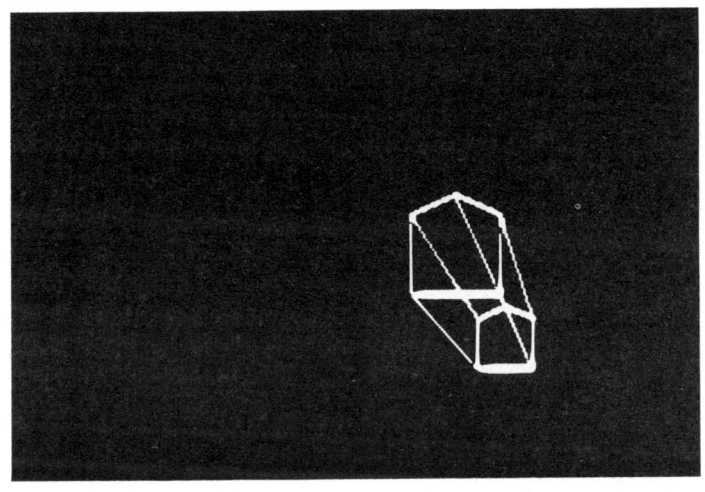

P58 Rotating House

Using the techniques developed in the previous programs we present here a program which shows an object continuously rotating about the origin. The object chosen is a line drawing of a house.

COMMANDS

Load in graphics module and RUN.
Key in program and RUN.

```
10 REM PROGRAM - ROTATING HOUSE
20 PRINT "[CS CD CD CD CD CD CD CD CD CD CD CD ]"
30 PRINT "            ROTATING HOUSE"
40 A=TI
50 IF TI<A+150 THEN GOTO 50
60 DIM H(10,3),S(10,3),P(10,3)
70 FOR I=1 TO 10
80 FOR J=1 TO 3
90 READ H(I,J):S(I,J)=H(I,J)
100 NEXT J
110 NEXT I
120 REM DATA FOR HOUSE
130 DATA 0,0,-100,50,0,-100,50,-40,-100,25,-50
140 DATA -100,0,-40,-100,0,0,-25,50 ,0,-25,50
150 DATA -40,-25,25,-50 ,-25,0,-40,-25
160 REM END OF DATA
170 SYS 50207:REM CLEAR BIT MAP
180 SYS 50210,1,0:REM COLOR BIT MAP
190 SYS50195 :REM BIT MAP ON
200 GOSUB 1000:REM CLEAR MAP AND DRAW HOUSE
210 VX=500:VY=-500:VZ=800:REM VIEW POINT
220 GOSUB 3000 :REM ROTATION MATRIX
230 REM LOOP BACK POINT
240 DATA 0,0,-100,50,0,-100,50,-40,-100,25,-50
250 REM PERSPECTIVE ROUTINE
260 FOR I=1 TO 10
270 PX=S(I,1)-VX
280 PY=S(I,2)-VY
290 PZ=S(I,3)-VZ
300 R=-VZ/PZ
310 QX=R*PX+VX
```

P58 Rotating House

```
320 QY=R*PY+VY
330 P(I,1)=QX
340 P(I,2)=QY
350 P(I,3)=0
360 NEXT I
370 FOR I=1 TO 10
380 FOR J=1 TO 3
390 H(I,J)=P(I,J)
400 NEXT J
410 NEXT I
420 GOSUB 1000:REM CLEAR BIT MAP AND DRAW HOUSE
430 GOSUB 4000 :REM ROTATE HOUSE
440 GOTO 230
450 END
900 READ H(I,J):S(I,J)=H(I,J)
990 REM CLEAR BIT MAP AND DRAW HOUSE
1000 REM CALLS SIMPLE CLIPPING SUBROUTINE
1010 SYS 50207
1020 K=1:GOSUB 2000
1030 SYS 50201,X,Y,1
1040 FOR J=2 TO 5
1050 K=J:GOSUB 2000
1060 SYS 50204,X,Y,1
1070 NEXT J
1080 K=1:GOSUB 2000
1090 SYS 50204,X,Y,1
1100 REM NEXT THE BACK OF THE HOUSE
1110 K=6:GOSUB 2000
1120 SYS 50201,X,Y,1
1130 FOR J=7 TO 10
1140 K=J:GOSUB 2000
1150 SYS 50204,X,Y,1
1160 NEXT J
1170 K=6:GOSUB 2000
1180 SYS 50204,X,Y,1
1190 REM NEXT JOIN THE BACK TO FRONT
1200 K=6:GOSUB 2000
1210 SYS 50201,X,Y,1
1220 K=1:GOSUB 2000
1230 SYS 50204,X,Y,1
1240 K=10:GOSUB 2000
1250 SYS 50201,X,Y,1
1260 K=5:GOSUB 2000
1270 SYS 50204,X,Y,1
1280 K=9:GOSUB 2000
1290 SYS 50201,X,Y,1
1300 K=4:GOSUB 2000
```

```
1310 SYS 50204,X,Y,1
1320 K=8:GOSUB 2000
1330 SYS 50201,X,Y,1
1340 K=3:GOSUB 2000
1350 SYS 50204,X,Y,1
1360 K=7:GOSUB 2000
1370 SYS 50201,X,Y,1
1380 K=2:GOSUB 2000
1390 SYS 50204,X,Y,1
1400 RETURN
1990 REM CLIPPING ROUTINE
2000 X=INT(H(K,1)+160)
2010 IF X>319 THEN X=319
2020 IF X<0 THEN X=0
2030 Y=INT(H(K,2)+100)
2040 IF Y>199 THEN Y=199
2050 IF Y<0 THEN Y=0
2060 RETURN
2990 REM ROTATION MATRIX
3000 C(1,1)=COS([]/10)
3010 C(1,2)=0
3020 C(1,3)=-SIN([]/10)
3030 C(2,1)=0
3040 C(2,2)=1
3050 C(2,3)=0
3060 C(3,1)=SIN([]/10)
3070 C(3,2)=0
3080 C(3,3)=COS([]/10)
3090 RETURN
3990 REM ROTATE HOUSE
4000 FOR I=1 TO 10
4010 T1=C(1,1)*S(I,1)+C(2,1)*S(I,2)+C(3,1)*S(I,3)
4020 T2=C(1,2)*S(I,1)+C(2,2)*S(I,2)+C(3,2)*S(I,3)
4030 T3=C(1,3)*S(I,1)+C(2,3)*S(I,2)+C(3,3)*S(I,3)
4040 S(I,1)=T1:S(I,2)=T2:S(I,3)=T3
4050 NEXT I
4060 RETURN
```

P59 Drawing Circles

When using the CBM-64 you have to make decisions when making up graphics. For example if you wish to draw a circle, you could draw it using:

    short line segments
    dots distributed round the edge
or a solid shaded circle, using dots.

This program shows the user all three methods of drawing circles.

The program also shows how we can set up arrays of the trigonometric functions to speed up the arithmetic of the program. (Note that because the PI symbol was not available at the time of printing this program we have used [PI] for PI.)

COMMANDS

Load in the graphics module and RUN.
Key in the program and RUN.
Select from the menu, and follow instructions.

```
10 REM PROGRAM   - DRAWING CIRCLES
20 PRINT"[CS ]"
30 PRINT"[CD CD CD CD CD CD CD CD ]"
40 PRINT "         DRAWING CIRCLES"
65 DIM S(200),C(200)
70 GOSUB 1000
80 SYS 50207:REM CLEAR BIT MAP
90 SYS 50210,0,1:REM COLOR BIT MAP
100 PRINT"[CS ]THIS PROGRAM SHOWS THE VARIOUS WAYS"
110 PRINT"IN WHICH WE CAN DRAW CIRCLES WITH THE"
120 PRINT "[CD ]1. SHORT LINE SEGMENTS ROUND THE EDGE"
140 PRINT "[CD ]2. DOTS DISTRIBUTED ROUND THE EDGE"
150 PRINT "[CD ]3. SHADED CIRCLE USING DOTS"
160 INPUT "ENTER CHOICE[]";C%
170 IF C%<1 OR C%>3 THEN PRINT "INVALID":GOTO 140
180 ON C% GOSUB 2000,3000,4000
190 GET A$:IF A$="" THEN GOTO 190
```

```
200 SYS 50198:REM TURN OFF BIT MAP
210 INPUT "ANOTHER GO?";R$
220 IF LEFT$(R$,1)="Y" THEN GOTO 80
230 END
980 REM SUBROUTINE TO SET UP ARRAYS OF
990 REM SINES AND COSINES
1000 REM DATA HELD IN S(I),C(I)
1010 FOR I=1 TO 200
1020 S(I)=SIN(I*2*[PI]/200)
1030 C(I)=COS(I*2*[PI]/200)
1040 NEXT I
1050 RETURN
1980 REM SUBROUTINE TO DRAW CIRCLES
1990 REM USING SHORT LINES
2000 PRINT "[CS ]"
2010 INPUT "ENTER RADIUS OF CIRCLE";RD
2020 PRINT "THE CIRCLE WILL BE CENTERED ON THE SCREEN"
2030 PRINT "PRESS ANY KEY TO DRAW CIRCLE"
2040 PRINT "WHEN CIRCLE HAS BEEN DRAWN, PRESS KEY"
2045 GET A$:IF A$="" THEN 2045
2050 SYS 50195
2060 X=INT(RD*S(1)+159)
2070 Y=INT(RD*C(1)+100)
2080 SYS 50201,X,Y,1
2100 FOR I=1 TO 200
2110 X=RD*S(I):Y=RD*C(I)
2120 X=X+159:Y=Y+100
2130 X=INT(X):Y=INT(Y)
2140 SYS 50204,X,Y,1
2150 NEXT I
2160 RETURN
2980 REM SUBROUTINE TO DRAW CIRCLES
2990 REM USING DOTS
3000 PRINT "[CS ]"
3010 INPUT "ENTER RADIUS OF CIRCLE";RD
3020 PRINT "THE CIRCLE WILL BE CENTERED ON THE SCREEN"
3030 INPUT"ENTER NUMBER OF DOTS 10-200";DT
3040 PRINT "PRESS ANY KEY TO DRAW CIRCLE"
3050 PRINT "WHEN CIRCLE HAS BEEN DRAWN, PRESS KEY"
3055 GET A$:IF A$="" THEN 3055
3060 SYS 50195
3070 FOR I=1 TO 200 STEP 200/DT
3080 X=RD*S(I):Y=RD*C(I)
3090 X=X+159:Y=Y+100
3100 X=INT(X):Y=INT(Y)
3110 SYS 50201,X,Y,1
3120 NEXT I
```

P59 Drawing Circles

```
3130 RETURN
3980 REM SUBROUTINE TO DRAW CIRCLES
3990 REM USING DOT SHADING
4000 PRINT "[CS ]"
4010 INPUT "ENTER RADIUS OF CIRCLE";RD
4020 PRINT "THE CIRCLE WILL BE CENTERED ON THE SCREEN"
4030 PRINT "ENTER THE ILLUMINATION CONSTANT"
4040 INPUT "(.05 TO .9) ";I
4050 PRINT "PRESS ANY KEY TO DRAW CIRCLE"
4060 PRINT "WHEN CIRCLE HAS BEEN DRAWN, PRESS KEY"
4065 GET A$:IF A$="" THEN 4065
4070 SYS 50195
4080 LN=2*RD
4090 N=LN*I
4100 DX=2*RD/N
4120 X=RD+DX
4130 REM LOOP BACK FOR REPEAT
4140 X=X-DX
4150 T=RD*RD-X*X
4160 IF T<0 THEN Y=0:GOTO 4180
4170 Y=SQR(T)
4180 D=2*Y
4190 DTS=D*I
4200 IF DTS=0 THEN DTS=1
4210 DY=2*Y/DTS
4220 FOR K=1 TO DTS
4230 J=-Y+K*DY
4240 X1=INT(X+159):J=INT(J+100)
4250 SYS50201,X1,J,1
4260 NEXT K
4270 IF X>-RD THEN GOTO 4140
4280 RETURN
```

P60 Four-Weekl ᴍ Moving Average

When attempting to measure trends in sales data it can be useful to plot the sales data along with a continually updated average of the last four weeks' sales.

This program performs such a task, with the sales data held in the form of data statements. Note that the data are terminated by an imaginary negative sale.

The program allows the user to see the data graphically; in order to do this the graphics utility must have been installed.

COMMANDS

Install the graphics utility.
Key in program and type RUN.
Follow instructions.

```
10 REM PROGRAM   - FOUR WEEKLY MOVING AVERAGE
20 PRINT "[CS CD CD CD CD CD CD CD CD CD CD ]"
30 PRINT "          FOUR WEEKLY MOVING"
40 PRINT:PRINT "              AVERAGE"
50 A=TI
60 IF TI<A+100 THEN GOTO 60
70 PRINT "[CS ]"
80 PRINT "THIS PROGRAM CAN BE USED TO HELP YOU"
90 PRINT "TO FORECAST SALES BASED ON A GRAPH OF"
100 PRINT "A 4-WEEK MOVING AVERAGE."
110 PRINT
120 PRINT "THIS CAN BE A FAIRLY USEFUL PROGRAM,"
130 PRINT "BUT BEAR IN MIND THAT IT DOES NOT"
140 PRINT "CONSIDER SEASONAL VARIATIONS."
150 PRINT:PRINT:PRINT
160 PRINT "DATA ARE HELD IN DATA STATEMENTS, AND"
170 PRINT "UP TO 52 WEEKS CAN BE HANDLED."
180 PRINT:PRINT
190 PRINT "IF NECESSARY, STOP THE PROGRAM AND ADD"
200 PRINT "TO OR CHANGE THE DATA."
210 PRINT:PRINT:PRINT
240 DIM SA(53),MA(50)
250 REM SCALE THE DATA
```

P60 Four-Weekly Moving Average

```
260 NO=0:MX=0
270 REM LOOP BACK POINT
280 NO=NO+1
290 READ SA(NO)
300 IF SA(NO)<0 THEN GOTO 330
310 IF MX<SA(NO) THEN MX=SA(NO)
320 GOTO 280
330 REM CALCULATE MOVING AVERAGES
340 FOR I=4 TO NO-1
350 MA(I-3)=(SA(I)+SA(I-1)+SA(I-2)+SA(I-3))/4
360 NEXT I
370 GOSUB 1000
380 I=1
390 REM LOOP BACK POINT
400 I=I+1:LI=LI+1
410 PRINT I,SA(I),,MA(I)
420 IF LI=18 THEN GOSUB 1000
430 IF SA(I)<0 THEN GOTO 450
440 GOTO 400
450 REM GRAPHICS ROUTINE
460 PRINT:PRINT
470 PRINT "PRESS ANY KEY TO SEE DATA DISPLAYED"
480 PRINT "GRAPHICALLY"
490 GET A$:IF A$="" THEN GOTO 490
500 REM CONSTRUCT GRAPH, USING GRAPHICS UTILITY
510 SYS 50195:REM TURN ON BIT MAP
520 SYS 50207:REM CLEAR BIT MAP
530 SYS 50210,1,0:REM COLOR BITMAP
540 REM DRAW AXES
550 SYS 50201,5,5,1
560 SYS 50204,5,190,1
570 SYS 50204,310,190,1
580 REM CALCULATE SCALING FACTOR
590 SCALE=180/MX
600 SYS 50201,5,5,1
610 REM PLOT SALES
620 FOR I=1 TO NO-1
630 X=5*I:Y=INT(SA(I)*SCALE)
640 SYS 50204,X,Y,1
650 NEXT I
660 X=10:Y=INT(MA(1)*SCALE)
670 SYS 50201,X,Y,0
680 FOR I=3 TO NO-4
690 X=5*I:Y=INT(MA(I)*SCALE)
700 SYS 50204,X,Y,0
710 NEXT I
720 GET A$:IF A$="" THEN 720
```

```
 730 SYS 50198
 740 END
1000 PRINT:PRINT "PRESS ANY KEY TO CONTINUE"
1010 GET A$:IF A$="" THEN 1010
1020 PRINT "[CS ]";
1030 PRINT"[RON ]            SALES DATA 1984
[ROF ]"
1040 PRINT
1050 LI=0
1060 PRINT "PERIOD     SALES VALUE    MOVING AVERAGE"
1070 RETURN
2000 DATA 112,224,115,212,118,215,113,214,115,216,112
2010 DATA 223,126,224,125,265,145,293,116,216,193,293
2020 DATA 187,315,220,354,232,367,198,354,267,365,287
2030 DATA 398,254,254,176,234,144,201,101,350,190,483
2040 DATA 190,190
2050 DATA -9
```

P61 Interfering Circles

It takes a little time for this program to finish, but we think that the effect is quite pretty.

COMMANDS

Load in graphics module and RUN.
Key in program and type RUN.

```
10 REM PROGRAM - CIRCLES
20 PRINT "[CS CD CD CD CD CD CD CD CD CD CD ]"
30 PRINT "            CIRCLES"
40 A=TI
50 IF TI<A+150 THEN GOTO 50
60 PRINT "[CS ]"
70 DIM S(63),C(63)
80 PRINT "[CD CD CD CD CD ]SETTING UP";
90 FOR I=1 TO 63
100 S(I)=SIN(I*.1)
110 C(I)=COS(I*.1)
120 PRINT ".";
130 NEXT I
140 SYS 50207
150 SYS 50210,1,0
160 SYS 50195
170 FOR R=2 TO 200 STEP 2
180 CX=120:CY=100
190 GOSUB 1000
200 CX=200:CY=100
210 GOSUB 1000
220 NEXT R
230 END
980 REM CIRCLE DRAWING ROUTINE
990 REM CENTER CX,CY RADIUS R
1000 X=CX:Y=R+CY
1010 IF X<0 THEN X=0
1020 IF X>319 THEN X=319
1030 IF Y<0 THEN Y=0
1040 IF Y>199 THEN Y=199
1050 SYS 50201,X,Y,1
1070 FOR I=1 TO 63
1080 X=INT(R*S(I)+CX):Y=INT(R*C(I)+CY)
```

```
1090 IF X<0 THEN X=0
1100 IF X>319 THEN X=319
1110 IF Y<0 THEN Y=0
1120 IF Y>199 THEN Y=199
1130 SYS 50204,X,Y,1
1140 NEXT I
1150 RETURN
```

P62 Zoom

One way of zooming in or out of a picture is to redraw the whole scene to a different size.

This program draws a cube and allows the user to zoom the cube into and out of the screen.

COMMANDS

Load in the graphics module and RUN.
Key in the program and type RUN.
Press key I to zoom in.
Press key O to zoom out.

```
10 REM PROGRAM - ZOOM
20 PRINT "[CS CD CD CD CD CD CD CD CD CD CD CR CR CR CR
CR CR CR CR CR CR CR CR CR CR CR CR ]";
30 PRINT "ZOOM"
40 A=TI
50 IF TI<A+150 THEN 50
60 SYS 50207
70 SYS 50210,1,0
80 SYS 50195
90 F=1:B=0
100 S=10:GOSUB 1000
110 GET A$:IF A$="" THEN 110
120 DS=(A$="I")-(A$="O")
130 SYS 50207:REMGOSUB 1000
140 S=S+DS:GOSUB 1000
150 GOTO 110
160 END
980 REM SUBROUTINE TO DRAW CUBE
990 REM OF SIDE LENGTH S
1000 IF S<0 THEN RETURN
1010 P=50201:P1=-S:P2=S:GOSUB 2000
1020 P=50204:P1=S:P2=S:GOSUB 2000
1030 P=50204:P1=S:P2=-S:GOSUB 2000
1040 P=50204:P1=S+S/2:P2=0:GOSUB 2000
1050 P=50204:P1=S+S/2:P2=2*S:GOSUB 2000
1060 P=50204:P1=S/1.25-S:P2=2*S:GOSUB 2000
1070 P=50204:P1=-S:P2=S:GOSUB 2000
```

```
1080 P=50204:P1=-S:P2=-S:GOSUB 2000
1090 P=50204:P1=S:P2=-S:GOSUB 2000
1100 P=50201:P1=S:P2=S:GOSUB 2000
1110 P=50204:P1=S+S/2:P2=2*S:GOSUB 2000
1120 RETURN
1980 REM SUBROUTINE TO CHECK OUT
1990 REM PLOTTING DATA
2000 X=INT(P1+160):Y=INT(P2+100)
2010 IF X<0 THEN X=0
2020 IF X>319 THEN X=319
2030 IF Y<0 THEN Y=0
2040 IF Y>199 THEN Y=199
2050 SYS P,X,Y,0
2060 RETURN
```

P63 Interference

This program generates an interference type pattern.

Once the pattern has been generated, the user can change the colors on the screen by pressing keys.

COMMANDS

Load in graphics module and RUN.
Key in program and RUN.
When pattern has been generated then press any key to change colors.

```
10 REM PROGRAM  - INTERFERENCE
20 SYS 50207
30 SYS 50210,0,1
40 SYS 50195
50 FOR I=0 TO 199
60 SYS 50201,0,I,1
70 X=319
80 Y=199-I
90 SYS 50204,X,Y,0
100 NEXT I
110 FOR I=319 TO 0 STEP -1
120 SYS 50201,I,0,1
130 Y=199
140 X=319-I
150 SYS 50204,X,Y,0
160 NEXT I
170 GET A$:IF A$="" THEN 170
180 F=INT(15*RND(0))
190 B=INT(15*RND(0))
200 IF B=F THEN 190
210 SYS 50210,F,B
220 BR=INT(15*RND(0))
230 IF BR=B OR BR=F THEN GOTO 220
240 POKE 53280,BR
250 GOTO 170
```

P64 Doodle

This program allows the user to use a joystick to doodle on the CBM-64 screen.

Full instructions for the program's use are presented to the user.

COMMANDS

Connect joystick to PORT 2.
Load in graphics module and RUN.
Key in program and RUN.
Follow instructions.

```
10 REM PROGRAM - DOODLE
20 PRINT "[CS CD CD CD CD CD CD CD CD CD CD ]"
30 PRINT "                    DOODLE"
40 A=TI
50 IF TI<A+150 THEN GOTO 50
60 PRINT "[CS ]"
70 PRINT "THIS PROGRAM ALLOWS THE USER TO DOODLE"
80 PRINT "ON THE SCREEN USING THE JOYSTICK"
90 PRINT "[CD ]MAKE SURE THAT YOUR JOYSTICK IS IN"
100 PRINT "PORT 2."
110 PRINT "[CD ]THE JOYSTICK NOW CONTROLS A DOT ON"
120 PRINT "THE SCREEN. THIS DOT CAN BE PLOTTED IN "
130 PRINT "VARIOUS COLORS - FOREGROUND, BACKGROUND"
140 PRINT "OR THE PRESENT COLOR CAN BE FLIPPED"
150 PRINT "[CD ]"
160 INPUT "WHAT FOREGROUND COLOR";F
170 INPUT "WHAT BACKGROUND COLOR";B
180 PRINT "USE JOYSTICK TO CONTROL DOT"
190 PRINT "USE FIRE TO SELECT COLOR"
200 PRINT "PRESS KEY F FOR FOREGROUND"
210 PRINT "         B FOR BACKGROUND"
220 PRINT "         R FOR REVERSE"
230 PRINT "         C TO CLEAR SCREEN"
240 PRINT "[CD CD ]PRESS ANY KEY TO CONTINUE"
250 GET A$:IF A$="" THEN GOTO 250
260 SYS 50207
270 SYS 50210,F,B
280 SYS 50195
```

P64 Doodle

```
290 X=160:Y=100:M=1
300 REM LOOP BACK POINT
310 SYS 50201,X,Y,M
320 A=PEEK(56320)
330 X=X+(A=123)-(A=119)+(A=122)+(A=121)-(A=118)-(A=117)
340 Y=Y+(A=126)-(A=125)+(A=122)+(A=118)-(A=117)-(A=121)
350 IF X>319 THEN X=319
360 IF X<0 THEN X=0
370 IF Y>199 THEN Y=199
380 IF Y<0 THEN Y=0
390 IF (PEEK(56320) AND 16)=0 GOTO 410
400 GOTO 310
410 GET A$:IF A$="" THEN GOTO 410
420 IF A$="F" THEN M=1
430 IF A$="B" THEN M=2
440 IF A$="R" THEN M=0
450 IF A$="C" THEN SYS 50207
460 GOTO 310
470 END
```

P65 Bar Chart

This program can draw a chart of up to thirty bars onto the screen. The bars are automatically scaled to fit onto the screen. The chart is not labelled. This is left as an exercise for the reader.

COMMANDS

Key in the program and type RUN.
Enter the number of bars, less than 30.
Enter the value of each bar as requested.

```
 10 REM PROGRAM - BAR CHART
 20 PRINT "[CS CD CD CD CD CD CD CD CD CD ]"
 30 PRINT "            BAR CHART"
 40 A=TI
 50 IF TI<A+150 THEN GOTO 50
 60 PRINT "[CS CD CD CD ]"
 70 PRINT "THIS PROGRAM CAN BE USED TO PRESENT DATA";
 80 PRINT "IN THE FORM OF A BAR CHART ON THE SCREEN";
 90 PRINT "UP TO 30 BARS CAN BE DISPLAYED ON THE"
100 PRINT "SCREEN."
110 PRINT "[CD ]PRESS ANY KEY TO CONTINUE[CD ]"
120 GET A$:IF A$="" THEN GOTO 120
130 INPUT "ENTER NUMBER OF BARS";BR
140 IF BR>30 THEN GOTO 130
150 IF BR<1 THEN GOTO 130
160 BR=INT(BR):MX=0
170 DIM V(BR)
180 PRINT
190 PRINT "NOW ENTER YOUR DATA ONE ELEMENT AT A "
200 PRINT "TIME."
210 FOR I=1 TO BR
220 PRINT "ENTER VALUE OF BAR ";I;
230 INPUT V(I)
240 IF V(I)>MX THEN MX=V(I)
250 NEXT I
255 INPUT "ENTER TITLE OF CHART";T$
260 PRINT "[CS ]"
270 SC=1
280 IF MX>20 THEN SC=MX/20
390 FOR I=1 TO BR
```

P65 Bar Chart

```
400 V(I)=INT(V(I)/SC)
410 NEXT I
420 REM DRAW SCALES
430 S=1108:C=55380
440 FOR I=0 TO 19
450 POKE S+I*40,66:POKE C+I*40,1
460 NEXT I
470 POKE S+20*40,91:POKE C+20*40,1
480 FOR I=1 TO 33
490 POKE S+20*40+I,67:POKE C+20*40+I,1
500 NEXT I
510 REM LABEL BAR CHART
520 L=LEN(T$)
530 PRINT "[CH CD ]";
540 FOR I=1 TO INT((40-L)/2)
550 PRINT "[CR ]";
560 NEXT I
570 PRINT T$;
580 FOR I=1 TO 20 STEP 2
590 T=INT(I*SC+.5)+INT(SC)
600 TP$=MID$(STR$(T),2)
610 FOR J=1 TO LEN(TP$)
620 POKE S+20*40-I*40-4+J,ASC(MID$(TP$,J,1)):
    POKE C+20*40-I*40-4+J,1
630 NEXT J
640 NEXT I
650 REM NOW PLOT THE BARS
660 CL=1
670 FOR I=1 TO BR
680 CL=CL+1:IF CL=16 THEN CL=1
690 FOR J=0 TO V(I)-1
700 POKE S+19*40+2+I-40*J,224:POKE C+19*40+2+I-40*J,CL
710 NEXT J
720 NEXT I
730 GET A$:IF A$="" THEN GOTO 730
```

P66 Mean and Standard Deviation

This program is used to find the mean and standard deviation of a list of data items.

COMMANDS

Key in the program and type RUN.
Follow instructions.

```
10 REM PROGRAM - MEAN AND STANDARD DEVIATION
20 PRINT "[CS CD CR CR CR CR CR ]";
30 PRINT "MEAN AND STANDARD DEVIATION"
40 PRINT "[CD ]THIS PROGRAM CAN BE USED TO FIND THE"
50 PRINT "MEAN AND STANDARD DEVIATION OF A SERIES"
60 PRINT "OF NUMERICAL VALUES. THIS PROGRAM CAN BE";
70 PRINT "OF GREAT USE IN THE LABORATORY."
80 PRINT
90 PRINT "THE PROGRAM ASKS YOU FIRST OF ALL TO"
100 PRINT "PRINT THE TITLE OF THE REPORT TO BE "
110 PRINT "WRITTEN, THEN THE NUMERICAL READINGS"
120 PRINT "ARE ENTERED ONE AT A TIME. THE PROGRAM"
130 PRINT "THEN PRINTS A REPORT OF THE DATA."
140 PRINT
150 PRINT "PRESS ANY KEY TO CONTINUE"
160 GET A$:IF A$="" THEN GOTO 160
170 PRINT "[CS ]"
180 PRINT "WHAT IS THE TITLE OF THE"
190 INPUT "REPORT";T$
200 PRINT
210 INPUT "HOW MANY DATA ITEMS ARE THERE";N
220 DIM D(N):S=0:D=0
230 PRINT
240 PRINT "PLEASE ENTER THE DATA ONE ITEM AT A TIME"
250 FOR I=1 TO N
260 INPUT "NEXT ITEM";D(I):S=S+D(I)
270 NEXT
280 M=S/N
290 PRINT "[CD ]CALCULATING.";
300 REM NOW DO THE CALCULATIONS
310 FOR I=1 TO N
320 PRINT ".";
330 D=D+(D(I)-M)^2
340 NEXT I
```

P66 Mean and Standard Deviation

```
350 VR=SQR(D/(N-1))
360 PRINT "[CS ]"
370 PRINT "                    ";T$
380 PRINT
390 PRINT
400 PRINT "THERE WERE ";N;" DATA ITEMS."
410 PRINT "[CD ]THE DATA ARE[CD ]"
420 FOR I=1 TO N
430 PRINT D(I);" ";
440 NEXT I
450 PRINT :PRINT:PRINT
460 PRINT "THE MEAN IS ";M
470 PRINT "THE STANDARD DEVIATION IS "VR
480 END
```

P67 Bubble Sort

This program is a demonstration of how the classical Bubble Sort works. The program sorts ten numbers on the screen.

COMMANDS

Key in the program and type RUN.
Follow instructions.

```
10 REM PROGRAM - BUBBLE SORT
20 DIM K(10):C=0:S=0
30 PRINT "[CS CD CD CD CD CD CD CD CD CD CD ]"
40 PRINT "             BUBBLE SORT"
50 A=TI
60 IF TI<A+100 THEN GOTO 60
70 PRINT "[CS ]":POKE 53280,0:POKE 53281,0
80 PRINT "[CD CD ]THIS PROGRAM EXHIBITS A SORTING
    ROUTINE"
90 PRINT "ON THE SCREEN."
100 PRINT: PRINT
110 PRINT "THE ROUTINE IS KNOWN AS THE BUBBLE SORT"
120 PRINT:PRINT:PRINT "PRESS ANY KEY TO CONTINUE"
130 GET A$:IF A$="" THEN GOTO 130
140 PRINT "[CS ]"
150 PRINT "THE PROGRAM SHOWS HOW THE COMPUTER"
160 PRINT "COMPARES AND SWAPS ITEMS IN A LIST OF"
170 PRINT "NUMBERS, IN ORDER TO OBTAIN A SORTED"
180 PRINT "LIST."
190 PRINT
200 PRINT "NUMBERS BEING COMPARED ARE SHOWN IN"
210 PRINT "RED, NUMBERS BEING SWAPPED ARE SHOWN"
220 PRINT "IN YELLOW."
230 PRINT:PRINT:PRINT "PRESS ANY KEY TO CONTINUE"
240 GET A$:IF A$="" THEN GOTO 240
250 PRINT "[CU CU ]THE PROGRAM ALLOWS THE USER TO ENTER"
260 PRINT "THE SPEED OF PROCESSING, IN THE RANGE"
270 PRINT "[CD ]1 TO 10, WITH 10 BEING FAST."
280 PRINT "THE PROGRAM PROMPTS THE USER TO ENTER"
290 PRINT "10 NUMBERS."
300 PRINT:PRINT
310 PRINT "FOR THE PURPOSES OF THIS DEMONSTRATION"
320 PRINT"ENSURE THAT ALL NUMBERS ENTERED HAVE"
```

P67 Bubble Sort

```
330 PRINT "THE SAME NUMBER OF DIGITS."
340 PRINT:PRINT:PRINT "PRESS ANY KEY TO CONTINUE"
350 GET A$:IF A$="" THEN GOTO 350
360 PRINT "[CS ]"
370 INPUT"SPEED OF PROCESSING";S
380 IF S>10 THEN S=10
390 IF S<1 THEN S=1
400 S=INT(11-S)*50
410 PRINT
420 PRINT "ENTER NUMBERS TO BE SORTED ONE AT A TIME"
430 INPUT "NUMBER";K(1)
440 L=LEN(STR$(K(1)))
450 FOR I=2 TO 10
460 INPUT "NUMBER";K(I)
470 IF LEN(STR$(K(I)))<>L THEN PRINT
    "PLEASE RE-ENTER":GOTO 460
480 NEXT I
490 GET A$:IF A$<>"" THEN 490:REM FLUSH BUFFER
500 PRINT "[CS RON ]                BUBBLE SORT
    [ROF ]"
510 PRINT "[CD CD CD CD CD CD CD CD CD CD CD CD
    CD CD CD CD CD CD CD RON ]
              [ROF ]";
520 SC=1239:CL=55511
530 FOR I=1 TO 10
540 FOR J=1 TO L
550 POKE SC+I*40+J,ASC(MID$(STR$(K(I)),J,1)):
    POKE CL+I*40+J,1
560 NEXT J
570 NEXT I
580 PRINT
    "[CH CD CD ]COMPARISONS=          SWAPS=";
590 REM SORTING ROUTINE
600 FOR I=1 TO 9
610 FOR K=I+1 TO 10
620 HU=2:GOSUB 1000
630 C=C+1
640 PRINT "[CH CD CD CR CR CR CR CR CR CR CR
    CR CR CR CR ]"C;
650 FOR Z=1 TO S:NEXT Z:REM DELAY
660 IF K(K)>K(I) THEN GOSUB 2000
670 HU=1:GOSUB 1000
680 NEXT K
690 NEXT I
700 END
990 REM SUBROUTINE TO COLOR TWO ITEMS
1000 FOR J=1 TO L
```

```
1010 POKE SC+I*40+J,ASC(MID$(STR$(K(I)),J,1)):
     POKE CL+I*40+J,HU
1020 POKE SC+K*40+J,ASC(MID$(STR$(K(K)),J,1)):
     POKE CL+K*40+J,HU
1030 NEXT J
1040 RETURN
1990 REM SWAP SUBROUTINE
2000 SW=SW+1
2010 HU=6:GOSUB 1000
2020 T=K(K)
2030 K(K)=K(I)
2040 K(I)=T
2050 HU=6:GOSUB 1000
2060 FOR Z=1 TO S:NEXT Z
2070 HU=1:GOSUB 1000
2080 PRINT "[CH CD CD CR CR CR CR CR CR CR CR CR
     CR CR CR CR CR CR CR CR CR CR CR CR CR CR
     CR CR CR CR CR CR CR CR CR CR ]"SW;
2090 RETURN
```

P68 Shell Sort

This is the classical fast Shell Sort routine. Similar to the Bubble Sort, the sorting is carried out on the screen. It can be a very useful exercise to try and figure out why the Shell routine works.

COMMANDS

Key in the program and type RUN.
Follow instructions.

```
10 REM PROGRAM - SHELL  SORT
20 DIM K(10):C=0:SW=0
30 PRINT "[CS CD CD CD CD CD CD CD CD CD CD ]"
40 PRINT "              SHELL  SORT"
50 A=TI
60 IF TI<A+100 THEN GOTO 60
70 PRINT "[CS ]":POKE 53280,0:POKE 53281,0
80 PRINT "[CD CD ]THIS PROGRAM EXHIBITS A SORTING
   ROUTINE"
90 PRINT "ON THE SCREEN."
100 PRINT: PRINT
110 PRINT "THE ROUTINE IS KNOWN AS THE SHELL SORT"
120 PRINT:PRINT:PRINT "PRESS ANY KEY TO CONTINUE"
130 GET A$:IF A$="" THEN GOTO 130
140 PRINT "[CS ]"
150 PRINT "THE PROGRAM SHOWS HOW THE COMPUTER"
160 PRINT "COMPARES AND SWAPS ITEMS IN A LIST OF"
170 PRINT "NUMBERS, IN ORDER TO OBTAIN A SORTED"
180 PRINT "LIST."
190 PRINT
200 PRINT "NUMBERS BEING COMPARED ARE SHOWN IN"
210 PRINT "RED, NUMBERS BEING SWAPPED ARE SHOWN"
220 PRINT "IN YELLOW."
230 PRINT:PRINT:PRINT "PRESS ANY KEY TO CONTINUE"
240 GET A$:IF A$="" THEN GOTO 240
250 PRINT "[CU CU ]THE PROGRAM ALLOWS THE USER TO ENTER"
260 PRINT "THE SPEED OF PROCESSING, IN THE RANGE"
270 PRINT "[CD ]1 TO 10, WITH 10 BEING FAST."
280 PRINT "THE PROGRAM PROMPTS THE USER TO ENTER"
290 PRINT "10 NUMBERS."
300 PRINT:PRINT
310 PRINT "FOR THE PURPOSES OF THIS DEMONSTRATION"
```

```
320 PRINT"ENSURE THAT ALL NUMBERS ENTERED HAVE"
330 PRINT "THE SAME NUMBER OF DIGITS."
340 PRINT:PRINT:PRINT "PRESS ANY KEY TO CONTINUE"
350 GET A$:IF A$="" THEN GOTO 350
360 PRINT "[CS ]"
370 INPUT"SPEED OF PROCESSING";S
380 IF S>10 THEN S=10
390 IF S<1 THEN S=1
400 S=INT(11-S)*50
410 PRINT
420 PRINT "ENTER NUMBERS TO BE SORTED ONE AT A TIME"
430 INPUT "NUMBER";K(1)
440 L=LEN(STR$(K(1)))
450 FOR I=2 TO 10
460 INPUT "NUMBER";K(I)
470 IF LEN(STR$(K(I)))<>L THEN PRINT
    "PLEASE RE-ENTER":GOTO 460
480 NEXT I
490 GET A$:IF A$<>"" THEN 490:REM FLUSH BUFFER
500 PRINT "[CS RON ]               SHELL    SORT
    [ROF ]"
510 PRINT "[CD CD CD CD CD CD CD CD CD CD CD CD
    CD CD CD CD CD CD CD RON ]
               [ROF ]";
520 SC=1239:CL=55511
530 FOR I=1 TO 10
540 FOR J=1 TO L
550 POKE SC+I*40+J,ASC(MID$(STR$(K(I)),J,1)):
    POKE CL+I*40+J,1
560 NEXT J
570 NEXT I
580 PRINT "[CH CD CD ]COMPARISONS=
    SWAPS=";
590 REM SORTING ROUTINE
595 D=4
600 FOR I=D+1 TO 10
610 FOR K=I-D TO 1 STEP -D
620 C=C+1:PRINT "[CH CD CD CR CR CR CR CR CR CR
    CR CR CR CR CR ]"C;
630 P=K+D:HU=2:GOSUB 1000
650 FOR Z=1 TO S:NEXT Z:REM DELAY
660 IF K(K)>K(P) THEN GOSUB 2000
670 HU=1:GOSUB 1000
680 NEXT K
690 NEXT I
700 D=INT(D/2)
710 IF D<>0 THEN GOTO 600
```

P68 Shell Sort

```
720 END
990 REM SUBROUTINE TO COLOR TWO ITEMS
1000 FOR J=1 TO L
1010 POKE SC+P*40+J,ASC(MID$(STR$(K(P)),J,1)):
     POKE CL+P*40+J,HU
1020 POKE SC+K*40+J,ASC(MID$(STR$(K(K)),J,1)):
     POKE CL+K*40+J,HU
1030 NEXT J
1040 RETURN
1990 REM SWAP SUBROUTINE
2000 SW=SW+1
2010 HU=6:GOSUB 1000
2020 T=K(K)
2030 K(K)=K(P)
2040 K(P)=T
2050 HU=6:GOSUB 1000
2060 FOR Z=1 TO S:NEXT Z
2070 HU=1:GOSUB 1000
2080 PRINT "[CH CD CD CR CR CR CR CR CR CR CR CR
     CR CR CR CR CR CR CR CR CR CR CR CR CR CR
     CR CR CR CR CR CR CR CR CR CR ]"SW;
2090 RETURN
```

P69 Merge

A common need in data processing is the ability to merge two sorted files to produce a third.

It is quicker to sort small files and then to merge the files to form larger ones. In this program, we mimic file handling by using arrays. The array elements are entered via the keyboard but the program could be amended to allow the elements to be entered via tape files.

COMMANDS

Key in the program and type RUN.
Enter the array elements when prompted in increasing order.

```
10 REM PROGRAM - MERGE
20 PRINT "[CS CD CD CD CD CD CD CD CD ]"
30 PRINT "                MERGE"
40 A=TI
50 IF TI<A+100 THEN GOTO 50
60 PRINT "[CS ]"
70 PRINT "THE BASIS OF MANY DISK BASED SORT"
80 PRINT "ROUTINES IS THE CAPABILITY OF MERGING"
90 PRINT "TOGETHER TWO LISTS SORTED PREVIOUSLY."
100 PRINT "THE DISK BASED SORT ROUTINE RECOGNIZES"
110 PRINT "THAT IT MIGHT BE IMPOSSIBLE TO READ A "
120 PRINT "WHOLE FILE INTO MEMORY FOR SORTING"
130 PRINT "WITH EITHER A BUBBLE OR SHELL SORT"
140 PRINT:PRINT
150 PRINT "PRESS ANY KEY TO CONTINUE"
160 GET A$:IF A$="" THEN GOTO 160
170 PRINT"[CU ]";
180 PRINT "THE FILE IS THEREFORE SPLIT INTO A"
190 PRINT "SERIES OF SUBFILES, SMALL ENOUGH TO READ";
200 PRINT "INTO MEMORY FOR SORTING."
210 PRINT
220 PRINT "THE SMALL SORTED SUBFILES ARE THEN "
230 PRINT "MERGED TO PRODUCE THE COMPLETELY "
240 PRINT "SORTED FILE.":PRINT
250 PRINT "PRESS ANY KEY TO CONTINUE"
260 GET A$:IF A$="" THEN GOTO 260
270 PRINT "[CS ]":PRINT:PRINT
280 PRINT
290 PRINT "THIS PROGRAM DEMONSTRATES A MERGE"
```

P69 Merge

```
300 PRINT "ROUTINE, BY MERGING TOGETHER TWO LISTS"
310 PRINT "OF NUMBERS EACH HOLDING UP TO 100 ITEMS"
320 PRINT:PRINT
330 PRINT "PRESS ANY KEY TO CONTINUE"
340 GET A$:IF A$="" THEN GOTO 340
350 DIM F(100),S(100),M(200)
360 PRINT "[CS ]":PRINT:PRINT
370 PRINT "ENTER THE FIRST LIST ONE ITEM AT A TIME"
380 PRINT:PRINT "MAKE SURE THAT THE DATA ITEMS ARE IN"
390 PRINT "INCREASING ORDER.":PRINT
400 PRINT "USE THE VALUE 0 TO TERMINATE THE LIST"
410 PRINT
420 PRINT "PRESS ANY KEY TO CONTINUE"
430 GET A$:IF A$="" THEN GOTO 430
440 I=1
450 PRINT "ENTER ELEMENT OF FIRST LIST";:INPUT F(I)
460 I=I+1
470 PRINT "ENTER ELEMENT OF FIRST LIST";:INPUT F(I)
480 IF F(I)<>0 AND NOT(F(I)<F(I-1)) AND I<101 THEN GOTO 460
490 IF F(I)=0 THEN GOTO 510
500 IF F(I)<F(I-1) THEN PRINT "OUT OF ORDER":GOTO 470
510 I=I-1
520 PRINT "FIRST LIST COMPLETE, THERE ARE "I"ITEMS IN THE LIST"
530 N1=I
540 PRINT:PRINT:PRINT
550 PRINT "PRESS ANY KEY TO CONTINUE"
560 GET A$:IF A$="" THEN GOTO 560
570 I=1
580 PRINT "ENTER ELEMENT OF SECOND LIST";:INPUT S(I)
590 I=I+1
600 PRINT "ENTER ELEMENT OF SECOND LIST";:INPUT S(I)
610 IF S(I)<>0 AND NOT(S(I)<S(I-1)) AND I<101 THEN GOTO 590
620 IF S(I)=0 THEN GOTO 640
630 IF S(I)<S(I-1) THEN PRINT "OUT OF ORDER":GOTO 600
640 I=I-1
650 PRINT "FIRST LIST COMPLETE, THERE ARE "I"ITEMS IN THE LIST"
660 N2=I
670 PRINT:PRINT:PRINT
680 PRINT "PRESS ANY KEY TO CONTINUE"
690 GET A$:IF A$="" THEN GOTO 690
700 PRINT "[CS ]"
710 I=1:J=1
720 PRINT "[CH CD CD CD ]FIRST LIST ELEMENT NUMBER ";
```

```
 730 PRINT I
 740 PRINT "VALUE ";F(I)
 750 PRINT "[CH CD CD CD CD CD CD ]SECOND LIST ELEMENT
 NUMBER ";
 760 PRINT J
 770 PRINT "VALUE "S(J)
 780 PRINT "[CH CD CD CD CD CD CD CD CD CD ]MERGE LIST
 ELEMENT NUMBER ";
 790 PRINT I+J-1
 800 PRINT "VALUE ";
 810 IF F(I)<S(J) THEN M(I+J-1)=F(I):PRINT
 M(I+J-1):I=I+1:GOTO 830
 820 IF NOT(F(I)<S(J)) THEN
 M(I+J-1)=S(J):PRINTM(I+J-1):J=J+1
 830 IF I=N1+1 THEN GOTO 860
 840 IF J=N2+1 THEN GOTO 980
 850 GOSUB 2000
 855 GOTO 720
 860 REM  RUNOUT J LIST
 870 FOR K=J TO N2
 875 GOSUB 2000
 880 M(K+I-1)=S(K)
 890 PRINT "[CH CD CD CD CD CD CD ]SECOND LIST ELEMENT
 NUMBER ";
 900 PRINT K
 910 PRINT "VALUE "S(K)
 920 PRINT "[CH CD CD CD CD CD CD CD CD CD ]MERGE LIST
 ELEMENT NUMBER ";
 930 PRINT I+K-1
 940 PRINT "VALUE "M(I+K-1)
 950 NEXT K
 960 GOTO 1070
 970 REM RUNOUT I
 980 FOR K=I TO N1
 985 GOSUB 2000
 990 M(K+J-1)=F(K)
1000 PRINT "[CH CD CD CD ]FIRST LIST ELEMENT NUMBER ";
1010 PRINT K
1020 PRINT "VALUE "F(K)
1030 PRINT "[CH CD CD CD CD CD CD CD CD CD ]MERGE LIST
 ELEMENT NUMBER ";
1040 PRINT J+K-1
1050 PRINT "VALUE "M(J+K-1)
1060 NEXT K
1070 INPUT "DISPLAY RESULT (Y/N)";R$
1080 IF R$="N" THEN STOP
1090 PRINT "[CS ]"
```

P69 Merge

```
1100 PRINT "FIRST LIST   SECOND LIST   MERGED LIST"
1110 FOR I=1 TO N1+N2
1120 PRINT F(I);TAB(14);S(I);TAB(28);M(I)
1130 NEXT I
1140 END
1990 REM DELAY SUBROUTINE
2000 PRINT "[CH CD CD CD CD CD CD CD CD CD CD CD CD CD
CD CD CD CD ]PRESS ANY KEY FOR NEXT ITEM"
2100 GET A$:IF A$="" THEN GOTO 2100
2110 PRINT "[CU ]                              "
2120 RETURN
```

P70 Permutations

This program can be used to find the number of permutations of n objects taken r at a time. This is a very useful routine in statistics.

COMMANDS

Key in the program and type RUN.
Follow instructions.

```
10 REM PROGRAM - PERMUTATIONS
20 PRINT "[CS CD CD CD CD CD CD CD CD ]"
30 PRINT "            PERMUTATIONS"
40 A=TI
50 IF TI<A+100 THEN GOTO 50
60 PRINT "[CS ]"
70 PRINT "THIS PROGRAM CAN BE USED TO FIND THE "
80 PRINT "NUMBER OF PERMUTATIONS OF N OBJECTS,"
90 PRINT"TAKEN R AT A TIME."
100 PRINT
110 PRINT "FOR EXAMPLE, SUPPOSE THAT THERE ARE 4"
120 PRINT "PEOPLE IN A RACE, THEN HOW MANY WAYS"
130 PRINT "CAN THE FIRST 3 POSITIONS BE FILLED?"
140 PRINT
150 PRINT "SUPPOSE THE RACERS ARE CALLED A,B,C AND"
160 PRINT "D, THEN POSSIBLE FINISHING POSITIONS"
170 PRINT "WOULD BE AS FOLLOWS:"
180 PRINT
190 PRINT"ABC ABD ACB ACD ADB ADC"
200 PRINT "BAC BAD BCA BCD BDA BDC"
210 PRINT "CAB CAD CBA CBD CDA CDB"
220 PRINT "DAB DAC DBA DBC DCA DCB"
230 PRINT
240 PRINT "IN THIS EXAMPLE THERE ARE 24 WAYS OF"
250 PRINT "PLACING THE FIRST 3 IN THE RACE."
260 PRINT:PRINT
270 PRINT "PRESS ANY KEY TO CONTINUE"
280 GET A$:IF A$="" THEN GOTO 280
290 PRINT"[CS ]"
300 PRINT "THIS PROGRAM WILL ALLOW THE USER TO"
310 PRINT "CALCULATE THE NUMBER OF PERMUTATIONS"
320 PRINT:PRINT
330 PRINT "PRESS ANY KEY TO CONTINUE"
340 GET A$:IF A$="" THEN GOTO 340
```

P70 Permutations

```
350 PRINT:PRINT
360 PRINT "HOW MANY OBJECTS ARE TO BE SELECTED"
370 INPUT "FROM";OB
380 PRINT
390 PRINT "HOW MANY OBJECTS ARE TO BE SELECTED";:INPUT SE
400 PERMS=1:N=OB
410 FOR I=1 TO SE
420 PERMS=PERMS*N
430 N=N-1
440 IF N=0 THEN GOTO 460
450 IF (10^38)/N<PERMS THEN PRINT "TOO BIG":STOP
460 NEXT I
470 PRINT:PRINT
480 PRINT "THE NUMBER OF WAYS OF SELECTING ";SE
490 PRINT "OBJECTS FROM ";OB;" OBJECTS IS"
500 PRINT PERMS
510 END
```

P71 Combinations

This program finds the number of combinations of n objects taken r at a time.

COMMANDS

Key in the program and type RUN.
Follow instructions.

```
10 REM PROGRAM - COMBINATIONS
20 PRINT "[CS CD CD CD CD CD CD CD CD ]"
30 PRINT "            COMBINATIONS"
40 A=TI
50 IF TI<A+100 THEN GOTO 50
60 PRINT "[CS ]"
70 PRINT "THIS PROGRAM CAN BE USED TO FIND THE "
80 PRINT "NUMBER OF COMBINATIONS OF N OBJECTS,"
90 PRINT"TAKEN R AT A TIME."
100 PRINT
110 PRINT "FOR EXAMPLE, SUPPOSE THAT WE WISH TO "
120 PRINT "MAKE UP A COMMITTEE OF 3 PEOPLE OUT "
130 PRINT "OF A POSSIBLE 4 PEOPLE. HOW MANY "
140 PRINT "WAYS CAN THIS BE DONE"
150 PRINT
160 PRINT "SUPPOSE THE PEOPLE ARE CALLED A,B,C AND"
170 PRINT "D, THEN POSSIBLE COMMITTEES WOULD BE"
180 PRINT "AS FOLLOWS:"
190 PRINT
200 PRINT"ABC ABD ACD BCD"
210 PRINT
220 PRINT "IN THIS EXAMPLE THERE ARE 4 WAYS OF"
230 PRINT "MAKING UP THE COMMITTEE."
240 PRINT:PRINT
250 PRINT "PRESS ANY KEY TO CONTINUE"
260 GET A$:IF A$="" THEN GOTO 260
270 PRINT"[CS ]"
280 PRINT "THIS PROGRAM WILL ALLOW THE USER TO"
290 PRINT "CALCULATE THE NUMBER OF PERMUTATIONS"
300 PRINT:PRINT
310 PRINT "PRESS ANY KEY TO CONTINUE"
320 GET A$:IF A$="" THEN GOTO 320
330 PRINT:PRINT
360 PRINT "HOW MANY OBJECTS ARE TO BE SELECTED"
```

P71 Combinations

```
370 INPUT "FROM";OB
380 PRINT
390 PRINT "HOW MANY OBJECTS ARE TO BE SELECTED";:INPUT
SE
400 N=OB:GOSUB 1000
410 FC=FT
420 N=SE:GOSUB 1000
430 FR=FT
440 N=OB-SE:GOSUB 1000
450 FM=FT
460 COMBS=FC/FR/FM
470 PRINT:PRINT
480 PRINT "THE NUMBER OF WAYS OF SELECTING ";SE
490 PRINT "OBJECTS FROM ";OB;" OBJECTS IS"
500 PRINT COMBS
510 END
970 REM FACTORIAL SUBROUTINE
980 REM THIS PROGRAM EVALUATES N! AND           PLACES
THE RESULT IN THE
990 REM PARAMETER FT
1000 IF N<1 THEN PRINT "GOTCHA! N<1":STOP
1010 IF INT(N)<>N THEN PRINT "GOTCHA! N NOT AN
INTEGER":STOP
1020 IF N>33 THEN PRINT "GOTCHA! TOO BIG FOR THE
MACHINE":STOP
1030 FT=1
1040 FOR I=1 TO N
1050 FT=FT*I
1060 NEXT I
1070 RETURN
```

P72 Least Squares

This program uses the method of least squares to find the best straight line through a set of data points.

The straight line found is in the form

$$Y=MX+B$$

When the equation is formed it is printed out.

COMMANDS

Key in the program and type RUN.
Enter the data items in the form X,Y.

```
10 REM PROGRAM - LEAST SQUARES
20 PRINT "[CS CD CD CD CD CD CD CD CD CD CD ]"
30 PRINT "              LEAST SQUARES"
40 A=TI
50 IF TI<A+100 THEN GOTO 50
60 PRINT "[CS ]"
70 PRINT "THIS PROGRAM IS USED TO FIND THE BEST"
80 PRINT "STRAIGHT LINE FIT TO A SET OF DATA "
90 PRINT "POINTS. THE BEST STRAIGHT LINE IS FOUND"
100 PRINT "BY THE METHOD OF LEAST SQUARES."
110 GOSUB 2000
120 PRINT "ENTER NUMBER OF DATA POINTS"
130 INPUT N
140 DIM X(N),Y(N)
150 PRINT:PRINT:PRINT
160 XS=0:SS=0:YS=0:XY=0
170 PRINT "ENTER DATA IN THE FORM OF NUMBER PAIRS"
180 PRINT "X AND Y"
190 FOR I= 1 TO N
200 PRINT "[CH CD CD CD CD CD CD CD CD CD CD CD CD CD CD CD ]X= ";
210 INPUT X(I)
220 INPUT "Y= ";Y(I)
230 XS=XS+X(I)
240 SS=SS+X(I)*X(I)
250 YS=YS+Y(I)
260 XY=XY+X(I)*Y(I)
270 NEXT I
280 D=N*SS-XS*XS
290 IF D=0 THEN PRINT "NO FIT POSSIBLE BY THIS
```

P72 Least Squares

```
    ROUTINE":STOP
300 M=(N*XY-XS*YS)/D
310 B=YS/N-M*XS/N
320 PRINT "LINE IS Y=";M;"*X+";B
330 END
1990 REM GET KEY SUBROUTINE
2000 PRINT:PRINT:PRINT
2010 PRINT "PRESS ANY KEY TO CONTINUE"
2020 GET A$:IF A$="" THEN GOTO 2020
2030 RETURN
```

P73 Number of Days

It can be interesting in many everyday problems to calculate the number of days between two dates. This program does this by calculating the number of days from day zero of the Gregorian Calendar for each date and then calculating the number of days between the two dates.

COMMANDS

Key in the program and type RUN.
Enter Gregorian dates when prompted.

```
10 REM PROGRAM - NUMBER OF DAYS
20 PRINT "[CS CD CD CD CD CD CD CD CD CD CD ]"
30 PRINT "         NUMBER OF DAYS "
40 A=TI
50 IF TI<A+100 THEN GOTO 50
60 PRINT "[CS ]"
70 PRINT "THIS PROGRAM EVALUATES THE NUMBER OF "
80 PRINT "DAYS BETWEEN TWO DATES."
90 PRINT :PRINT
100 PRINT "THE PROGRAM USES THE GREGORIAN CALENDER"
110 PRINT:PRINT
120 PRINT "ENTER FIRST DAY OF INTEREST"
130 INPUT "MONTH (1 TO 12)";M1
140 INPUT "DAY (1 TO 31)";D1
150 INPUT "YEAR";Y1
160 MM=M1:DD=D1:YY=Y1
170 GOSUB 2000
180 N1=DYS
190 PRINT:PRINT
200 PRINT "ENTER SECOND DAY OF INTEREST"
210 INPUT "MONTH (1 TO 12)";M2
220 INPUT "DAY (1 TO 31)";D2
230 INPUT "YEAR";Y2
240 MM=M2:DD=D2:YY=Y2
250 GOSUB 2000
260 N2=DYS
270 PRINT"[CS CD CD CD CD CD CD ]"
280 PRINT "THE NUMBER OF DAYS FROM":PRINT
290 PRINT M1;"/";D1;"/";Y1;"   TO":PRINT
300 PRINT M2;"/";D2;"/";Y2;"   IS":PRINT
```

P73 Number of Days

```
 310 PRINT N2-N1;"DAYS"
 320 END
1900 REM SUBROUTINE TO CALCULATE NUMBER
1910 REM OF DAYS SINCE DAY 0 OF GREGORIAN
1920 REM CALENDAR
1930 REM DATE IS ENTERED AS DAY=DD%, MONTH=MM% AND YEAR=YY%
1940 REM NUMBER OF DAYS SINCE 0 IS
1950 REM RETURNED AS DYS
1960 REM THE DATA HELD IN THE DATA
1970 REM STATEMENT ARE THE NUMBER OF
1980 REM DAYS FROM THE BEGINNING OF THE
1990 REM YEAR TO THE 1ST OF THE MONTH
2000 RESTORE
2010 IF MM>12 OR MM<1 THEN PRINT "ERROR IN MONTH":STOP
2020 IF DD>31 OR DD<1 THEN PRINT "ERROR IN DAY":STOP
2030 FOR I=1 TO MM
2040 READ TYS
2050 NEXT I
2060 DATA 0,31,59,90,120,151,181,212,243,273,304,334
2070 TYS=TYS+DD
2080 DYS=TYS+YY*365+INT(YY/4)+1-INT(YY/100)+INT(YY/400)
2090 IF YY=INT(YY/4)*4 AND MM<3 THEN DYS=DYS-1
2100 RETURN
```

P74 Encoder

This program can be used to code a secret message. The system used for the encoding is very simple. You are asked for a key word, the characters of which are used to offset the characters of the secret message. The program uses all the normal printable characters of the Commodore-64, so that characters such as space, full stop and comma, etc are also encoded.

COMMANDS

Press shift and Commodore keys together. This allows you to enter the program in upper and lower case characters.
Key in the program and type RUN.
Follow instructions.

```
10 rem program - encoder
20 print "[cs cd cd cd cd cd cd cd cd cd cd ]"
30 print "              encoder"
40 a=ti
50 if ti<a+100 then goto 50
60 print "[cs ]"
70 print chr$(14):rem switch to allow lower case
80 print "This program can be used to produce a"
90 print "coded version of a secret message."
100 print
110 print "The program bases the encoding on a key"
120 print "word which you can specify."
130 print:print:print
140 print "Press any key to continue"
150 get a$:if a$="" then goto 150
160 print:print:print
170 print "Note that in this program we use the "
180 print "normal uppercase-lowercase character set"
190 print:print:print
200 print "Enter the secret message"
210 m$=""
220 get a$:if a$="" then goto 220
230 if asc(a$)<>13 then m$=m$+a$:goto 220
240 print "[cs cd cd cd cd cd ]"
250 print "Do you wish to see the secret message"
260 print "to check it before encoding";
270 input "(y/n)";r$
280 if left$(r$,1)="n" then goto 370
290 print:print:print
```

P74 Encoder

```
300 print "Press space bar to see message"
310 get a$:if a$="" then goto 310
320 print:print:print
330 print m$
340 print:print:print
350 print "Press space bar to hide message"
360 get a$:if a$="" then goto 360
370 print "[cs ]"
380 print "[cs cd cd cd cd cd ]"
390 print "Enter the key word"
400 k$=""
410 get a$:if a$="" then goto 410
420 if asc(a$)<>13 then k$=k$+a$:goto 410
430 print "[cs cd cd cd cd cd ]"
440 print "Do you wish to see the key word to"
450 print "check it before encoding";
460 input "(y/n)";r$
470 if left$(r$,1)="n" then goto 560
480 print:print:print
490 print "Press space bar to see key word"
500 get a$:if a$="" then goto 500
510 print:print:print
520 print k$
530 print:print:print
540 print "Press space bar to hide key word"
550 get a$:if a$="" then goto 550
560 print "[cs cd cd cd cd cd ]"
570 print "Are both the message and the key word"
580 print "all right";:input r$
590 if r$="n" then goto 10
600 print:print:print
610 rem encoding algorithm
620 dim p(25),c(255),d(255)
630 for i=1 to len(k$)
640 p(i)=asc(mid$(k$,i,1))-32
650 next i
660 for i=1 to len(m$)
670 c(i)=asc(mid$(m$,i,1))-32
680 next i
690 c$=""
700 j=0
710 for i=1 to len(m$)
720 d(i)=(c(i)+p(j+1))
730 d(i)=d(i)-int(d(i)/93)*93
740 c$=c$+chr$(d(i)+32)
750 j=j+1
760 j=j-int(j/len(k$))*len(k$)
```

```
770 next i
780 print:print:print
790 print "Your coded message is....":print:print
800 print c$
810 print:print:print
820 print "Press space bar to hide message"
830 get a$:if a$="" then goto 830
840 print "[cs ]"
850 end
```

P75 Decoder

This program can be used to decode the secret message found using the encoder program. You need to have the secret message plus the key word to find the original message.

COMMANDS

Press the Commodore and shift keys together. This allows you to enter the program as shown below.
Key in program and type RUN.
Follow instructions

```
10 rem program - decoder
20 print "[cs cd cd cd cd cd cd cd cd cd cd ]"
30 print "          decoder"
40 a=ti
50 if ti<a+100 then goto 50
60 print "[cs ]"
70 print chr$(14):rem switch to allow lower case
80 print "This program can be used to produce a"
90 print "decoded version of a secret message."
100 print
110 print "The program bases the decoding on a key"
120 print "word which you can specify."
130 print:print:print
140 print "Press any key to continue"
150 get a$:if a$="" then goto 150
160 print:print:print
170 print "Note that in this program we use the "
180 print "normal uppercase-lowercase character set"
190 print:print:print
200 print "Enter the coded message"
210 c$=""
220 get a$:if a$="" then goto 220
230 if asc(a$)<>13 then c$=c$+a$:goto 220
240 print "[cs cd cd cd cd cd ]"
250 print "Do you wish to see the coded message"
260 print "to check it before decoding";
270 input "(y/n)";r$
280 if left$(r$,1)="n" then goto 370
290 print:print:print
300 print "Press space bar to see message"
310 get a$:if a$="" then goto 310
320 print:print:print
```

```
330 print c$
340 print:print:print
350 print "Press space bar to hide message"
360 get a$:if a$="" then goto 360
370 print "[cs ]"
380 print "[cs cd cd cd cd cd ]"
390 print "Enter the key word"
400 k$=""
410 get a$:if a$="" then goto 410
420 if asc(a$)<>13 then k$=k$+a$:goto 410
430 print "[cs cd cd cd cd cd ]"
440 print "Do you wish to see the key word to"
450 print "check it before encoding";
460 input "(y/n)";r$
470 if left$(r$,1)="n" then goto 560
480 print:print:print
490 print "Press space bar to see key word"
500 get a$:if a$="" then goto 500
510 print:print:print
520 print k$
530 print:print:print
540 print "Press space bar to hide key word"
550 get a$:if a$="" then goto 550
560 print "[cs cd cd cd cd cd ]"
570 print "Are both the message and the key word"
580 print "all right";:input r$
590 if r$="n" then goto 10
600 print:print:print
610 rem decoding algorithm
620 dim p(25),c(255),d(255)
630 for i=1 to len(k$)
640 p(i)=asc(mid$(k$,i,1))-32
650 next i
660 for i=1 to len(c$)
670 c(i)=asc(mid$(c$,i,1))-32
680 next i
690 m$=""
700 j=0
710 for i=1 to len(c$)
720 d(i)=(c(i)-p(j+1))
730 if d(i)<0 then d(i)=d(i)+93
740 m$=m$+chr$(d(i)+32)
750 j=j+1
760 j=j-int(j/len(k$))*len(k$)
770 next i
780 print:print:print
790 print "Your coded message is....":print:print
```

P75 Decoder

```
800 print m$
810 print:print:print
820 print "Press space bar to hide message"
830 get a$:if a$="" then goto 830
840 print "[cs ]"
850 end
```

P76 Dog Race

In this program we introduce you to the Commodore dog track. It can be useful to play the part of the bookie when running the program.

The program makes use of the user-defined characters of the Commodore-64.

COMMANDS

Key in the program and type RUN.
Follow instructions.

```
10 REM PROGRAM - DOG RACE
20 PRINT "[CS CD CD CD CD CD CD CD CD CD ]"
30 PRINT "                DOG RACE"
40 A=TI
50 IF TI<A+150 THEN GOTO 50
60 POKE 52,48:POKE 56,48:CLR:
   REM RESERVE RAM AREA FOR CHARACTERS
70 RO=53248:REM START OF CHARACTER ROM
80 RA=12288:REM START OF CHARACTER RAM
90 IT=56334:REM INTERRUPT TIMER
100 CC=53272:
    REM CONTROLS CHARACTER LOCATION
110 SC=1024:REM START OF SCREEN MEMORY
120 POKE 53280,6:REM BLUE BORDER
130 POKE 53281,1:REM WHITE SCREEN
140 PRINT CHR$(142):REM UPPER CASE
150 POKE IT,PEEK (IT) AND 254:
    REM DISABLE INTERRUPT TIMER
160 POKE 1,PEEK (1) AND 251:
    REM SWITCH FROM I/O TO CHAR. ROM
170 PRINT "[CS ]":PRINT:PRINT
180 PRINT "              RACE NIGHT                "
190 PRINT:PRINT:PRINT
200 PRINT "       GOOD EVENING FOLKS"
210 PRINT "          WELCOME TO THE "
220 PRINT "        COMMODORE DOG TRACK"
230 FOR N=0 TO 511:POKE N+RA,PEEK (N+RO)
    :NEXT:REM TRANSFER CHARACTERS
240 POKE 1,PEEK (1) OR 4:
```

P76 Dog Race

```
         REM SWITCH FROM CHAR. TO I/O ROM
250 POKE IT,PEEK (IT) OR 1:
         REM ENABLE INTERRUPT TIMER
260 POKE CC,(PEEK (CC) AND 240)+12:
         REM CONTROL OF CHARACTERS TO RAM
270 REM****************************
280 REM NOW WE REDEFINE CHR$(33) AS THE
         DOG SHAPE
290 REM CHR$(34) AS THE CLOSED TRAP
300 REM CHR$(35) AS THE OPEN TRAP
310 FOR N=33 TO 35
320 FOR K=0 TO 7
330 READ A
340 POKE RA+K+N*8,A
350 NEXT:NEXT
360 PRINT:PRINT:PRINT
370 PRINT "PRESS ANY KEY TO CONTINUE"
380 GET A$:IF A$="" THEN GOTO 380
390 PRINT "[CS ]"
400 DIM C(10):REM COLOUR ARRAY FOR DOGS
410 FOR I=1 TO 10
420 READ C(I)
430 NEXT I
440 REM PLACE THE TRAPS
450 FOR I=1 TO 10
455 I$=MID$(STR$(I),2):IF LEN(I$)=1 THEN I$=" "+I$
460 PRINT:PRINT CHR$(C(I));I$+" ";CHR$(34);SPC(34);"."
470 NEXT I
480 PRINT:PRINT "PRESS RETURN TO START"
490 GET A$:IF A$="" THEN GOTO 490
500 IF ASC(A$)<>13 THEN GOTO 490
505 PRINT "[CU ]                         ";
510 PRINT "[CH ]"
520 FOR I=1 TO 10
530 PRINT:PRINT "[CR CR ] ";CHR$(C(I));CHR$(35);CHR$(33)
540 NEXT I
550 DIM D(10),P(10)
560 FOR I=1 TO 10:D(I)=5:NEXT I
570 FIN=0
580 P=INT(RND(0)*10)+1
590 G=0
600 FOR I=1 TO 10
610 IF P=P(I) THEN G=1
620 NEXT I
630 IF G=1 THEN GOTO 580
640 X=2*P-1:Y=D(P):GOSUB 3000
650 PRINT " ";CHR$(C(P));CHR$(33);
```

```
660 D(P)=D(P)+1
670 IF D(P)=38 THEN P(FIN+1)=P:FIN=FIN+1
680 IF FIN<10 THEN GOTO 580
690 X=21:Y=0:GOSUB 3000
700 PRINT "PRESS ANY KEY FOR PLACINGS"
710 GET A$:IF A$="" THEN GOTO 710
720 PRINT "[CS ]"
730 PRINT:PRINT:PRINT "THE RESULTS WERE"
740 PRINT:PRINT:PRINT
750 PRINT "            1ST DOG - ";P(1)
760 PRINT "            2ND DOG - ";P(2)
770 PRINT "            3RD DOG - ";P(3)
780 :PRINT:PRINT
790 PRINT "IN ORDER THE REST WERE":PRINT:PRINT
800 FOR I=4 TO 10
810 PRINT "            DOG ";P(I)
820 NEXT I
830 END
1000 REM DATA FOR SHAPES
1010 REM DOG
1020 DATA 4,6,132,252,124,202,169,169
1030 REM CLOSED TRAP
1040 DATA 240,240,240,240,240,240,240,
          240
1050 REM OPEN TRAP
1060 DATA 255,255,255,240,240,240,240,
          240
1070 END
2000 REM COLOR DATA
2010 DATA 28,30,144,149,150,153,154,156,
158,159
2990 REM PRINT AT SUBROUTINE
3000 PRINT "[CH ]"
3005 IF X=0 THEN GOTO 3020
3010 FOR I=1 TO X:PRINT:NEXT I
3015 IF Y=0 THEN GOTO 3030
3020 FOR I=1 TO Y-1:PRINT"[CR ]";:NEXT I
3030 RETURN
```

P77 Magic Matrix

This program is based on an interesting idea presented in Martin Gardener's book "Mathematical Puzzles and Diversions", (Bell, 1964).

The program generates a matrix which is not a magic square but which has some interesting properties.

We have found that this is an amusing party trick, even if the matrix is simply drawn out on a piece of paper. The basic idea is rather simple, see if you can work it out.

COMMANDS

Press the shift and Commodore keys together to go into lower case mode.
Key in program and type RUN.
Follow instructions.

```
10 rem program - magic matrix
20 cl$=chr$(147):home$=chr$(19):down$=chr$(17):acros$=chr$(29)
30 print cl$;
40 x=10:y=13:gosub 5000
50 print "magic matrix"
60 a=ti
70 if ti<a+150 then goto 70
80 rem set up screen display
90 brder=53280:screen=53281
100 purple=4:yellow=7:red$=chr$(28):black$=chr$(144)
105 case$=chr$(142):uncase$=chr$(14)
110 poke brder,yellow
120 poke screen,purple
130 print cl$+black$+uncase$
140 x=3:y=3:gosub 5000
150 print "This program produces a square array"
160 print "   with an interesting property."
170 x=7:y=3:gosub 5000
180 print "You are asked to choose any number"
190 print "   in the square. You indicate "
200 print "   your choice by a row and column "
210 print "   number."
220 x=13:y=3:gosub 5000
230 print "The computer will then block out"
240 print "   all other numbers in that row"
```

```
250 print "    and column. This continues until"
260 print "    all the numbers are either chosen"
270 print "    or deleted."
280 x=20:y=3:gosub 5000
290 print "Press any key to continue";
300 get a$:if a$="" then goto 300
310 print cl$;
320 x=3:y=3:gosub 5000
330 print "Whatever numbers are chosen, the "
340 print "    sum of the chosen numbers will be"
350 print "    equal to the number the computer"
360 print "    will print at the bottom of the "
370 print "    screen before you start."
380 x=20:y=3:gosub 5000
390 print "Press any key to continue";
400 get a$:if a$="" then goto 400
410 dim x(5,2)
420 sum=0
430 for i=1 to 5
440 x(i,1)=int(rnd(0)*31)
450 x(i,2)=int(rnd(0)*31)
460 sum=sum+x(i,1)+x(i,2)
470 next i
480 dim a(5,5),row(5),col(5)
485 print cl$+red$+"[ron ]                    [rof ]"+black$
490 for n=1 to 5
500 for k=1 to 5
510 a(n,k)=x(n,2)+x(k,1)
520 p=a(n,k):gosub 4000
530 x=3+2*n:y=4+4*k:gosub 5000
540 print p$;
550 next k:next n
560 s$=""
570 x=20:y=1:gosub 5000
580 print "Sum = "sum
590 for j=1 to 5
600 x=21:y=1:gosub 5000
610 input "Row = ";rw
620 input "Column = ";cl
630 if row(rw)>0 or col(cl)>0 then 600
640 row(rw)=1:col(cl)=1
650 print red$
655 :
660 for i=0 to 4
670 x=5+i*2:y=5+4*cl:gosub 5000
680 print " . ";
690 x=3+2*rw:y=9+4*i:gosub 5000
```

P77 Magic Matrix

```
700 print " . "
710 next i
715 :
720 print black$;
730 s$=s$+" "+str$(a(rw,cl))
740 x=3+2*rw:y=35:gosub 5000
750 print a(rw,cl);
760 next j
770 x=24:y=1:gosub 5000
780 print mid$(s$,2)+"=";sum;
790 get a$:if a$="" then goto 790
800 print cl$+case$
810 end
3990 rem format subroutine
4000 p$=str$(p)
4010 if len(p$)>=3 then goto 4040
4020 p$=" "+p$
4030 goto 4010
4040 return
4990 rem subroutine to place cursor at position x,y
5000 print home$;
5010 if x=1 then 5030
5020 for r=1 to x:print down$;:next r
5030 if y=1 then 5050
5040 for c=1 to y:print across$;:next c
5050 return
```

```
                    MAGIC MATRIX

              .   30   19    .    8
              .    .    .    .    .    18
              .   29   18    .    7
              .    .    .    .    .    16
              .   31   20    .    9


Sum  =   91
Row  = ? 2
Column = ? 4
```

P78 Shuffle

This program shuffles a deck of cards on the screen. The program uses the Commodore card characters.

You could consider this program to be the kernel of any card based game.

COMMANDS

Key in program and type RUN.

```
10 REM PROGRAM  -  SHUFFLE
20 CL$=CHR$(147):HOME$=CHR$(19):
   DOWN$=CHR$(17):ACROS$=CHR$(29)
30 H$=CHR$(115):C$=CHR$(120):
   D$=CHR$(122):S$=CHR$(97)
40 PRINT CL$;
50 X=10:Y=16:GOSUB 5000
60 PRINT "SHUFFLE"
70 A=TI
80 IF TI<A+150 THEN GOTO 80
90 REM SET UP SCREEN DISPLAY
100 BRDER=53280:SCREEN=53281
110 PURPLE=4:YELLOW=7:RED$=CHR$(28):
    BLACK$=CHR$(144)
120 CASE$=CHR$(142):UNCASE$=CHR$(14)
130 POKE BRDER,YELLOW
140 POKE SCREEN,PURPLE
150 FOR I=2 TO 9
160 HR$=HR$+MID$(STR$(I),2)+H$
170 CB$=CB$+MID$(STR$(I),2)+C$
180 DI$=DI$+MID$(STR$(I),2)+D$
190 SP$=SP$+MID$(STR$(I),2)+S$
200 NEXT I
210 HR$="A"+H$+HR$+"T"+H$+"J"+H$+"Q"+H$+"K"+H$
220 CB$="A"+C$+CB$+"T"+C$+"J"+C$+"Q"+C$+"K"+C$
230 DI$="A"+D$+DI$+"T"+D$+"J"+D$+"Q"+D$+"K"+D$
240 SP$="A"+S$+SP$+"T"+S$+"J"+S$+"Q"+S$+"K"+S$
250 PACK$=HR$+CB$+DI$+SP$
260 PRINT CL$+BLACK$
270 PRINT "[RON ]                SHUFFLING
    [ROF ]"
280 FOR Z=1 TO 10:PRINT DOWN$:NEXT Z
290 PRINT "[RON ]
    [ROF ]";
```

P78 Shuffle

```
300 SHUFFLED$=""
310 FOR I=1 TO 50
320 P=(INT(RND(0)*(53-I))+1)*2-1
330 SHUFFLED$=SHUFFLED$+MID$(PACK$,P,2)
340 PACK$=LEFT$(PACK$,P-1)+MID$(PACK$,P+2)
350 T$=SHUFFLED$+PACK$
360 PRINT HOME$+DOWN$+DOWN$+DOWN$+DOWN$+DOWN$
370 FOR J=1 TO 4
380 HN$=MID$(T$,(J-1)*26+1,26)
390 PRINT " ";
400 FOR K=0 TO 12
410 CD$=MID$(HN$,K*2+1,2)
420 S$=RIGHT$(CD$,1)
430 IF S$=H$ OR S$=D$ THEN PRINT RED$;CD$;" ";:GOTO 450
440 IF S$=C$ OR S$=S$ THEN PRINT BLACK$;CD$;" ";
450 NEXT K
460 PRINT:PRINT
470 NEXT J
480 FOR Z=1 TO 50:NEXT Z
490 NEXT I
500 END
5000 PRINT HOME$;
5010 IF X=1 THEN 5030
5020 FOR R=1 TO X:PRINT DOWN$;:NEXT R
5030 IF Y=1 THEN 5050
5040 FOR C=1 TO Y:PRINT ACROS$;:NEXT C
5050 RETURN
```

P79 Recipes

In this program, we have recorded some of our favorite recipes. These are based on recipes in "Favourite Family Cookbook" by Norma Macmillan (Octopus, 1978).

Although we have included our own recipes, it would perhaps be better if you replaced our data statements with your own.

COMMANDS

Key in program and type RUN.
Follow the menus as presented.

```
10 REM PROGRAM FOR RECIPES
20 PRINT "[CS ]";
30 PRINT "[RON ]              RECIPES           [ROF ]"
40 PRINT:PRINT:PRINT:PRINT
50 PRINT "      1. [RON ]HORS D'OEUVRES[ROF ]"
60 PRINT "      2. [RON ]SOUPS         [ROF ]"
70 PRINT "      3. [RON ]FISH          [ROF ]"
80 PRINT "      4. [RON ]MEAT          [ROF ]"
90 GOSUB 1000
100 IF CH<1 OR CH>4 THEN GOTO 10
110 RESTORE
120 REM SELECT SUB MENU
125 IF CH=1 THEN GOTO 185
130 FOR M=1 TO CH-1
140 READ T$
150 FOR I=1 TO 4
160 READ T1$
170 NEXT I
180 NEXT M
185 READ T$
190 PRINT "[CS ]":PRINT:PRINT:PRINT
200 PRINT TAB(20-LEN(T$)/2); CHR$(18);T$; CHR$(146)
210 PRINT:PRINT:PRINT
220 FOR M=1 TO 4
230 READ M$
240 PRINT TAB(5);M;" ";M$
250 NEXT M
260 IF CH=4 THEN GOTO 330
270 FOR M=CH+1 TO 4
```

```
280 READ S$
290 FOR N=1 TO 4
300 READ S$
310 NEXT N
320 NEXT M
330 REM WE HAVE NOW READ PAST ALL TITLE      PAGES
340 C=CH
350 GOSUB 1000
360 REM NOW WE CALCULATE WHERE TO READ FROM
370 REM C=RECIPE TYPE:CH=CHOICE WITHIN TYPE
380 REM THEREFORE RECIPE NUMBER IS (C-1)*4+CH
390 REM EACH RECIPE IS HELD IN 21 DATA ITEMS
400 REM THUS WE HAVE TO READ PAST
410 REM ((C-1)*4+CH-1)*21 ITEMS TO GET
420 REM TO RECIPE
430 E=((C-1)*4+CH-1)*21
440 FOR I=1 TO E
450 READ S$
460 NEXT I
470 REM NOW WE ARE AT THE CORRECT RECIPE
480 READ T$
490 PRINT "[CS ]";
TAB(20-LEN(T$)/2);CHR$(18);T$;CHR$(146):PRINT:PRINT
500 FOR I=1 TO 19
510 READ L$
520 PRINT L$
530 NEXT I
540 PRINT "PRESS ANY KEY TO RETURN TO MENU"
550 GET A$:IF A$="" THEN GOTO 550
560 RUN
999 END
1000 PRINT:PRINT:PRINT
1010 PRINT "ENTER THE APPROPRIATE NUMBER"
1020 PRINT "FOR THE RECIPE OF YOUR CHOICE ";
1030 INPUT CH
1040 RETURN
2000 DATA H O R S  D' O E U V R E S,KIPPER PATE,EGG
MAYONNAISE
2010 DATA MUSHROOMS A LA GRECQUE,GRILLED GRAPEFRUIT
2020 DATA S O U P S,BORSCH,PEA SOUP,OXTAIL SOUP,FRENCH
ONION SOUP
2030 DATA F I S H,TROUT WITH ALMONDS,SALMON
STEAKS,FINNAN HADDIE
2040 DATA SCALLOPS AND BACON
2050 DATA M E A T,NEAPOLITAN STEAK,WEINER SCHNITZEL,LAMB
CURRY,PORK 'N ORANGE
2999 REM HORS D'OEUVRES
```

```
3000 REM K I P P E R    P A T E
3001 DATA ,K I P P E R    P A T E
3002 DATA 2TBLESPOON UNSALTED BUTTER
3003 DATA 1/2 LB KIPPER FILLETS
3004 DATA 1 CUP CREAM CHEESE
3005 DATA 1/2 GARLIC CLOVE - CRUSHED
3006 DATA JUICE OF 1/2 LEMON
3007 DATA BLACK PEPPER,,,
3011 DATA MELT BUTTER IN FRYING PAN
3012 DATA ADD THE KIPPERS AND COOK TILL SOFT
3013 DATA REMOVE FISH AND COOL THEN FLAKE FISH
3014 DATA BLEND FISH CHEESE ETC UNTIL SMOOTH
3015 DATA SERVE CHILLED WITH PEPPER,,,,
3100 DATA E G G    M A Y O N N A I S E
3101 DATA 4 LARGE LETTUCE LEAVES
3102 DATA 8 SPRIGS WATERCRESS
3103 DATA 4 EGGS - HARD BOILED AND HALVED
3104 DATA 1 AND 1/4 CUPS OF MAYONNAISE
3105 DATA PINCH OF PAPRIKA,,,
3112 DATA PUT A LETTUCE LEAF ON EACH PLATE
3113 DATA ADD 2 SPRIGS OF WATERCRESS TO EACH
3114 DATA PLACE EGGS IN CENTER FLAT SIDE DOWN
3115 DATA POUR OVER MAYONNAISE AND ADD PAPRIKA,,,,,,,,
3200 DATA MUSHROOMS A LA GRECQUE
3201 DATA 1 AND 1/4 CUPS WATER
3202 DATA SMALL ONION CHOPPED
3203 DATA 1 TEASPOON TOMATO PASTE
3204 DATA SALT AND PEPPER TO TASTE
3205 DATA BOUQUET GARNI
3206 DATA LEMON JUICE TO TASTE
3207 DATA 3 CUPS OF SMALL BUTTON MUSHROOMS
3208 DATA PARSLEY TO GARNISH,,,
3209 DATA PUT ALL EXCEPT MUSHROOMS AND GARNISH
3210 DATA INTO SAUCEPAN AND SIMMER FOR 5 MINUTES
3211 DATA ADD MUSHROOMS AND SIMMER FOR 10 MINS
3212 DATA REMOVE MUSHROOMS
3213 DATA BOIL LIQUID UNTIL 3-4 TABLESPOONS LEFT
3214 DATA POUR OVER MUSHROOOMS AND SERVE WITH
3215 DATA PARSLEY,,
3300 DATA GRILLED GRAPEFRUIT
3301 DATA 2 LARGE GRAPEFRUIT - HALVED
3302 DATA 4 TEASPOONS OF MEDIUM SHERRY
3303 DATA 4 TABLESPOONS OF BROWN SUGAR
3304 DATA 1 TABLESPOON OF BUTTER - CUT INTO FOUR,,,,
3305 DATA LOOSEN SEGMENTS OF GRAPEFRUIT AND
3306 DATA REMOVE SEEDS. DRAIN HALVES ONTO KITCHEN
```

P79 Recipes

```
3307 DATA PAPER FOR A FEW MINUTES. PLACE
3308 DATA GRAPEFRUIT HALVES IN GRILL PAN CUT
3309 DATA SIDES UP. SPRINKLE EACH WITH SUGAR AND
3310 DATA SHERRY. TOP EACH WITH BUTTER AND GRILL
3311 DATA UNTIL BUBBLING.,,,,,,
4000 DATA B O R S C H
4001 DATA 2 TABLESPOONS OF BUTTER
4002 DATA LARGE ONION - PEELED AND SLICED
4003 DATA LARGE CARROT - PEELED AND GRATED
4004 DATA 2 LARGE COOKED BEETROOTS - SLICED
4005 DATA 1/2 SMALL HEAD RED CABBAGE - SHREDDED
4006 DATA 1 TABLESPOON OF TOMATO PASTE
4007 DATA 1 TABLESPOON OF VINEGAR AND 1 OF SUGAR
4008 DATA SALT AND PEPPER TO TASTE
4009 DATA 5 CUPS OF BEEF STOCK
4010 DATA 1 AND 1/4 CUPS OF SOUR CREAM TO SERVE,,,
4011 DATA MELT BUTTER IN PAN AND COOK VEGETABLES
4012 DATA GENTLY FOR 5 MINUTES. STIR IN OTHER
4013 DATA INGREDIENTS AND SIMMER FOR 20-30 MINS
4014 DATA UNTIL VEG ARE TENDER. SERVE WITH CREAM.,,,
4100 DATA P E A   S O U P
4101 DATA 2 TABLESPOONS OF BUTTER AND 1 OF OIL
4102 DATA 1 ONION AND 2 CELERY STALKS - CHOPPED
4103 DATA 2 CUPS OF SHELLED PEAS
4104 DATA 1 SMALL HAM BONE
4105 DATA 2 CUPS OF CHICKEN STOCK
4106 DATA 1 TABLESPOON OF CORNFLOUR
4107 DATA 1 AND 1/4 CUPS OF MILK
4108 DATA SALT AND PEPPER TO TASTE,,,
4109 DATA MELT BUTTER AND OIL IN PAN - FRY CELERY
4110 DATA AND ONION. COOK PEAS FOR 5 MINS. ADD
4111 DATA BONE AND STOCK THEN BOIL FOR 40 MINS.
4112 DATA REMOVE BONE AND PUREE SOUP. DISSOLVE
4113 DATA FLOUR IN MILK AND ADD TO SOUP. SIMMER
4114 DATA UNTIL THICK.,,,
4200 DATA O X T A I L    S O U P
4201 DATA 4 TABLESPOONS OF OLIVE OIL
4202 DATA 4 AND 1/2 PINTS OF WATER
4203 DATA 1 OXTAIL - CUT INTO PIECES
4204 DATA 2 ONIONS AND 2 CARROTS - CHOPPED
4205 DATA 2 CELERY STALKS AND 1 TURNIP - CHOPPED
4206 DATA SALT AND PEPPER
4207 DATA ONE 14 OZ CAN OF TOMATOES
4208 DATA 2 TABLESPOONS OF FLOUR AND 4 OF SHERRY.,,,
4209 DATA BROWN OXTAIL AND FRY VEG TILL SOFT. ADD
4210 DATA TO WATER WITH SALT AND PEPPER. SIMMER
4211 DATA FOR 4 HOURS. REMOVE OXTAILS AND CUT
```

```
4212 DATA MEAT FROM BONES. REMOVE FAT FROM SOUP
4213 DATA AND RETURN MEAT. THICKEN WITH SHERRY
4214 DATA AND FLOUR. SERVE HOT.,,,
4300 DATA F R E N C H   O N I O N   S O U P
4301 DATA 2 TABLESPOONS BUTTER
4302 DATA 2 TABLESPOONS OF OLIVE OIL
4303 DATA 1 GARLIC CLOVE - CRUSHED
4304 DATA 3 LARGE SLICED ONIONS
4305 DATA 5 CUPS OF BEEF STOCK
4306 DATA SALT AND PEPPER
4307 DATA 8-12 SLICES OF FRENCH BREAD
4308 DATA 3/4 CUP OF CHEESE.,,,
4309 DATA FRY GARLIC AND ONION FOR 20 MINS - DO
4310 DATA NOT BROWN TOO MUCH. ADD TO STALK WITH
4311 DATA SALT AND PEPPER. SIMMER FOR 30 MINS.
4312 DATA TOAST BREAD. SERVE SOUP HOT WITH TOAST
4313 DATA AND CHEESE.,,,,
5000 DATA T R O U T    W I T H    A L M O N D S
5001 DATA 1/4 CUP PLAIN FLOUR
5002 DATA SALT AND PEPPER
5003 DATA 4 LARGE TROUT - CLEANED
5004 DATA 1/3 CUP BUTTER
5005 DATA 1/2 CUP ALMOND FLAKES
5006 DATA 2 TEASPOONS OF LEMON JUICE
5007 DATA LEMON AND PARSLEY TO GARNISH,,,
5008 DATA MIX FLOUR WITH SALT AND PEPPER AND COAT
5009 DATA THE TROUT. MELT BUTTER IN PAN AND BROWN
5010 DATA TROUT QUICKLY ON BOTH SIDES. COOK TROUT
5011 DATA UNTIL TENDER. REMOVE FISH AND KEEP HOT.
5012 DATA COOK ALMONDS IN PAN UNTIL GOLDEN. STIR
5013 DATA IN LEMON JUICE. POUR LIQUID AND
5014 DATA ALMONDS OVER FISH AND GARNISH.,,,
5100 DATA S A L M O N    S T E A K S
5101 DATA 4 SALMON STEAKS
5102 DATA 1/4 CUP OF BUTTER CUT INTO FOUR
5103 DATA 4 HALF BAY LEAVES AND 4 ONION SLICES
5104 DATA 4 SLIVERS LEMON RIND AND 4 SPRIGS THYME
5105 DATA 4 PARLSEY SPRIGS
5106 DATA SALT AND PEPPER TO TASTE,,,,
5107 DATA DIVIDE INGREDIENTS INTO INDIVIDUAL
5108 DATA PORTIONS. WRAP EACH IN FOIL AND BAKE
5109 DATA IN A MODERATE OVEN (180 C:350 F GAS
5110 DATA MARK 4). FOR 15-20 MINUTES. SERVE
5111 DATA STEAKS HOT WITHOUT HERBS.,,,,,
5200 DATA F I N N A N    H A D D I E
5201 DATA 1 AND 1/2 LB SMOKED HADDOCK - CHOPPED
5202 DATA 1 AND 1/4 CUPS OF MILK
```

P79 Recipes

```
5203 DATA 2/3 CUP OF SINGLE CREAM
5204 DATA 2 TABLESPOONS BUTTER
5205 DATA PEPPER
5206 DATA 6 EGGS,,,
5207 DATA PLACE FISH IN BAKING DISH. PUT MILK AND
5208 DATA CREAM AND BUTTER IN PAN AND HEAT UNTIL
5209 DATA BUTTER IS MELTED. POUR OVER FISH. BAKE
5210 DATA IN MODERATE OVEN (180C : 350F : GAS 4)
5211 DATA FOR 20 MINS. POACH EGGS 5 MINS BEFORE
5212 DATA FISH IS READY. TOP FISH MIXTURE WITH
5213 DATA EGGS AND SERVE.,,,,
5300 DATA S C A L L O P S   A N D   B A C O N
5301 DATA 16-20 SHELLED SCALLOPS
5302 DATA SALT AND PEPPER AND LEMON JUICE
5303 DATA 16-20 SLICES OF BACON,,,,
5304 DATA SPRINKLE SCALLOPS WITH SALT AND PEPPER
5305 DATA AND LEMON JUICE. STRETCH BACON WITH
5306 DATA FLAT KNIFE. WRAP RASHER ROUND EACH
5307 DATA SCALLOP AND SECURE WITH COCKTAIL STICK.
5308 DATA GRILL SLOWLY TILL COOOKED - 5 MINS
5309 DATA AND SERVE WITH TARTARE SAUCE.,,,,,,,,
6000 DATA N E A P O L I T A N    S T E A K
6001 DATA 4 SIRLOIN STEAKS
6002 DATA 3 CUPS PEELED AND CHOPPED TOMATOES
6003 DATA 2 TABLESPOONS OLIVE OIL
6004 DATA 2 CHOPPED GARLIC CLOVES
6005 DATA 1 TABLESPOON CHOPPED PARSLEY
6006 DATA 1/2 TEASPOON OREGANO
6007 DATA 1 TEASPOON OF SUGAR
6008 DATA SALT AND PEPPER.,,,
6009 DATA BOIL TOMATOES OIL GARLIC PARSLEY SUGAR
6010 DATA SALT AND PEPPER. SIMMER FOR 5 MINS.
6011 DATA GRILL STEAKS AND POUR SAUCE OVER.
6012 DATA SERVE HOT.,,,,,,
6100 DATA W I E N E R   S C H N I T Z E L
6101 DATA 4 VEAL ESCALOPES POUNDED THIN
6102 DATA JUICE OF 2 LEMONS
6103 DATA SALT AND PEPPER AND LARGE BEATEN EGG
6104 DATA 1 CUP OF DRY BREADCRUMBS
6105 DATA 3 TABLESPOONS BUTTER
6106 DATA LEMON WEDGES TO GARNISH,,,
6107 DATA MARINATE VEAL IN LEMON WITH SALT AND
6108 DATA PEPPER FOR 1 HOUR. DIP VEAL IN EGG AND
6109 DATA COAT WITH BREADCRUMBS. FRY VEAL IN
6110 DATA BUTTER TILL GOLDEN BROWN.,,,,,,,,
6200 DATA L A M B    C U R R Y
6201 DATA 2LB LEAN LAMB CUBED
```

```
6202 DATA 2/3 CUP YOGHURT
6203 DATA 2 TEASPOONS OF GARAM MASALA
6204 DATA 1 TABLESPOON CURRY POWDER
6205 DATA 2 TABLESPOONS OF BUTTER
6206 DATA 2 TABLESPOONS OF OLIVE OIL
6207 DATA 2 CHOPPED ONIONS
6208 DATA 1 CRUSHED GARLIC CLOVE
6209 DATA SALT PEPPER AND LEMON JUICE TO TASTE
6210 DATA 2/3 CUP DRIED FRUIT
6211 DATA 2 TABLESPOONS OF ALMONDS,
6212 DATA MIX YOGHURT WITH GARAM MASALA AND CURRY
6213 DATA ADD LAMB CUBES AND MARINATE FOR 4 HOURS
6214 DATA FRY ONIONS AND GARLIC TILL SOFT. STIR
6215 DATA IN LAMB AND YOGHURT WITH SALT,PEPPER &
6216 DATA LEMON JUICE. COOK FOR 5 MINS THEN ADD
6217 DATA FRUIT AND ALMONDS. SIMMER TILL TENDER.,,
6300 DATA P O R K    'N   O R A N G E
6301 DATA 1/4 CUP PLAIN FLOUR
6302 DATA 1 AND 1/2LB PORK FILLET CUT INTO CUBES
6303 DATA 2 TABLESPOONS OF BUTTER
6304 DATA 1 SMALL CHOPPED ONION
6305 DATA 1 CHOPPED GREEN PEPPER- NO PITH OR SEED
6306 DATA GRATED RIND AND JUICE OF 2 ORANGES
6307 DATA 1 TABLESPOON OF WORCESTERSHIRE SAUCE
6308 DATA 2/3 CUPS OF BEEF STOCK
6309 DATA 1 PEELED SEGMENTED ORANGE,,
6310 DATA MIX FLOUR SALT AND PEPPER IN BAG. ADD
6311 DATA PORK CUBES AND SHAKE TO COAT. FRY ONION
6312 DATA AND PEPPER IN BUTTER TILL SOFT. BROWN
6313 DATA PORK. STIR IN ORANGE RIND AND JUICE ADD
6314 DATA STOCK AND SAUCE. SIMMER FOR 10 MINS.
6315 DATA ADD ORANGE SEGS AND COOK FOR 2 MINS.
6316 DATA SERVE HOT,,,
6317 REM END OF PROGRAM DATA
```

P80 Kitchen Timer

A useful program for the kitchen here - it lets you know how long it will be before a meal is ready. At the end of the period specified an alarm sounds.

COMMANDS

Key in the program and RUN.

Enter the delay required when prompted.

Press any key to stop the alarm.

```
10 REM KITCHEN TIMER
20 REM ************
30 REM
100 CL$=CHR$(147):REM TO CLEAR SCREEN
110 UP$=CHR$(145):REM UP CURSOR
120 S$=CHR$(32)
130 FOR N=0 TO 2:S$=S$+S$+S$:NEXT:
    REM S$ CONTAINS 27 SPACES
140 POKE 53280,0:REM BLACK BORDER
150 POKE 53281,0:REM BLACK SCREEN
160 PRINT CHR$(30):REM GREEN INK
170 REM*************************
180 PRINT CL$:PRINT:PRINT
190 PRINT TAB(14)"KITCHEN TIMER"
200 PRINT TAB(14)"+++++++++++++"
210 PRINT:PRINT
220 PRINT TAB(5)
    "WHAT SETTING DO YOU REQUIRE?"
230 PRINT
240 PRINT TAB(11):INPUT"HOURS";H%
250 IF H%<0 OR H%>23 THEN
    PRINT UP$+S$+UP$:GOTO 240
260 PRINT
270 PRINT TAB(11):INPUT"MINUTES";M%
280 IF M%<0 OR M%>60 THEN
    PRINT UP$+S$+UP$:GOTO 270
290 PRINT
300 PRINT TAB(11):INPUT"SECONDS";S%
```

```
310 IF S%<0 OR S%>60 THEN
    PRINT UP$+S$+UP$:GOTO 300
320 TI$="000000":REM RESET CLOCK
330 DL=H%*3600+M%*60+S%
340 PRINT CL$
350 FOR N=0 TO 8:PRINT:NEXT
360 PRINT TAB(12)"TIME REMAINING":PRINT
370 REM***************************
380 REM PRINT TIME REMAINING
390 A$=STR$(H%):IF LEN(A$)=2 THEN
    A$="0"+RIGHT$(A$,1)
400 IF LEN(STR$(H%))=3 THEN
    A$=RIGHT$(STR$(H%),2)
410 B$=STR$(M%):IF LEN(B$)=2 THEN
    B$="0"+RIGHT$(B$,1)
420 IF LEN(STR$(M%))=3 THEN
    B$=RIGHT$(STR$(M%),2)
430 C$=STR$(S%):IF LEN(C$)=2 THEN
    C$="0"+RIGHT$(C$,1)
440 IF LEN(STR$(S%))=3 THEN
    C$=RIGHT$(STR$(S%),2)
450 D$=A$+":"+B$+":"+C$
460 PRINT TAB(15)D$:PRINT UP$+UP$
470 REM***************************
480 REM CALCULATE DELAY
490 T=DL-INT(TI/60):IF T<=0 THEN 550
500 H%=T/3600:T=T-H%*3600
510 M%=T/60:
520 S%=T-M%*60
530 GOTO 380
540 REM***************************
550 REM TIME UP
560 PRINTCL$
570 FOR N=0 TO 8:PRINT:NEXT
580 PRINT TAB(15)"TIME UP"
590 FOR N=0 TO 5:PRINT:NEXT
600 PRINT TAB(8)"PRESS ANY KEY TO STOP"
610 REM***************************
620 REM ALARM
630 S=54272:REM START OF SOUND CHIP
640 POKE S+1,160
650 POKE S+5,8
660 POKE S+15,40
670 POKE S+24,15
680 POKE S+4,0:POKE S+4,21
690 FOR DE=0 TO 100:NEXT
```

```
700 POKE S+4,20
710 FOR DE=0 TO 10:NEXT
720 GET A$:IF A$="" THEN 680
730 POKE S+4,0:POKE S+24,0
740 END
750 REM***************************
760 REM***************************
```

P81 School Report

This program prepares a school report for a student. The program could be developed to store data on a tape or disk file and handle more than one student.

COMMANDS

Key in program and type RUN.
Enter details as requested.

```
10 REM PROGRAM - SCHOOL REPORT
20 PRINT "[CS CD CD CD CD CD CD CD CD CD CD ]"
30 PRINT "           SCHOOL REPORT"
40 A=TI
50 IF TI<A+100 THEN GOTO 50
60 GOSUB 1000
70 PRINT "    PLEASE ENSURE THAT YOUR PRINTER"
80 PRINT "    HAS BEEN SET UP CORRECTLY."
90 PRINT:PRINT:PRINT
100 PRINT "    PRESS ANY KEY WHEN READY"
110 GET A$:IF A$="" THEN 110
120 GOSUB 1000
130 PRINT "WHAT IS NAME OF SCHOOL ";
140 INPUT SC$
150 INPUT "ENTER STUDENT'S NAME ";N$
160 OPEN 1,4:REM OPEN PRINTER
170 PRINT#1,TAB((60-LEN(SC$))/2);SC$
180 PRINT#1:PRINT#1:PRINT#1
190 INPUT "SESSION";S$
200 PRINT#1,"SESSION - ";S$
210 PRINT#1,"NAME - ":N$
220 PRINT#1:PRINT#1:PRINT#1
230 PRINT#1,"   SUBJECT    !ATTEND!GRADE!POSITION!COMMENT"
240 PRINT#1,SPC(14);"! P   A !       !IN CLASS!"
250 PRINT#1,"---------------!------!-----!--------!----------------"
260 REM LOOP BACK POINT
265 GOSUB 1000
270 INPUT "SUBJECT (999  TO END);SB$
280 IF SB$="999" THEN 480
290 INPUT "POSSIBLE ATTENDANCE ";P$
300 INPUT "ACTUAL ATTENDANCE ";A$
```

P81 School Report

```
310 INPUT "GRADE ";GR$
320 INPUT "POSITION IN CLASS ";PO$
330 INPUT "TEACHER'S COMMENT";CO$
340 IF LEN(SB$)>14 THEN SB$=LEFT$(SB$,14):GOTO 360
350 FOR Z=LEN(SB$) TO 13:SB$=SB$+" ":NEXT Z
360 IF LEN(P$)>3 THEN P$=LEFT$(P$,3):GOTO 380
370 FOR Z=LEN(P$) TO 2:P$=P$+" ":NEXT Z
380 IF LEN(A$)>3 THEN A$=LEFT$(A$,3):GOTO 400
390 FOR Z=LEN(A$) TO 2:A$=A$+" ":NEXT Z
400 IF LEN(GR$)>5 THEN GR$=LEFT$(GR$,5):GOTO 420
410 FOR Z=LEN(GR$) TO 4:GR$=GR$+" ":NEXT Z
420 IF LEN(PO$)>8 THEN PO$=LEFT$(PO$,8):GOTO 440
430 FOR Z=LEN(PO$) TO 7:PO$=PO$+" ":NEXT Z
440 IF LEN(CO$)>20 THEN CO$=LEFT$(CO$,20):GOTO 460
450 FOR Z=LEN(CO$) TO 19:CO$=CO$+" ":NEXT Z
460 PRINT#1,SB$+"!"+P$+"!"+A$+"!"+GR$+"!"+PO$+"!"+CO$
470 GOTO 265
480 GOSUB 1000
490 PRINT#1:PRINT#1:PRINT#1
500 INPUT "OVERALL ASSESSMENT ";OV$
510 PRINT#1,"OVERALL ASSESSMENT"
520 PRINT#1,"=================="
530 PRINT#1
540 PRINT#1,OV$
550 PRINT#1:PRINT#1:PRINT#1
560 PRINT#1,"SIGNATURE OF PARENT OR GUARDIAN"
570 PRINT#1,"-------------------------------"
580 GOSUB 1000
590 INPUT "ANOTHER (Y/N) ";R$
600 IF R$="Y" THEN GOTO 10
610 END
1000 PRINT "[CS ]";
1010 PRINT "[RON ]            SCHOOL REPORT
   [ROF ]"
1020 PRINT:PRINT:PRINT
1030 RETURN
```

P82 Language Tutorial

This program gives the French implementation of a language vocabulary tutorial. It could easily be adapted for other languages. The data are in the form of word pairs which may be inserted by the teacher as data statements in lines 1000 onwards. The last item of data must be EOF.

The program gives the student up to three attempts at each word. After the tutorial is finished statistics are returned.

The program could be extended so that several alternative answers may be accepted for some words.

COMMANDS

Key in the program and RUN.

Follow the instructions.

```
10 REM LANGUAGE TUTORIAL
20 REM *****************
30 REM
100 CL$=CHR$(147):REM TO CLEAR SCREEN
110 POKE 53280,9:REM BROWN BORDER
120 POKE 53281,1:REM WHITE SCREEN
130 PRINT CHR$(31):REM BLUE INK
140 PRINT CL$:PRINT:PRINT
150 PRINT TAB(12)"FRENCH TUTORIAL"
160 PRINT TAB(12)"==============="
170 PRINT:PRINT
190 PRINT TAB(4)
    "THIS PROGRAM TESTS YOUR KNOWLEDGE"
200 PRINT TAB(4)
    "OF FRENCH VOCABULARY. ENGLISH"
210 PRINT TAB(4)
    "WORDS ARE PUT ON THE SCREEN ONE AT"
220 PRINT TAB(4)
    "A TIME AND YOU ARE ASKED FOR THE"
230 PRINT TAB(4)
    "FRENCH EQUIVALENTS. YOU ARE"
```

```
240 PRINT TAB(4)
    "ALLOWED THREE ATTEMPTS AT EACH"
250 PRINT TAB(4)"WORD."
260 PRINT:PRINT
270 PRINT TAB(8)CHR$(18)
    " PRESS ANY KEY TO START "
280 GET A$:IF A$="" THEN 280:REM
    NO SPACE BETWEEN INVERTED COMMAS
290 REM*******************************
300 RESTORE
310 CLR:CL$=CHR$(147)
320 REM*******************************
330 READ E$
340 IF E$="EOF" THEN 620:REM FINISH
350 READ F$
360 F=0
370 FOR N=1 TO 3
380 PRINT CL$:PRINT:PRINT
390 PRINT TAB(14)CHR$(18)" ATTEMPT"
    STR$(N)+CHR$(32)
400 PRINT:PRINT
410 PRINT TAB(7)
    "TYPE IN THE FRENCH WORD"
420 PRINT TAB(7)
    "THEN PRESS THE RETURN KEY."
430 PRINT:PRINT
440 PRINT TAB(7)"ENGLISH WORD IS - "E$
450 PRINT:PRINT
460 PRINT TAB(8):INPUT
    "FRENCH WORD IS ";T$
470 IF T$=F$ THEN R(N)=R(N)+1:F=1:N=3
480 NEXT
490 REM*******************************
500 PRINT:PRINT
510 IF F=1 THEN PRINT TAB(15)CHR$(18)
    " CORRECT ":GOTO 580
520 REM*******************************
530 REM WRONG ANSWER
540 R(4)=R(4)+1
550 PRINT TAB(7)
    "CORRECT ANSWER IS - "F$
560 FOR K=1 TO LEN(F$):PRINT TAB(26+K)
    "-";:NEXT:REM UNDERLINE
570 REM*******************************
580 FOR DE=0 TO 2000:NEXT:REM DELAY
600 GOTO 330
610 REM*******************************
```

```
620 REM FINISH
630 PRINT CL$:PRINT:PRINT
640 PRINT TAB(8)
    "NUMBER CORRECT AT FIRST"
650 PRINT TAB(8)"ATTEMPT WAS";R(1)
660 PRINT
670 PRINT TAB(8)
    "NUMBER CORRECT AT SECOND"
680 PRINT TAB(8)"ATTEMPT WAS";R(2)
690 PRINT
700 PRINT TAB(8)
    "NUMBER CORRECT AT THIRD"
710 PRINT TAB(8)"ATTEMPT WAS";R(3)
720 PRINT
730 PRINT TAB(8)"NUMBER OF UNKNOWN"
740 PRINT TAB(8)"ANSWERS WAS";R(4)
750 PRINT:PRINT
760 PRINT TAB(10):INPUT
    "ANOTHER GO (Y/N)";Y$
770 IF ASC(Y$)=89 THEN 300
780 END
790 REM*****************************
800 REM*****************************
810 REM
820 REM PUT IN AS MANY ENGLISH WORDS AS
830 REM YOU WISH (EACH FOLLOWED BY ITS
840 REM FRENCH EQUIVALENT) IN LINES
850 REM 1000 ONWARDS. TERMINATE THE
860 REM DATA WITH EOF AS SHOWN. A FEW
870 REM SIMPLE WORDS ARE GIVEN AS
880 REM EXAMPLES.
890 REM
900 REM*****************************
910 REM*****************************
920 REM
930 REM             ********
940 REM             *
950 REM             * DATA
960 REM             *
970 REM             ********
980 REM
990 REM*****************************
1000 DATA YES,OUI,NO,NON,END,FIN,EOF
```

P83 Counting

This program could be useful for the very young schoolchild. It displays up to nine monsters on the screen. The user is required to count the monsters and press the appropriate numeric key. The RETURN key is not used.

The program could be expanded so that several groups of items (say monsters, flowers and automobiles) appear on the screen at the same time and the user is asked to count the numbers in one particular group.

Multicolor mode user defined characters are used in this program.

COMMANDS

Key in the program and RUN.

Stop the program by pressing the RUN/STOP and RESTORE keys simultaneously.

```
10 REM COUNTING
20 REM ********
30 REM
40 POKE 52,48:POKE 56,48:CLR:
   REM RESERVE RAM AREA FOR CHARACTERS
50 REM RAM RESERVED BEFORE MAIN PROGRAM
        STARTS AS VARIABLES ARE CLEARED
60 REM***************************
100 CL$=CHR$(147):REM TO CLEAR SCREEN
110 RO=53248:REM START OF CHARACTER ROM
120 RA=12288:REM START OF CHARACTER RAM
130 IT=56334:REM INTERRUPT TIMER
140 CC=53272:
    REM CONTROLS CHARACTER LOCATION
150 SC=1024:REM START OF SCREEN MEMORY
160 POKE 53280,14:REM BLUE BORDER
170 POKE 53281,0:REM BLACK SCREEN
180 PRINT CHR$(158):REM YELLOW INK
190 REM***************************
200 PRINT CL$:PRINT:PRINT
```

```
210 PRINT TAB(18)"WAIT"
220 PRINT CHR$(142):REM UPPER CASE
230 POKE IT,PEEK (IT) AND 254:
    REM DISABLE INTERRUPT TIMER
240 POKE 1,PEEK (1) AND 251:
    REM SWITCH FROM I/O TO CHAR. ROM
250 FOR N=0 TO 511:POKE N+RA,PEEK (N+RO)
    :NEXT:REM TRANSFER CHARACTERS
260 POKE 1,PEEK (1) OR 4:
    REM SWITCH FROM CHAR. TO I/O ROM
270 POKE IT,PEEK (IT) OR 1:
    REM ENABLE INTERRUPT TIMER
280 POKE CC,(PEEK (CC) AND 240)+12:
    REM CONTROL OF CHARACTERS TO RAM
290 REM****************************
300 REM DEFINE CHARACTERS
310 FOR N=27 TO 30
320 FOR K=0 TO 7
330 READ A:POKE RA+8*N+K,A
340 NEXT:NEXT
350 REM****************************
360 REM MULTICOLOR MODE
370 POKE 53282,15:REM SCREEN #1 GRAY 3
380 POKE 53283,11:REM SCREEN #2 GRAY 1
390 POKE 53270,PEEK(53270) OR 16:
    REM MULTICOLOR MODE ON********
400 CM=55296:REM COLOR MEMORY
410 REM****************************
420 REM PRINT MONSTERS IN BACKGROUND
    COLOR
430 PRINT CL$:FOR N=0 TO 21:PRINT:NEXT
440 MN%=9*RND(1):REM NUMBER OF MONSTERS
    WILL BE MN%+1
450 FOR K=0 TO MN%
460 X(K)=1+INT(37*RND(1))
470 Y(K)=1+INT(18*RND(1))
480 L=1024+40*Y(K)+X(K)
490 M=1024+40*(Y(K)+1)+X(K)
500 IF PEEK(L)<>32 OR PEEK(L+1)<>32
    THEN 460
510 IF PEEK(M)<>32 OR PEEK(M+1)<>32
    THEN 460
520 POKE L,27:POKE L+1,28:POKE M,29:
    POKE M+1,30
530 NEXT
540 REM****************************
550 REM COLOR THEM IN
```

```
560 FOR K=0 TO MN%
570 N=CM+40*Y(K)+X(K)
580 P=CM+40*(Y(K)+1)+X(K)
590 POKE N,11:POKE N+1,11:POKE P,11:
    POKE P+1,11
600 NEXT
610 REM***************************
620 S=54272:REM START OF SOUND CHIP
630 POKE S,255:POKE S+1,2:POKE S+5,76:
    POKE S+6,32:POKE S+24,0
640 REM***************************
650 PRINT TAB(10)"HOW MANY MONSTERS?"
660 M$=RIGHT$(STR$(MN%+1),1)
670 FOR K=11 TO 15
680 POKE 53282,K:POKE 53283,26-K
690 FOR J=0 TO 50 :GET A$:IF A$<>""
    THEN K=15:J=50:REM NO SPACE
700 NEXT:NEXT
710 POKE S+4,0:POKE S+24,0
720 IF A$="" THEN 670:REM NO SPACE
730 IF ASC(A$)<48 OR ASC(A$)>57
    THEN 670
740 IF A$<>M$ THEN POKE S+4,0:
    POKE S+24,15:POKE S+4,129:GOTO 670
750 REM***************************
760 REM CORRECT ANSWER
770 PRINT CHR$(145)CHR$(145)
780 PRINT TAB(10)"  THAT'S RIGHT!!  "
790 FOR N=11 TO 0 STEP -1
800 POKE 53281,N:POKE 53280,14-N
810 POKE 53281,N:POKE 53280,14-N
820 POKE S+4,0:POKE S+24,15:POKE S+4,17
830 FOR K=10 TO 150 STEP 5
840 POKE S+1,K
850 NEXT :NEXT
860 POKE S+4,0:POKE S+15,0
870 GOTO 410:REM MORE MONSTERS
880 REM***************************
890 REM***************************
1000 REM DATA FOR CHARACTERS
1010 DATA 1,1,5,5,34,34,42,42
1020 DATA 64,64,80,80,136,136,168,168
1030 DATA 4,4,49,48,192,192,192,192
1040 DATA 16,16,76,12,3,3,3,3
1050 REM***************************
1060 REM***************************
```

P84 Spelling

This program may be used as a spelling aid for young children. The instructions for using the program are included in the code.

The idea of the program is to provide positive feedback by making a game out of spelling. The instructor can determine the vocabulary by typing in data in lines 6000 onwards. As many words as required (up to the limit of computer memory) may be entered. The last data entry must be EOF.

The program could be developed as a teaching package by including an instruction-to-teacher section and a results section.

Both character sets are used in this program. The lower case character set is transferred to RAM and three characters in this set are redefined. The upper case character set is obtained from character ROM in the standard way.

COMMANDS

Key in the program and RUN.

Enter the level of difficulty – 9 is the hardest.

Instructions for moving and firing the gun are included in the program.

```
10 REM SPELLING
20 REM ********
30 REM
40 POKE 52,48:POKE 56,48:CLR:
   REM RESERVE RAM AREA FOR CHARACTERS
50 REM RAM RESERVED BEFORE MAIN PROGRAM
        STARTS AS VARIABLES ARE CLEARED
60 REM***************************
100 CL$=CHR$(147):REM TO CLEAR SCREEN
110 RO=55296:REM START OF CHARACTER
        SET 2 IN ROM
120 RA=12288:REM START OF CHARACTER RAM
```

P84 Spelling

```
130 IT=56334:REM INTERRUPT TIMER
140 CC=53272:
    REM CONTROLS CHARACTER LOCATION
150 SC=1024:REM START OF SCREEN MEMORY
160 POKE 53280,3:REM CYAN BORDER
170 POKE 53281,6:REM BLUE SCREEN
180 PRINT CHR$(5):REM WHITE INK
190 REM***************************
200 PRINT CL$:PRINT:PRINT
210 PRINT TAB(18)"WAIT"
220 PRINT CHR$(142):REM UPPER CASE
230 POKE IT,PEEK (IT) AND 254:
    REM DISABLE INTERRUPT TIMER
240 POKE 1,PEEK (1) AND 251:
    REM SWITCH FROM I/O TO CHAR. ROM
250 FOR N=0 TO 511:POKE N+RA,PEEK (N+RO)
    :NEXT:REM TRANSFER CHARACTERS
260 POKE 1,PEEK (1) OR 4:
    REM SWITCH FROM CHAR. TO I/O ROM
270 POKE IT,PEEK (IT) OR 1:
    REM ENABLE INTERRUPT TIMER
280 POKE 650,128:REM KEY REPEAT
290 REM***************************
300 REM REDEFINE CHARACTERS
310 FOR N=27 TO 29
320 FOR K=0 TO 7
330 READ A
340 POKE RA+K+N*8,A
350 NEXT:NEXT
360 REM***************************
370 REM SET UP SOUNDS
380 S=54272:REM START OF SOUND CHIP-
    ALSO GIVES COLOR DISPLACEMENT
390 POKE S,255:POKE S+1,100:POKE S+5,7:
    POKE S+6,0
400 POKE S+7,5:POKE S+8,90:POKE S+12,9:
    POKE S+13,0
410 POKE S+14,25:POKE S+15,30:
    POKE S+19,12:POKE S+20,0
420 POKE S+24,15
430 REM***************************
440 PRINT CL$:PRINT
450 PRINT TAB(16)"SPELLING"
460 PRINT TAB(16)"--------"
470 PRINT
480 PRINT TAB(5)
    "THIS PROGRAM CAN BE USED AS A"
```

```
490 PRINT TAB(5)
    "SPELLING AID FOR YOUNG CHILDREN."
500 PRINT TAB(5)
    "THE USER WILL SEE A WORD FOR"
510 PRINT TAB(5)
    "SIX SECONDS AND WILL THEN HAVE"
520 PRINT TAB(5)
    "TO SHOOT THE LETTERS OF THE"
530 PRINT TAB(5)
    "WORD FROM AN ALPHABET AT THE"
540 PRINT TAB(5)
    "TOP OF THE SCREEN. IF THE WORD"
550 PRINT TAB(5)
    "IS SPELLED CORRECTLY A SPACESHIP"
560 PRINT TAB(5)
    "WILL CROSS THE SCREEN, TO BE"
570 PRINT TAB(5)
    "SHOT DOWN BY THE USER. POINTS"
580 PRINT TAB(5)
    "ARE SCORED FOR EACH CORRECT"
590 PRINT TAB(5)
    "LETTER AND FOR SHOOTING DOWN"
600 PRINT TAB(5)"THE SPACESHIP."
610 REM***************************
620 PRINT:PRINT
630 PRINT TAB(6)CHR$(18)
    " PRESS ANY KEY TO CONTINUE "
640 GET A$:IF A$="" THEN 640
650 REM NO SPACE BETWEEN COMMAS
660 REM***************************
670 PRINT CL$
680 PRINT:PRINT
690 PRINT TAB(7)
    "KEY M MOVES GUN TO RIGHT"
700 PRINT:PRINT
710 PRINT TAB(7)
    "KEY N MOVES GUN TO LEFT"
720 PRINT:PRINT
730 PRINT TAB(7)
    "KEY Z FIRES GUN"
740 PRINT:PRINT:PRINT
750 PRINT TAB(4):INPUT
    "LEVEL OF DIFFICULTY (1 TO 9)";D$
760 IF D$="" THEN D$="1":REM RETURN KEY
    PRESSED WITHOUT ANY ENTRY
770 IF ASC(D$)<49 OR ASC(D$)>57
    THEN D$="1":REM DEFAULT ENTRY
```

```
780 REM***************************
790 POKE 53272,23:REM LOWER CASE
800 PRINT CL$:PRINT:PRINT
810 RT=PEEK(CC):REM REMEMBERS ORIGINAL
    VALUE IN CHARACTER CONTROL REGISTER
820 POKE CC,(RT AND 240)+12:
    REM CONTROL OF CHARACTERS TO RAM
830 PRINT TAB(7)
    "ABCDEFGHIJKLMNOPQRSTUVWXYZ"
840 X=7:REM X POSITION OF GUN
850 Y=ASC(D$)-43:REM Y POSITION OF GUN
860 FOR N=0 TO 16:PRINT:NEXT
870 SR=0:REM SCORE
880 RESTORE:FOR N=1 TO 24:READ A:NEXT:
    REM POINT TO START OF WORD DATA
890 REM***************************
900 REM GET WORDS
910 PRINT TAB(16)CHR$(145)"SCORE";SR;
    "    "
920 READ WD$:IF WD$="EOF" THEN 1390:
    REM FINISH
930 FOR N=1 TO LEN(WD$)
940 POKE SC+727+N,ASC(MID$(WD$,N,1))-64
950 POKE S+SC+727+N,7:NEXT:
    REM PRINT WORD
960 FOR DE=0 TO 3000:NEXT:REM DELAY
970 FOR N=1 TO LEN(WD$)
980 POKE SC+727+N,32:NEXT:
    REM DELETE WORD
990 REM***************************
1000 REM SPELL WORD
1010 FOR N=1 TO LEN(WD$)
1020 POKE SC+X+40*Y,28
1030 POKE S+SC+X+40*Y,3
1040 GET A$:IF A$="" THEN 1040:REM
     NO SPACE BETWEEN INVERTED COMMAS
1050 IF A$<>"N" AND A$<>"M" AND A$<>"Z"
     THEN 1040
1060 IF A$="N" THEN DX=-1:GOSUB 3000:
     GOTO 1020:REM MOVE LEFT
1070 IF A$="M" THEN DX=1:GOSUB 3000:
     GOTO 1020:REM MOVE RIGHT
1080 GOSUB 4000:REM FIRE
1090 IF ASC(MID$(WD$,N,1))=X+58 THEN
     SP=0:GOSUB 5000:GOTO 1110:REM HIT
1100 N=N-1:SR=SR-1:IF SR<0 THEN SR=0:
     REM MISS
```

```
1110 PRINT TAB(16)CHR$(145)"SCORE";SR;
     "      "
1120 NEXT
1130 REM**************************
1140 REM SPACESHIP
1150 FOR N=0 TO 39
1160 TI$="000000"
1170 POKE SC+160+N,27
1180 POKE S+SC+160+N,1
1190 GET A$:IF A$="" THEN 1270:REM
     NO SPACE BETWEEN INVERTED COMMAS
1200 IF A$<>"N" AND A$<>"M" AND A$<>"Z"
     THEN 1190
1210 IF A$="N" THEN DX=-1:GOSUB 3000:
     REM MOVE LEFT
1220 IF A$="M" THEN DX=1:GOSUB 3000:
     REM MOVE RIGHT
1230 IF A$="Z" THEN GOSUB 4000:REM FIRE
1240 IF X=N AND A$="Z" THEN SP=1:
     GOSUB 5000:N=39:GOTO 1290:REM HIT
1250 POKE SC+40*Y+X,28
1260 POKE S+SC+40*Y+X,3
1270 IF TI<15 THEN 1190
1280 POKE SC+160+N,32
1290 PRINT TAB(16)CHR$(145)"SCORE";SR;
     "      "
1300 NEXT
1310 REM**************************
1320 REM DELETE WORD
1330 FOR N=1 TO LEN(WD$)
1340 POKE SC+727+N,32
1350 NEXT
1360 FOR DE=0 TO 1000:NEXT:REM DELAY
1370 GOTO 900:REM GET NEXT WORD
1380 REM**************************
1390 REM FINISH
1400 PRINT CL$:PRINT:PRINT
1410 POKE CC,RT:REM CONTROL OF
     CHARACTERS BACK TO ROM
1420 GET A$:IF A$<>"" THEN 1420:REM
     NO SPACE BETWEEN INVERTED COMMAS
1430 REM FLUSH KEYBOARD BUFFER
1440 POKE 53272,20:REM UPPER CASE
1450 PRINT TAB(13)"FINAL SCORE";SR
1460 PRINT:PRINT:PRINT
1470 PRINT TAB(8):INPUT
     "WANT ANOTHER GO (Y/N)";Y$
```

```
1480 IF Y$="" THEN Y$="N":REM NO SPACE
     BETWEEN INVERTED COMMAS
1490 IF ASC(Y$)=89 THEN 670
1500 POKE S+24,0
1510 END
1520 REM**************************
1530 REM**************************
2000 REM DATA FOR GRAPHICS
2010 DATA 0,60,126,171,255,126,36,36
2020 DATA 24,24,24,24,24,255,255,255
2030 DATA 0,0,24,24,24,24,0,0
2040 REM**************************
2050 REM**************************
2500 REM
2510 REM          ***************
2520 REM          *
2530 REM          * SUBROUTINES
2540 REM          *
2550 REM          ***************
2560 REM
3000 REM MOVE
3010 IF X+DX=40 OR X+DX=-1 THEN 3040
3020 POKE SC+X+40*Y,32
3030 X=X+DX
3040 RETURN
3050 REM**************************
3060 REM**************************
4000 REM FIRE
4010 POKE S+4,0:POKE S+4,129
4020 FOR R=1 TO Y-4
4030 POKE SC+X+40*(Y-R),29
4040 POKE S+SC+X+40*(Y-R),0
4050 FOR DE=0 TO 30:NEXT
4060 POKE SC+X+40*(Y-R),32
4070 NEXT
4080 RETURN
4090 REM**************************
4100 REM**************************
5000 REM HIT
5010 IF SP=0 THEN POKE SC+727+N,X-6:
     POKE S+11,0:POKE S+11,17
5020 IF SP=1 THEN POKE S+18,0:
     POKE S+18,129
5030 SR=SR+1+9*SP
5040 RETURN
5050 REM**************************
5060 REM**************************
```

```
5500 REM
5510 REM             *************
5520 REM             *
5530 REM             * WORD DATA
5540 REM             *
5550 REM             *************
5560 REM
5600 REM *******************************
5610 REM
5620 REM    PUT AS MANY WORDS AS YOU WISH
5630 REM    AS DATA IN LINES 6000 ON.
5640 REM    ENSURE THAT THE FINAL DATA
5650 REM    ENTRY IS EOF. A FEW SIMPLE
5660 REM    WORDS ARE GIVEN AS EXAMPLES.
5670 REM
5680 REM *******************************
5690 REM
6000 DATA CAT,DOG,HOUSE,COMPUTER,EOF
10000 REM**************************
10010 REM**************************
```

P85 Number Base Conversion

This is a very useful program for work in a computing laboratory. It allows you to convert numbers from one base to another.

COMMANDS

Key in the program and RUN.

Select the conversion you require.

```
10 REM NUMBER BASE CONVERSION
20 REM **********************
30 REM
100 CL$=CHR$(147):REM TO CLEAR SCREEN
110 PRINT CL$
120 POKE 53280,14:REM BLUE BORDER
130 POKE 53281,11:REM GRAY SCREEN
140 PRINT CHR$(159):REM CYAN INK
150 PRINT:PRINT
160 PRINT TAB(9)"NUMBER BASE CONVERSION"
170 PRINT TAB(9)"**********************"
180 PRINT:PRINT
190 PRINT TAB(4)
    "THIS PROGRAM DEALS WITH POSITIVE"
200 PRINT TAB(4)
    "INTEGER NUMBERS ONLY."
210 GOSUB 7000:REM ANYKEY
220 REM***********************
230 REM DISPLAY MENU
240 PRINT CL$:PRINT:PRINT:PRINT
250 PRINT TAB(8)"1. HEX TO DECIMAL"
260 PRINT
270 PRINT TAB(8)"2. DECIMAL TO HEX"
280 PRINT
290 PRINT TAB(8)"3. BINARY TO DECIMAL"
300 PRINT
310 PRINT TAB(8)"4. DECIMAL TO BINARY"
320 PRINT
330 PRINT TAB(8)"5. ENDS PROGRAM"
340 PRINT:PRINT
```

```
350 PRINT TAB(8)"ENTER 1,2,3,4 OR 5"
360 PRINT:PRINT TAB(8);:INPUT
    "WHAT IS YOUR SELECTION";X$
370 A=ASC(X$)-48
380 IF A<1 OR A>5 THEN 230
390 IF A=5 THEN END
400 ON A GOSUB 1000,2000,3000,4000
410 GOTO 230:REM DISPLAY MENU
420 REM***********************
430 REM***********************
900 REM
910 REM        ***************
920 REM        *
930 REM        * SUBROUTINES
940 REM        *
950 REM        ***************
960 REM
1000 REM HEX TO DECIMAL
1010 PRINT CL$:PRINT:PRINT:PRINT
1020 PRINT TAB(12)"HEX TO DECIMAL"
1030 PRINT TAB(12)"**************"
1040 PRINT:PRINT
1050 PRINT TAB(4)
     "PLEASE USE CAPITAL LETTERS FOR"
1060 PRINT TAB(4)
     "HEX SYMBOLS A TO F."
1070 PRINT:PRINT
1080 PRINT TAB(4);:INPUT
     "WHAT IS THE HEX NUMBER";H$
1090 DEC=0
1100 FOR N=1 TO LEN(H$)
1110 HEX=ASC(MID$(H$,N,1))
1120 ERR=1
1130 IF HEX>47 AND HEX<58 THEN
     HEX=HEX-48:ERR=0:REM 0 TO 9
1140 IF HEX>64 AND HEX<71 THEN
     HEX=HEX-55:ERR=0:REM A TO F
1150 IF ERR=1 THEN 1000:REM IGNORE
     INVALID ENTRY
1160 D=HEX*16^(LEN(H$)-N)
1170 DEC=DEC+D
1180 NEXT
1190 PRINT:PRINT
1200 PRINT TAB(4)
     "DECIMAL NUMBER IS";DEC
1210 GOSUB 7000:REM ANYKEY
1220 RETURN
```

P85 Number Base Conversion

```
1230 REM*********************
1240 REM*********************
2000 REM DECIMAL TO HEX
2010 PRINT CL$:PRINT:PRINT:PRINT
2020 PRINT TAB(12)"DECIMAL TO HEX"
2030 PRINT TAB(12)"**************"
2040 PRINT:PRINT
2050 PRINT TAB(4)
     "WHAT IS THE DECIMAL NUMBER"
2060 PRINT TAB(4);:INPUT D$
2070 H$="":REM NO SPACE
2080 FOR N=1 TO LEN(D$)
2090 DEC=ASC(MID$(D$,N,1))
2100 IF DEC<48 OR DEC>57 THEN 2000:
     REM IGNORE INVALID ENTRY
2110 NEXT
2120 DC=VAL(D$)
2130 REM*********************
2140 REM CALCULATE LOOP (HEX)
2150 D=16*(DC/16-INT(DC/16))
2160 IF DC<16 THEN D=DC
2170 DC=INT(DC/16)
2180 D=D+48:IF D>57 THEN D=D+7:
     REM CONVERT D TO ASCII
2190 H$=CHR$(D)+H$
2200 IF DC>0 THEN 2140:
     REM CALCULATE LOOP (HEX)
2210 REM*********************
2220 PRINT:PRINT
2230 PRINT TAB(4)
     "HEXADECIMAL NUMBER IS ";H$
2240 GOSUB 7000:REM ANYKEY
2250 RETURN
2260 REM*********************
2270 REM*********************
3000 REM BINARY TO DECIMAL
3010 PRINT CL$:PRINT:PRINT:PRINT
3020 PRINT TAB(10)"BINARY TO DECIMAL"
3030 PRINT TAB(10)"*****************"
3040 PRINT:PRINT
3050 PRINT TAB(4)
     "WHAT IS THE BINARY NUMBER"
3060 PRINT TAB(4):INPUT B$
3070 DEC=0
3080 FOR N=1 TO LEN(B$)
3090 BIN=ASC(MID$(B$,N,1))-48
3100 IF BIN<0 OR BIN>1 THEN 3000
```

```
3110 REM IGNORE INVALID ENTRY
3120 D=BIN*2^(LEN(B$)-N)
3130 DEC=DEC+D
3140 NEXT
3150 PRINT:PRINT
3160 PRINT TAB(4)
     "DECIMAL NUMBER IS";DEC
3170 GOSUB 7000:REM ANYKEY
3180 RETURN
3190 REM**********************
3200 REM**********************
4000 REM DECIMAL TO BINARY
4010 PRINT CL$:PRINT:PRINT:PRINT
4020 PRINT TAB(10)"DECIMAL TO BINARY"
4030 PRINT TAB(10)"*****************"
4040 PRINT:PRINT
4050 PRINT TAB(4)
     "WHAT IS THE DECIMAL NUMBER"
4060 PRINT TAB(4);:INPUT D$
4070 B$="":REM NO SPACE
4080 FOR N=1 TO LEN(D$)
4090 DEC=ASC(MID$(D$,N,1))
4100 IF DEC<48 OR DEC>57 THEN 2000:
     REM IGNORE INVALID ENTRY
4110 NEXT
4120 DC=VAL(D$)
4130 REM**********************
4140 REM CALCULATE LOOP (BIN)
4150 D=2*(DC/2-INT(DC/2))
4160 IF DC<2 THEN D=DC
4170 DC=INT(DC/2)
4180 D=D+48:REM CONVERT D TO ASCII
4190 B$=CHR$(D)+B$
4200 IF DC>0 THEN 4140:
     REM CALCULATE LOOP (BIN)
4210 REM**********************
4220 PRINT:PRINT
4230 PRINT TAB(4)
     "BINARY NUMBER IS "
4240 PRINT TAB(4);B$
4250 GOSUB 7000:REM ANYKEY
4260 RETURN
4270 REM**********************
4280 REM**********************
7000 REM ANYKEY
7010 PRINT:PRINT
```

```
7020 PRINT TAB(4)
     "PRESS ANY KEY TO GET MENU"
7030 GET A$:IF A$="" THEN 7030
7040 REM NO SPACE BETWEEN INVERTED
         COMMAS
7050 RETURN
7060 REM***********************
7070 REM***********************
```

P86 Color Codes for Resistors

This program could be useful in an electronics laboratory. It allows you to calculate the value of a resistor from its color code, or to calculate the color code from its value. The program deals only with resistors coded by color bands as shown below:

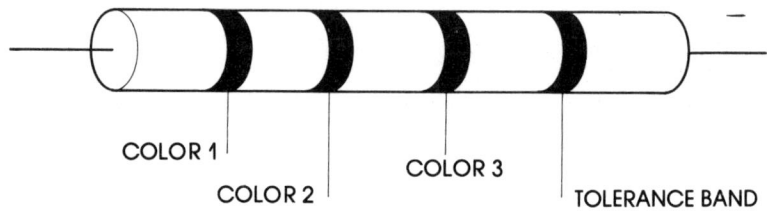

COLOR 1
COLOR 2
COLOR 3
TOLERANCE BAND

COMMANDS

Key in the program and RUN.

Follow the instructions.

```
10 REM COLOR CODES FOR RESISTORS
20 REM ************************
30 REM
100 CL$=CHR$(147):REM TO CLEAR SCREEN
110 PRINT CL$
120 POKE 53280,10:REM PINK BORDER
130 POKE 53281,10:REM PINK SCREEN
140 PRINT CHR$(144):REM BLACK INK
150 PRINT TAB(10)"RESISTOR COLOR CODES"
160 PRINT TAB(10)"********************"
170 PRINT:PRINT:PRINT
180 PRINT TAB(4)
    "THIS PROGRAM MAY BE USED TO"
```

P86 Color Codes for Resistors

```
190 PRINT TAB(4)
    "DETERMINE THE VALUE OF A RESISTOR"
200 PRINT TAB(4)
    "FROM ITS COLOR CODE, OR TO"
210 PRINT TAB(4)
    "DETERMINE ITS COLOR CODE FROM ITS"
220 PRINT TAB(4)"RESISTANCE VALUE."
230 DIM B$(12):REM HOLDS COLORS
240 FOR N=0 TO 12
250 READ A$:B$(N)=A$
260 NEXT
270 REM********************
280 DATA BLACK,BROWN,RED,ORANGE,YELLOW
290 DATA GREEN,BLUE,VIOLET,GRAY,WHITE
300 DATA GOLD,SILVER,NONE
310 REM********************
320 GOSUB 3000:REM ANY KEY
330 REM
340 REM
350 REM
360 REM
370 REM********************
380 REM********************
390 REM ANOTHER
400 PRINT CL$:PRINT:PRINT:PRINT
410 PRINT TAB(4)
    "DO YOU WISH TO FIND RESISTANCE"
420 PRINT TAB(4) "VALUE OR COLOR CODE?"
430 PRINT:PRINT
440 PRINT TAB(8)"PRESS KEY 1 FOR VALUE"
450 PRINT
460 PRINT TAB(8)"PRESS KEY 2 FOR CODE"
470 PRINT
480 PRINT TAB(8)"PRESS KEY 3 TO END"
490 GET A:IF A=0 THEN 490
500 PRINT CL$
510 IF A=3 THEN END
520 ON A GOSUB 1000,2000
530 GOTO 390:REM GO TO ANOTHER
540 REM
900 REM         **************
910 REM         *
920 REM         * SUBROUTINES
930 REM         *
940 REM         **************
950 REM
1000 REM VALUE
```

```
1010 PRINT TAB(12)"COLORS ARE:"
1020 PRINT
1030 FOR N=0 TO 9
1040 PRINT,B$(N),"=";N
1050 NEXT
1060 PRINT:PRINT
1070 PRINT TAB(3)
     "ENTER THE THREE COLOR BANDS AS"
1080 PRINT TAB(3)
     "THREE NUMBERS FOLLOWED BY THE"
1090 PRINT TAB(3)"RETURN KEY."
1100 PRINT:PRINT
1110 PRINT TAB(3)"FOR EXAMPLE:"
1120 PRINT TAB(3)"RED-BLACK-ORANGE=203"
1130 PRINT
1140 PRINT TAB(3);:INPUT
     "WHAT ARE THE COLORS";COL$
1150 REM CHECK ENTRY
1160 FOR N=1 TO 3
1170 D(N)=ASC(MID$(COL$,N,1))-48
1180 IF D(N)<0 OR D(N)>9 THEN
     PRINT CL$:GOTO 1000
1190 NEXT
1200 REM*********************
1210 REM GET TOLERANCE
1220 PRINT CL$
1230 PRINT:PRINT
1240 PRINT TAB(3)
     "THE THIRD BAND INDICATES"
1250 PRINT TAB(3)
     "TOLERANCE. THE ALTERNATIVES ARE:"
1260 PRINT:PRINT
1270 FOR N=10 TO 12
1280 PRINT,N-9,B$(N)
1290 NEXT
1300 PRINT:PRINT
1310 PRINT TAB(3)
     "ENTER 1,2 OR 3 TO SELECT"
1320 PRINT TAB(3)
     "TOLERANCE COLOR. ANY OTHER ENTRY"
1330 PRINT TAB(3)
     "WILL BE TREATED AS NO FOURTH"
1340 PRINT TAB(3)"BAND."
1350 PRINT:PRINT
1360 PRINT TAB(3);:INPUT"SELECTION";T$
1370 IF T$<>"1" AND T$<>"2" THEN T$="3"
1380 T=ASC(T$)-48
```

P86 Color Codes for Resistors

```
1390 T=T*5
1400 REM*********************
1410 REM CALCULATE RESISTANCE
1420 RES =(D(1)*10+D(2))*10^D(3)
1430 PRINT CL$
1440 PRINT:PRINT:PRINT
1450 PRINT TAB(4)
     "RESISTANCE IS";RES ;"OHM"
1460 PRINT:PRINT:PRINT
1470 PRINT TAB(4)
     "TOLERANCE IS";T;"%"
1480 GOSUB 3000:REM ANY KEY
1490 RETURN
1500 REM*********************
1510 REM*********************
2000 REM GET CODE
2010 PRINT:PRINT:PRINT
2020 PRINT TAB(4)
     "PLEASE ENTER RESISTANCE IN OHM."
2030 PRINT TAB(4)
     "PLEASE ENTER NUMBERS ONLY."
2040 PRINT TAB(4)
     "ANY OTHER SYMBOLS, INCLUDING"
2050 PRINT TAB(4)
     "DECIMAL POINTS WILL NOT BE"
2060 PRINT TAB(4)
     "ACCEPTED. PLEASE DO NOT START"
2070 PRINT TAB(4)
     "THE ENTRY WITH A ZERO."
2080 PRINT
2090 PRINT TAB(4)
     "RESISTORS WITH VALUES LESS THAN"
2100 PRINT TAB(4)
     "10 OHM OR GREATER THAN"
2110 PRINT TAB(4)
     "99000000000 OHM ARE NOT COVERED"
2120 PRINT TAB(4)"BY THIS PROGRAM."
2130 PRINT:PRINT
2140 PRINT TAB(4);:INPUT
     "RESISTANCE VALUE IN OHM";RST$
2150 FOR N=1 TO LEN(RST$)
2160 T=ASC(MID$(RST$,N,1))
2170 IF T>57 OR T<48-(N=1) THEN
     PRINT CL$:GOTO 2000
2180 NEXT
2190 IF LEN(RST$)>11 OR LEN(RST$)<2
     THEN PRINT CL$:GOTO 2000
```

```
2200 REM*********************
2210 PRINT CL$
2220 REM GET TOLERANCE
2230 PRINT:PRINT:PRINT
2240 PRINT TAB(4)
     "ENTER 1,2 OR 3 DEPENDING ON"
2250 PRINT TAB(4)
     "WHETHER THE TOLERANCE IS 5%,10%"
2260 PRINT TAB(4)"OR 20% RESPECTIVELY."
2270 PRINT
2280 PRINT TAB(4)
     "ALL ENTRIES OTHER THAN 1 OR 2"
2290 PRINT TAB(4)
     "WILL BE ASSUMED TO MEAN 20%"
2300 PRINT TAB(4)"TOLERANCE."
2310 PRINT:PRINT
2320 PRINT TAB(4);:INPUT
     "TOLERANCE (1,2 OR 3)";TL$
2330 IF TL$<>"1" AND TL$<>"2" THEN
     TL$="3"
2340 REM*********************
2350 REM DISPLAY BANDS
2360 PRINT CL$
2370 PRINT:PRINT:PRINT
2380 A(1)=ASC(LEFT$(RST$,1))-48
2390 A(2)=ASC(MID$(RST$,2,1))-48
2400 A(3)=LEN(RST$)-2
2410 A(4)=ASC(TL$)-39
2420 FOR N=1 TO 4
2430 PRINT TAB(4)
     "BAND";N;"IS",B$(A(N))
2440 PRINT
2450 NEXT
2460 GOSUB 3000:REM ANY KEY
2470 RETURN
2480 REM*********************
2490 REM*********************
3000 REM ANY KEY
3010 PRINT:PRINT:PRINT
3020 PRINT TAB(4)
     "PRESS ANY KEY FOR INSTRUCTIONS"
3030 GET A$:IF A$="" THEN 3030
3040 REM NO SPACE BETWEEN INVERTED
     COMMAS
3050 REM WAIT FOR A KEY
3060 RETURN
3070 REM*********************
```

P87 Volumes of Solids

This program calculates the volumes of spheres cylinders and cones or pyramids.

It could be extended to calculate the volumes of other regular solids.

COMMANDS

Key in the program and RUN.

Follow the instructions.

```
10 REM VOLUMES OF SOLIDS
20 REM ****************
30 REM
100 CL$=CHR$(147):REM TO CLEAR SCREEN
110 PRINT CL$
120 POKE 53280,8:REM ORANGE BORDER
130 POKE 53281,8:REM ORANGE SCREEN
140 PRINT CHR$(144):REM BLACK INK
150 PRINT TAB(10)"VOLUMES OF SOLIDS"
160 PRINT TAB(10)"*****************"
170 PRINT:PRINT:PRINT
180 PRINT TAB(5)
    "PRESS KEY 1 FOR SPHERE"
190 PRINT
200 PRINT TAB(5)
    "PRESS KEY 2 FOR CYLINDER"
210 PRINT
220 PRINT TAB(5)
    "PRESS KEY 3 FOR CONE OR PYRAMID"
230 PRINT
240 PRINT TAB(5)
    "PRESS KEY 4 TO FINISH"
250 GET A:IF A=0 THEN 250
260 IF A=4 THEN END
270 PRINT CL$
280 ON A GOSUB 1000,2000,3000
290 RUN
```

```
 300 REM
 310 REM          ***************
 320 REM          *
 330 REM          *  SUBROUTINES
 340 REM          *
 350 REM          ***************
 360 REM
1000 REM SPHERE
1010 PRINT TAB(10)"VOLUME OF A SPHERE"
1020 PRINT TAB(10)"******************"
1030 PRINT:PRINT:PRINT
1040 INPUT"WHAT IS THE RADIUS";R
1050 PRINT:PRINT:PRINT
1060 VOL=4*π*R*R*R/3
1070 PRINT
     "THE VOLUME OF A SPHERE OF RADIUS";R
1080 PRINT:PRINT"IS";VOL
1090 GOSUB 4000
1100 RETURN
1110 REM***************************
1120 REM***************************
2000 REM CYLINDER
2010 PRINT TAB(9)"VOLUME OF A CYLINDER"
2020 PRINT TAB(9)"********************"
2030 PRINT:PRINT:PRINT
2040 INPUT"WHAT IS THE HEIGHT";H
2050 PRINT:PRINT
2060 INPUT"WHAT IS THE BASE RADIUS";R
2070 PRINT:PRINT:PRINT
2080 VOL=π*R*R*H
2090 PRINT
     "THE VOLUME OF A CYLINDER OF"
2100 PRINT
2110 PRINT"BASE RADIUS";R;"AND HEIGHT";H
2120 PRINT:PRINT"IS";VOL
2130 GOSUB 4000
2140 RETURN
2150 REM***************************
2160 REM***************************
3000 REM CONE
3010 PRINT TAB(11)"VOLUME OF A CONE"
3020 PRINT TAB(11)"****************"
3030 PRINT:PRINT:PRINT
3040 INPUT
     "DO YOU KNOW THE BASE AREA (Y/N)";Y$
3050 IF ASC(Y$)=89 OR ASC(Y$)=121 THEN
     GOSUB 5000:GOTO 3500
```

P87 Volumes of Solids

```
3060 PRINT:PRINT
3070 PRINT
     "SELECT BASE SHAPE BY PRESSING:"
3080 PRINT
3090 PRINT
     "KEY 1 FOR EQUILATERAL TRIANGLE"
3100 PRINT TAB(4)"2 FOR SQUARE"
3110 PRINT TAB(4)"3 FOR CIRCLE"
3120 PRINT
3130 GET B:IF B=0 THEN 3130
3140 IF B>3 OR B<1 THEN 3130
3150 ON B GOSUB 6000,7000,8000
3160 REM*********************
3500 REM CONE VOLUME
3510 PRINT CL$
3520 PRINT TAB(11)"VOLUME OF A CONE"
3530 PRINT TAB(11)"****************"
3540 PRINT:PRINT:PRINT
3550 INPUT"WHAT IS THE HEIGHT";H
3560 PRINT:PRINT:PRINT
3570 PRINT
     "THE VOLUME OF A CONE OF BASE"
3580 PRINT
3590 PRINT
     "AREA";AR;"AND HEIGHT";H
3600 PRINT
3610 PRINT"IS";AR*H/3
3620 GOSUB 4000
3630 RETURN
3640 REM**************************
3650 REM**************************
4000 REM ANY KEY
4010 PRINT:PRINT:PRINT
4020 PRINT"PRESS ANY KEY TO RETURN"
4030 GET A$:IF A$="" THEN 4030
4040 REM
     NO SPACE BETWEEN INVERTED COMMAS
4050 RETURN
4060 REM**************************
4070 REM**************************
5000 REM GET BASE AREA
5010 PRINT:PRINT
5020 INPUT"WHAT IS THE BASE AREA";AR
5030 RETURN
5040 REM**************************
5050 REM**************************
6000 REM TRIANGLE
```

```
6010 INPUT
     "LENGTH OF SIDE OF TRIANGLE";S
6020 AR=.5*S*S*SIN(π/3)
6030 RETURN
6040 REM*************************
6050 REM*************************
7000 REM SQUARE
7010 INPUT
     "LENGTH OF SIDE OF SQUARE";S
7020 AR=S*S
7030 RETURN
7040 REM*************************
7050 REM*************************
8000 REM CIRCLE
8010 INPUT"RADIUS OF CIRCLE";R
8020 AR=π*R*R
8030 RETURN
8040 REM*************************
8050 REM*************************
```

P88 Physics Experiment 1

The next two programs are an attempt to show how a micro could be used within a physics laboratory to take some of the drudgery out of experimentation.

The programs are based on two experiments in F. Tyler's "A Laboratory Manual of Physics" (Edward Arnold, 1966).

COMMANDS

Use Work Sheets and programs to perform the experiments.

EXPERIMENT 1 - MOMENT OF INERTIA

Work Sheet 1

Determination of the moment of inertia of a flywheel

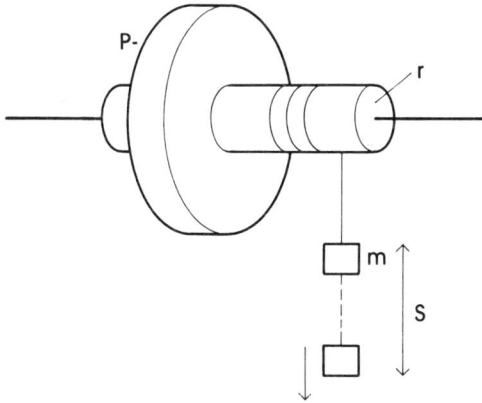

Apparatus

Wall supported flywheel of standard pattern: a weight is attached to a length of fine cord which is wrapped round the axle, the free end being passed through a hole in the axle. The length of the cord is adjusted so that the cord detaches itself from the axle when the weight reaches the ground.

Callipers, stop watch, meter rule.

Method

The value of m is obtained by weighing; the radius r of the axle is found by using callipers.

The weight (m) is allowed to fall through a measured distance (s) to the ground, and the time of descent (t) is taken by a stop-watch. The number of revolutions (n) of the wheel during this time is taken by observing a mark made on the circumference of the wheel at P. The further revolutions (p) made by the wheel before coming to rest after m is detached are also counted by reference to the mark P. The experiment is repeated three times for the same distance (s).

Perform the experiment as follows:

Power on microcomputer.
Load program.
Take measurements m, r and s.
RUN the program.
Perform the experiment as directed, and enter values as prompted.

```
10 REM MOMENT OF INERTIA
20 REM *****************
30 REM
100 CL$=CHR$(147):REM TO CLEAR SCREEN
110 UP$=CHR$(145):REM UP CURSOR
120 S$=CHR$(32):REM ONE SPACE
130 D$="-"
140 POKE 53280,2:REM RED BORDER
150 POKE 53281,7:REM YELLOW SCREEN
160 PRINT CHR$(144):REM BLACK INK
170 PRINT CL$:PRINT
180 FOR N=0 TO 9
```

```
190 SP$=SP$+S$+S$:DS$=DS$+D$+D$
200 NEXT:REM SP$ CONTAINS 20 SPACES
            DS$ CONTAINS 20 DASHES
210 PRINT TAB(10)CHR$(18)DS$
220 PRINT TAB(10)CHR$(18)
    "  MOMENT OF INERTIA  "
230 PRINT TAB(10)CHR$(18)
    "        OF A         "
240 PRINT TAB(10)CHR$(18)
    "      FLYWHEEL       "
250 PRINT TAB(10)CHR$(18)DS$
260 PRINT
270 PRINT TAB(10)"PHYSICS EXPERIMENT 1"
280 PRINT TAB(10)DS$
290 PRINT
300 PRINT TAB(10)CHR$(18)DS$
310 PRINT TAB(10)CHR$(18)
    "   SEE WORK SHEET    "
320 PRINT TAB(10)CHR$(18)DS$
330 PRINT:PRINT
340 REM***********************
350 SP$=MID$(SP$+SP$,2):REM 39 SPACES
360 PRINT TAB(4):INPUT
    "RADIUS OF AXLE (METERS)";R
370 IF R<=0 THEN PRINT UP$+SP$+UP$:
    GOTO 360
380 PRINT TAB(4):INPUT
    "MASS OF WEIGHT (KG)";M
390 IF M<=0 THEN PRINT UP$+SP$+UP$:
    GOTO 380
400 PRINT TAB(4):INPUT
    "DISTANCE TO GROUND (METERS)";S
410 IF S<=0 THEN PRINT UP$+SP$+UP$:
    GOTO 400
420 REM***********************
430 TT=0:NN=0:PP=0
440 FOR K=1 TO 3
450 PRINT CL$:PRINT:PRINT
460 PRINT TAB(10)CHR$(18)
    "  PERFORM EXPERIMENT  "
470 PRINT:PRINT
480 PRINT TAB(17)"RUN";K
490 PRINT TAB(17)"====="
500 PRINT
510 PRINT TAB(10):INPUT"TIME (SECS)";T
```

```
520 IF T<=0 THEN PRINT UP$+SP$+UP$:
    GOTO 510
530 PRINT
540 PRINT TAB(10):INPUT"N (REVS)";N
550 IF N<=0 THEN PRINT UP$+SP$+UP$:
    GOTO 540
560 PRINT
570 PRINT TAB(10):INPUT"P (REVS)";P
580 IF P<=0 THEN PRINT UP$+SP$+UP$:
    GOTO 570
590 TT=TT+T:NN=NN+N:PP=PP+P
600 NEXT
610 REM***********************
620 T=TT/3:N=NN/3:P=PP/3
630 G=9.81:REM ACCELERATION DUE TO
    GRAVITY
640 IT=M*R*R*(G*T*T/2/S-1)*(P/(P+N))
650 IT=INT(IT*100+.5)/100
660 IT$=MID$(STR$(IT),2):IF IT<1 THEN
    IT$="0"+IT$
670 PRINT CL$:PRINT:PRINT:PRINT:PRINT
680 PRINT TAB(10)"MOMENT OF INERTIA ="
690 PRINT
700 PRINT TAB(10)IT$" KG-(METER)^2"
710 PRINT TAB(10)"-------------------"
720 REM***********************
730 PRINT:PRINT
740 Y$="N":PRINT TAB(7):INPUT
    "ANOTHER EXPERIMENT (Y/N)";Y$
750 IF ASC(Y$)=89 THEN PRINT CL$:PRINT:
    PRINT:GOTO 360
760 END
770 REM***********************
780 REM***********************
```

P89   Physics Experiment 2

EXPERIMENT 2 - FOCAL LENGTH

Work Sheet 2

Determination of the focal length of a concave mirror

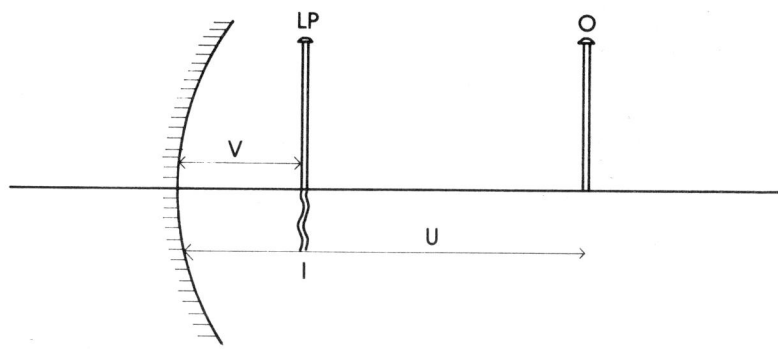

Apparatus

Concave mirror in stand, two retort stands with clamps and pins, meter rule.

Method

The object pin O is placed a given distance (U) from the concave mirror. The position of the image I formed by reflection in the mirror is located by the method of non-parallax using the second pin (locating pin LP). The distance (V) of the locating pin from the mirror is measured. O and I are said to be conjugate points. A series of values of V for a given range of values of u are obtained.

The computer program is used to calculate the focal length of the mirror from each measurement. The average of these values, and their standard deviation, are calculated and presented on the screen.

```
10 REM FOCAL LENGTH
20 REM ************
30 REM
100 CL$=CHR$(147):REM TO CLEAR SCREEN
110 UP$=CHR$(145):REM UP CURSOR
120 S$=CHR$(32):REM ONE SPACE
130 D$="-"
140 POKE 53280,2:REM RED BORDER
150 POKE 53281,7:REM YELLOW SCREEN
160 PRINT CHR$(144):REM BLACK INK
170 PRINT CL$:PRINT
180 FOR N=0 TO 3
190 S$=S$+S$:D$=D$+D$
200 NEXT:REM S$ CONTAINS 16 SPACES
              D$ CONTAINS 16 DASHES
210 PRINT TAB(12)CHR$(18)D$
220 PRINT TAB(12)CHR$(18)
    "  FOCAL LENGTH  "
230 PRINT TAB(12)CHR$(18)
    "      OF A      "
240 PRINT TAB(12)CHR$(18)
    " CONCAVE MIRROR "
250 PRINT TAB(12)CHR$(18)D$
260 PRINT
270 PRINT TAB(10)"PHYSICS EXPERIMENT 2"
280 PRINT TAB(10)"----"+D$
290 PRINT
300 PRINT TAB(12)CHR$(18)D$
310 PRINT TAB(12)CHR$(18)
    " SEE WORK SHEET "
320 PRINT TAB(12)CHR$(18)D$
330 PRINT:PRINT
340 REM***********************
350 PRINT TAB(9);:INPUT
    "HOW MANY MEASUREMENTS";MEAS%
360 PRINT TAB(7) UP$+S$+S$+UP$
370 IF MEAS%<1 THEN 350
380 FOR N=1 TO MEAS%
390 PRINT TAB(13)"MEASUREMENT";N
400 PRINT
410 PRINT TAB(16);:INPUT"U = ";U
420 PRINT
430 PRINT TAB(16):INPUT"V = ";V
440 PRINT UP$+UP$+UP$+UP$+UP$+UP$
450 FOR K=0 TO 4
460 PRINT TAB(13)S$
470 NEXT
```

```
480 PRINT UP$+UP$+UP$+UP$+UP$+UP$
490 T=1/(1/V+1/U)
500 SQ=SQ+T*T
510 NEXT
520 REM*********************
530 MN=SM/MEAS%
540 DV=SQR(SQ/MEAS%-MN*MN)
550 PRINT TAB(4)
    "AVERAGE FOCAL LENGTH =";MN
560 PRINT
570 PRINT TAB(4)
    "STANDARD DEVIATION   =";DV
580 PRINT
590 PRINT TAB(4):INPUT
    "WANT TO REPEAT THE EXPERIMENT";Y$
600 IF ASC(Y$)=89 THEN RUN
610 REM*********************
620 REM*********************
```

P90 Resistors

300

This program computes the resultant resistance of an electric circuit of the following type:

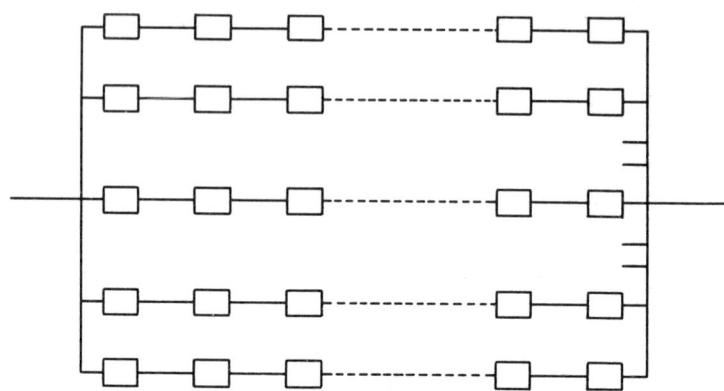

COMMANDS

Key in the program and RUN.

Follow the instructions, entering the resistance values as required.

```
10 REM RESISTORS
20 REM *********
30 REM
100 PRINT CHR$(147):REM CLEAR SCREEN
110 POKE 53281,0:REM BLACK SCREEN
120 POKE 53280,0:REM BLACK BORDER
130 PRINT CHR$(158):REM YELLOW INK
140 PRINT
150 PRINT TAB(15)"RESISTORS"
160 PRINT:PRINT:PRINT
170 PRINT TAB(5)
    "THIS PROGRAM COMPUTES THE TOTAL"
```

```
180 PRINT TAB(5)
    "RESISTANCE OF A CIRCUIT"
190 PRINT TAB(5)
    "CONSISTING OF SEVERAL BRANCHES"
200 PRINT TAB(5)
    "CONNECTED IN PARALLEL, EACH"
210 PRINT TAB(5)
    "BRANCH CONSISTING OF ONE OR"
220 PRINT TAB(5)
    "MORE SERIES RESISTORS."
230 PRINT:PRINT:PRINT
240 PRINT TAB(5)
    "PRESS ANY KEY TO CONTINUE"
250 GET A$:IF A$="" THEN 250
260 REM NO SPACE BETWEEN INVERTED
        COMMAS
270 REM WAIT FOR A KEY
280 REM********************
290 REM********************
300 REM ANOTHER
310 PRINT CHR$(147):REM CLEAR SCREEN
320 INPUT"NUMBER OF BRANCHES";BR%
330 IF BR%<1 THEN 300
340 DIM R(BR%)
350 REM********************
360 REM********************
370 FOR N=1 TO BR%
380 GOSUB 1000:REM PRINT BRANCH NUMBER
390 INPUT"NUMBER OF RESISTORS";RS%
400 IF RS%<1 THEN 380
410 REM********************
420 REM********************
430 GOSUB 1000:REM PRINT BRANCH NUMBER
440 FOR K=1 TO RS%
450 PRINT"VALUE OF RESISTOR";K;
460 INPUT VL
470 IF VL<0 THEN PRINT
    "POSITIVE VALUE PLEASE":GOTO 450
480 REM********************
490 GOSUB 1000:REM PRINT BRANCH NUMBER
500 R(N)=R(N)+VL
510 NEXT
520 IF R(N)=0 THEN TTL=0:GOTO 600
530 REM ZERO RESISTANCE BRANCH
540 CN=CN+1/R(N)
550 REM ADD CONDUCTANCES OF BRANCHES
560 NEXT
```

```
570 REM*********************
580 REM*********************
590 TTL=1/CN:REM TOTAL RESISTANCE
600 REM DISPLAY TOTAL RESISTANCE
610 PRINT CHR$(147):REM CLEAR SCREEN
620 PRINT:PRINT:PRINT:PRINT
630 PRINT:PRINT:PRINT:PRINT
640 PRINT TAB(9)"TOTAL RESISTANCE IS"
650 PRINT
660 PRINT TAB(9) TTL;"OHM"
670 PRINT TAB(9)"=================="
680 PRINT:PRINT:PRINT:PRINT:PRINT:PRINT
690 INPUT"ANOTHER CIRCUIT";Y$
700 IF ASC(Y$)=89 THEN CLR:GOTO 300:
    REM ANOTHER
710 END
900 REM          *****************
910 REM          *
920 REM          *
930 REM          *   SUBROUTINES
940 REM          *
z50 REM          *
960 REM          *****************
970 REM
1000 PRINT CHR$(147):REM CLEAR SCREEN
1010 PRINT:PRINT:PRINT
1020 PRINT TAB(15)"BRANCH";N
1030 PRINT:PRINT
1040 RETURN
1050 REM*********************
1060 REM*********************
```

P91 Calculator

There are many occasions when you need the capability of a simple calculator rather than a complex computer. This program simulates a simple four function (+,-,*,/) calculator.

The program could be expanded to provide memory-add, memory-subtract and memory-read features.

COMMANDS

Key in the program and RUN.

Use the numeric keys and +, -, * and / to perform arithmetic. Use '.' for decimal point and '=' to get final answer. Use the C, A, and S keys as instructed.

```
10 REM CALCULATOR
20 REM *********
30 REM
100 CL$=CHR$(147):REM TO CLEAR SCREEN
110 UP$=CHR$(145):REM UP CURSOR
120 POKE 53280,8:REM ORANGE BORDER
130 POKE 53281,7:REM YELLOW SCREEN
140 PRINT CHR$(31):REM BLUE INK
150 REM **********************
160 PRINT CL$
170 PRINT:PRINT:PRINT
180 PRINT TAB(14)CHR$(18)"CALCULATOR"
190 PRINT:PRINT:PRINT
200 PRINT TAB(7)
    "KEY C CLEARS CURRENT ENTRY"
210 PRINT
220 PRINT TAB(7)
    "KEY A CLEARS ALL ENTRIES"
230 PRINT
240 PRINT TAB(7)
    "KEY S STOPS PROGRAM"
250 PRINT:PRINT:PRINT:PRINT
260 REM**********************
270 S$=CHR$(32):REM SPACE
```

```
280 FOR N=0 TO 4
290 S$=S$+S$
300 NEXT:
310 REM S$ CONTAINS 32 SPACES
320 E$="":REM NO SPACE
330 REM***********************
340 REM CLEAR ALL
350 A$=E$:F$=E$:R=0
360 REM***********************
370 REM REPEAT
380 GET B$:IF B$=E$ THEN 380
390 REM***********************
400 REM DECODE
410 IF ASC(B$)>47 AND ASC(B$)<58
    THEN GOSUB 1000
420 IF B$="." THEN GOSUB 1000
430 IF B$="+" OR B$="-" OR B$="*"
    OR B$="/" OR B$="=" THEN GOSUB 2000
440 IF B$="A" OR B$="C" THEN GOSUB 3000
450 IF B$="A" OR B$="=" THEN 340:
    REM CLEAR ALL
460 IF B$="S" THEN END
470 GOTO 370:REM REPEAT
480 REM
900 REM            ***************
910 REM            *
920 REM            * SUBROUTINES
930 REM            *
940 REM            ***************
950 REM
1000 REM NUMBER OR DECIMAL POINT
1010 IF LEN(A$)=8 THEN 1050:
     REM 8 DIGITS MAXIMUM ENTRY
1020 A$=A$+B$
1030 PRINT UP$+S$:PRINTUP$+UP$
1040 PRINT TAB(21-LEN(A$)) A$
1050 RETURN
1060 REM*********************
1070 REM*********************
2000 REM OPERATOR
2010 IF F$="+" OR F$=E$ THEN R=R+VAL(A$)
2020 IF F$="-" THEN R=R-VAL(A$)
2030 IF F$="*" THEN R=R*VAL(A$)
2040 IF F$="/" AND VAL(A$)<>0
     THEN R=R/VAL(A$)
2050 PRINT UP$+S$:PRINT UP$+UP$
```

```
2060 IF F$="/" AND VAL(A$)=0 THEN 2080:
     REM IGNORE DIVISION BY ZERO
2070 F$=B$: IF F$="=" THEN
     F$=CHR$(146)+CHR$(32)
2080 PRINT TAB(21-LEN(STR$(R)))R;
     TAB(33) CHR$(18)+F$
2090 A$=E$
2100 RETURN
2110 REM********************
2120 REM********************
3000 REM CLEAR
3010 PRINT UP$+S$
3020 IF B$="A" THEN PRINT TAB(33)
     UP$+CHR$(32)
3030 A$=E$
3040 RETURN
3050 REM********************
3060 REM********************
```

P92 Coordinate Conversion

It can happen quite often that you have points plotted on a graph in the rectangular (x,y) format and wish to convert the coordinates of these points to the polar (r,θ) format, or vice versa, as in the following figure:

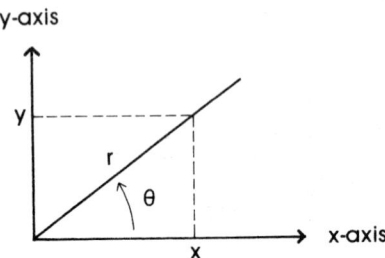

The conversion formulae are:

x=r*COS(θ)
y=r*SIN(θ)
r=x^2+y^2
θ=ARC TAN(y/x)

This is a demonstration program and the formulae used are accurate only for the first quadrant. The special case when x=0 has not been dealt with, nor has any 'trap' been set for entry of negative values of r. The program, extended to incorporate all these features, could be a valuable tool for mathematicians.

COMMANDS

Key in the program and RUN.

Follow the instructions.

P92 Coordinate Conversion

```
10 REM COORDINATE CONVERSION
20 REM **********************
30 REM
100 CL$=CHR$(147):REM TO CLEAR SCREEN
110 UP$=CHR$(145):REM UP CURSOR
120 S$=CHR$(32):REM ONE SPACE
130 D$="-"
140 POKE 53280,9:REM BROWN BORDER
150 POKE 53281,1:REM WHITE SCREEN
160 PRINT CHR$(31):REM BLUE INK
170 PRINT CL$:PRINT
180 FOR N=0 TO 3
190 S$=S$+S$:D$=D$+D$
200 NEXT:REM S$ CONTAINS 16 SPACES
             D$ CONTAINS 16 DASHES
210 PRINT TAB(12)CHR$(18)D$
220 PRINT TAB(12)CHR$(18)
    "   COORDINATE   "
230 PRINT TAB(12)CHR$(18)S$
240 PRINT TAB(12)CHR$(18)
    "   CONVERSION   "
250 PRINT TAB(12)CHR$(18)D$
260 PRINT:PRINT:PRINT
270 REM***********************
280 REM SELECT DEGREES OR RADIANS
290 PRINT TAB(4)
    "DO YOU WISH ANGLES TO BE IN:"
300 PRINT
310 PRINT TAB(12)"1. RADIANS?"
320 PRINT
330 PRINT TAB(12)"2. DEGREES?"
340 PRINT:PRINT
350 PRINT TAB(4):INPUT
    "WHAT IS YOUR CHOICE (1 OR 2)";A$
360 B=ASC(A$)-48
370 IF B<1 OR B>2 THEN GOSUB 3000:
    GOTO 280
380 IF B=1 THEN DEF FNA1(A)=A:
    DEF FNA2(A)=A:T$="RADIANS"
390 IF B=2 THEN DEF FNA1(A)=A*180/π:
    DEF FNA2(A)=A*π/180:T$="DEGREES"
400 GOSUB 3000:REM CLEAR
410 REM***********************
420 REM MENU

430 PRINT TAB(4)
    "KEY 1. RECTANGULAR TO POLAR"
```

```
440 PRINT
450 PRINT TAB(4)
    "KEY 2. POLAR TO RECTANGULAR"
460 PRINT
470 PRINT TAB(4)
    "KEY 3. STOPS THE PROGRAM"
480 PRINT:PRINT
490 PRINT TAB(4):INPUT
    "ENTER YOUR CHOICE (1,2 OR 3)";C$
500 C=ASC(C$)-48
510 IF C<1 OR C>3 THEN GOSUB 3000:
    GOTO 420
520 IF C=3 THEN END
530 ON C GOSUB 1000,2000
540 GOSUB 3000:REM CLEAR
550 PRINT:PRINT:PRINT:PRINT:PRINT
560 PRINT TAB(4):INPUT
    "WANT TO ALTER ANGLE UNITS";Y$
570 PRINT:PRINT:GOSUB 3000
580 IF ASC(Y$)=89 OR ASC(Y$)=121
    THEN 280:REM DEGREES OR RADIANS
590 GOTO 420:REM MENU
600 REM
900 REM        ***************
910 REM        *
920 REM        * SUBROUTINES
930 REM        *
940 REM        ***************
950 REM
1000 REM RECTANGULAR TO POLAR
1010 GOSUB 3000:REM CLEAR
1020 PRINT TAB(8):INPUT
     "WHAT IS X-COORDINATE";X
1030 PRINT
1040 PRINT TAB(8):INPUT
     "WHAT IS Y-COORDINATE";Y
1050 PRINT
1060 R=SQR(X*X+Y*Y)
1070 A=ATN(Y/X)
1080 PRINT TAB(8)"RADIAL VALUE =";R
1090 PRINT
1100 PRINT TAB(8)"ANGLE =";FNA1(A);T$
1110 PRINT
1120 PRINT TAB(12)CHR$(18)
     "PRESS ANY KEY";
1130 GET A$:IF A$="" THEN 1130
1140 RETURN
```

```
1150 REM************************
1160 REM************************
2000 REM POLAR TO RECTANGULAR
2010 GOSUB 3000:REM CLEAR
2020 PRINT TAB(8):INPUT
     "WHAT IS RADIAL VALUE";R
2030 PRINT
2040 PRINT TAB(8):INPUT
     "WHAT IS ANGLE";A
2050 PRINT
2060 A=FNA2(A)
2070 X=R*COS(A):Y=R*SIN(A)
2080 PRINT TAB(8)"X COORDINATE =";X
2090 PRINT
2100 PRINT TAB(8)"Y COORDINATE =";Y
2110 PRINT
2120 PRINT TAB(12)CHR$(18)
     "PRESS ANY KEY";
2130 GET A$:IF A$="" THEN 2130
2140 RETURN
2150 REM************************
2160 REM************************
3000 REM CLEAR
3010 PRINT UP$+UP$+UP$+UP$+UP$+UP$+UP$+
         UP$+UP$
3020 FOR K=0 TO 8
3030 PRINT TAB(4)S$+S$
3040 NEXT
3050 PRINT UP$+UP$+UP$+UP$+UP$+UP$+UP$+
         UP$+UP$+UP$
3060 RETURN
3070 REM************************
3080 REM************************
```

P93 Vector Multiplication

This is a rather simple program which can be used to find the dot and cross products of vectors. The vectors used have only three components.

The program would have been more complex if it had been written for general vectors. We believe, however, that this is a useful routine to have in any program library.

COMMANDS

Key in the program and RUN.

Enter vectors when prompted.

```
10 REM VECTOR MULTIPLICATION
20 REM *********************
30 REM
100 CL$=CHR$(147):REM TO CLEAR SCREEN
110 POKE 53280,6:REM BLUE BORDER
120 POKE 53281,1:REM WHITE SCREEN
130 PRINT CHR$(144):REM BLACK INK
140 PRINT CL$:PRINT:PRINT
150 PRINT TAB(9)"VECTOR MULTIPLICATION"
160 PRINT TAB(9)"*********************"
170 PRINT:PRINT
180 PRINT TAB(4)
    "THIS PROGRAM COMPUTES BOTH THE"
190 PRINT TAB(4)
    "DOT AND THE CROSS PRODUCTS OF"
200 PRINT TAB(4)"TWO VECTORS."
210 PRINT
220 PRINT TAB(4)
    "THE VECTORS ARE ENTERED IN"
230 PRINT TAB(4)
    "COMPONENT FORM AND THEIR PRODUCTS"
240 PRINT TAB(4)"ARE THEN GIVEN."
250 PRINT
260 PRINT TAB(4)
    "THE VECTORS MUST BE IN 3D SPACE."
270 PRINT:PRINT:PRINT
```

P93 Vector Multiplication

```
280 PRINT TAB(4)
    "PRESS ANY KEY TO CONTINUE."
290 GET A$:IF A$="" THEN 290:REM
    NO SPACE BETWEEN INVERTED COMMAS
300 REM*****************************
310 PRINT CL$:PRINT:PRINT:PRINT:PRINT
320 PRINT TAB(4)
    "ENTER COMPONENTS OF FIRST VECTOR"
330 PRINT:PRINT:PRINT
340 FOR N=0 TO 2
350 PRINT TAB(8)"COMPONENT";N+1;:
    INPUT U(N)
360 PRINT
370 NEXT
380 REM*****************************
390 PRINT CL$:PRINT:PRINT:PRINT:PRINT
400 PRINT TAB(4)
    "ENTER COMPONENTS OF SECOND VECTOR"
410 PRINT:PRINT:PRINT
420 FOR N=0 TO 2
430 PRINT TAB(8)"COMPONENT";N+1;:
    INPUT V(N)
440 PRINT
450 NEXT
460 REM*****************************
470 REM DOT PRODUCT
480 FOR N=0 TO 2
490 D=D+U(N)*V(N)
500 NEXT
510 REM*****************************
520 REM CROSS PRODUCT
530 W(0)=U(1)*V(2)-U(2)*V(1)
540 W(1)=U(2)*V(0)-U(0)*V(2)
550 W(2)=U(0)*V(1)-U(1)*V(0)
560 REM*****************************
570 PRINT CL$:PRINT:PRINT
580 PRINT TAB(13)"CROSS PRODUCT"
590 PRINT TAB(13)"*************"
600 PRINT
610 PRINT TAB(4)"VECTOR 1"SPC(4)
    "VECTOR 2"SPC(4)"PRODUCT"
620 PRINT TAB(4)"--------"SPC(4)
    "--------"SPC(4)"-------"
630 FOR N=0 TO 2
640 PRINT TAB(4);U(N);TAB(16);V(N);
    TAB(28);W(N)
650 NEXT
```

```
660 PRINT:PRINT:PRINT
670 PRINT TAB(14)"DOT PRODUCT"
680 PRINT TAB(14)"***********"
690 PRINT
700 PRINT TAB(8)"DOT PRODUCT IS";D
710 PRINT:PRINT:PRINT
720 PRINT TAB(8):INPUT
    "ANOTHER PRODUCT (Y/N)";Y$
730 IF ASC(Y$)=89 THEN CLR:
    CL$=CHR$(147):GOTO 300
740 END
750 REM******************************
760 REM******************************
```

P94 Quadratic Equations

In this program we have to solve:

$$Ax^2 + Bx + C = 0 \quad \ldots\ldots\ldots\ldots\ldots\ldots\ldots\ldots\ldots\ldots\ldots\ldots(I)$$

To do this we use the formula:

$$x = (-B \pm SQR(B*B - 4*A*C))/2/A \quad \ldots\ldots\ldots\ldots(II)$$

This gives the two roots of (I). There are, however, some problems:

1. If A=0 we have division by zero in equation (II).
   In this case the solution is x = C/B.

2. If B*B - 4*A*C = 0 we have only one root.
   In this case the solution is x = -B/(2*A).

3. If B*B - 4*A*C < 0 we have complex roots.

COMMANDS

Key in the program and RUN.

Enter the coefficients in the correct order when prompted.

```
10 REM QUADRATIC EQUATIONS
20 REM *******************
30 REM
100 CL$=CHR$(147):REM TO CLEAR SCREEN
110 POKE 53280,6:REM BLUE BORDER
120 POKE 53281,1:REM WHITE SCREEN
130 PRINT CHR$(144):REM BLACK INK
140 PRINT CL$:PRINT:PRINT
150 PRINT TAB(11)"QUADRATIC EQUATIONS"
160 PRINT TAB(11)"==================="
170 PRINT:PRINT
```

```
180 PRINT TAB(4)
    "THIS PROGRAM SOLVES EQUATIONS OF"
190 PRINT TAB(4)"THE FORM:"
200 PRINT
210 PRINT TAB(13)"A*X^2+B*X+C=0"
220 PRINT
230 PRINT TAB(4)
    "ENTER THE THREE PARAMETERS IN THE"
240 PRINT TAB(4)"CORRECT ORDER."
250 PRINT
260 PRINT TAB(4):INPUT
    "COEFFICIENT OF X^2 (A)=";A
270 PRINT TAB(4):INPUT
    "COEFFICIENT OF X  (B) =";B
280 PRINT TAB(4):INPUT
    "CONSTANT TERM (C)     =";C
290 IF A=0 AND B=0 THEN 140:
    REM NOT A SENSIBLE CONDITION
300 REM****************************
310 IF A<>0 THEN A$=STR$(A)+"*X^2"
320 IF B>0 THEN B$=MID$(STR$(B),2)+"*X"
330 IFA<>0 AND B>0 THEN B$="+"+B$
340 IF B<0 THEN B$=STR$(B)+"*X"
350 IF C>0 THEN C$="+"+MID$(STR$(C),2)
360 IF C<0 THEN C$=STR$(C)
370 E$=A$+B$+C$+"=0"
380 PRINT
390 PRINT TAB(4)"EQUATION IS "E$
400 PRINT
410 PRINT TAB(4):INPUT
    "IS THIS CORRECT (Y/N)";Y$
420 IF ASC(Y$)<>121 AND ASC(Y$)<>89
    THEN 140
430 REM****************************
440 PRINT CL$:PRINT:PRINT:PRINT
450 PRINT TAB(4)"EQUATION IS "E$
460 PRINT:PRINT
470 IF A=0 THEN PRINT TAB(4)
    "SOLUTION IS: X =";-C/B:GOTO 550
480 REM****************************
490 D=B*B-4*A*C:REM DISCRIMINANT
500 IF D=0 THEN GOSUB 1000
510 IF D>0 THEN GOSUB 2000
530 IF D<0 THEN GOSUB 3000
540 REM****************************
550 PRINT:PRINT TAB(9)
    "*******************"
```

P94 Quadratic Equations

```
560 PRINT:PRINT:PRINT
570 PRINT TAB(4):INPUT
    "WANT TO SOLVE ANOTHER (Y/N)";Y$
580 IF ASC(Y$)=89 THEN 140
590 END
600 REM****************************
610 REM****************************
700 REM
710 REM          ***************
730 REM          *
740 REM          * SUBROUTINES
750 REM          *
760 REM          ***************
770 REM
1000 REM EQUAL ROOTS
1010 PRINT TAB(4)
     "WE HAVE EQUAL ROOTS"
1020 PRINT:PRINT
1030 PRINT TAB(4)
     "THE SOLUTION IS: X =";-B/2/A
1040 RETURN
1050 REM****************************
2000 REM REAL ROOTS
2010 PRINT TAB(4)
     "WE HAVE TWO REAL ROOTS"
2020 PRINT:PRINT
2030 PRINT TAB(4)
     "ROOT 1 IS: X =";(-B+SQR(D))/2/A
2040 PRINT
2050 PRINT TAB(6)
     "ROOT 2 IS: X =";(-B-SQR(D))/2/A
2060 RETURN
2070 REM****************************
3000 REM COMPLEX ROOTS
3010 PRINT TAB(4)
     "WE HAVE COMPLEX ROOTS"
3020 PRINT:PRINT
3030 PRINT TAB(4)"ROOT 1 IS:"
3040 PRINT TAB(4)"X =";
     -B/2/A;"+I*(";SQR(-D)/2/A;")"
3050 PRINT
3060 PRINT TAB(4)"ROOT 2 IS:"
3070 PRINT TAB(4)"X =";
     -B/2/A;"-I*(";SQR(-D)/2/A;")"
3080 RETURN
3090 REM****************************
3100 REM****************************
```

P95 Factorization

This program finds the prime factors of positive integers. Any positive integer N may be expressed in terms of prime numbers and indices. The index of a prime number is the power to which that number is raised in the factorization of N.

For example:

$$180 = 2^2 * 3^2 * 5$$

We use a method of repeated division to find the set of factors for N.

Let us consider an example - find the prime factors of 180.

The first possible factor of 180 is 2, and we can write:

$$180 = 2*90 = 2*2*45$$

Thus 2 is a factor of 180 and of 90, but it is not a factor of 45. That is to say that dividing 45 by two gives a remainder which is not zero.

We can now try 3:

$$180 = 2*2*3*15 = 2*2*3*3*5$$

Trying the next prime, 5, gives a result on division of 1. This indicates that all the factors have been found.

Thus:

$$180 = 2*2*3*3*5*1 = 2^2 * 3^3 * 5$$

The program presented here uses this algorithm.

COMMANDS

Key in the program and RUN.

Enter the number to be factorized.

P95 Factorization

```
10 REM FACTORIZATION
20 REM ************
30 REM
100 CL$=CHR$(147):REM TO CLEAR SCREEN
110 POKE 53280,6:REM BLUE BORDER
120 POKE 53281,1:REM WHITE PAPER
130 PRINT CHR$(144):REM BLACK INK
140 PRINT CL$:PRINT:PRINT
150 PRINT TAB(13)"FACTORIZATION"
160 PRINT TAB(13)"*************"
170 PRINT:PRINT
180 PRINT TAB(4)
    "THIS PROGRAM CAN BE USED TO"
190 PRINT TAB(4)
    "FACTORIZE A POSTIVE INTEGER INTO"
200 PRINT TAB(4)"PRIME FACTORS."
210 PRINT
220 PRINT TAB(4)
    "IN ITS PRESENT FORM THE PROGRAM"
230 PRINT TAB(4)
    "USES ONLY THE PRIMES LESS THAN"
240 PRINT TAB(4)"100."
250 PRINT:PRINT
260 PRINT TAB(4):INPUT
    "NUMBER TO BE FACTORIZED";N
270 IF N<2 THEN 140:REM TRIVIAL ENTRIES
    OF 1 OR 2 IGNORED
280 N=INT(ABS(N)):Q=N
290 D=100:REM CHANGE THIS LINE TO ALTER
    THE RANGE OF THE PROGRAM.
300 DIM F(D):DIM I(D)
310 REM******************************
320 REM FIND THE INDICES OF THE FACTORS
330 FOR K=2 TO D
340 T=Q-INT(Q/K)*K
350 IF T=0 THEN F(K)=1:I(K)=I(K)+1:
    Q=INT(Q/K):GOTO 340
360 NEXT
370 REM IF THERE IS A 1 IN THE KTH
380 REM POSITION OF THE FACTOR ARRAY
390 REM THEN K IS A FACTOR AND I(K) IS
400 REM THE INDEX OF THAT FACTOR.
410 REM******************************
420 REM THE NEXT SECTION OF CODE WRITES
430 REM OUT THE FACTORIZATION. NOTE
440 REM THAT THE FIRST 1 IS WRITTEN
```

```
450 REM JUST TO TIDY UP THE DISPLAY,
460 REM EVEN THOUGH IT MIGHT NOT BE
470 REM CONSIDERED A PRIME NUMBER.
480 PRINT CL$:PRINT:PRINT
490 C=1:A$="1"
500 FOR K=2 TO D
510 IF F(K)=1 THEN A$=A$+" *"+STR$(K)+
    "^"+MID$(STR$(I(K)),2):C=C*K^I(K)
520 NEXT
530 REM******************************
540 IF C=>N THEN GOSUB 1000
550 IF C<N THEN GOSUB 2000
560 PRINT:PRINT
570 PRINT TAB(8):INPUT
    "ANOTHER RUN (Y/N)";Y$
580 IF ASC(Y$)=89 THEN RUN
590 END
600 REM******************************
610 REM******************************
900 REM
910 REM          ***************
920 REM          *
930 REM          * SUBROUTINES
940 REM          *
950 REM          ***************
960 REM
1000 REM FACTORIZATION OK
1010 PRINT TAB(4)
     "THE PRIME FACTORIZATION OF"
1020 PRINT
1030 PRINT TAB(3)N
1040 PRINT
1050 PRINT TAB(4)"IS:"
1060 PRINT

1070 PRINT TAB(4)A$
1080 RETURN
1090 REM*****************************
1100 REM*****************************
2000 REM FACTORIZATION INCORRECT
2010 PRINT TAB(4)
     "EITHER THE NUMBER HAS A PRIME"
2020 PRINT TAB(4)
     "FACTOR GREATER THAN 100 OR THE"
2030 PRINT TAB(4)
     "ROUNDING ERRORS OF THE MICRO"
```

```
2040 PRINT TAB(4)
     "HAVE MUDDLED THE CALCULATION."
2050 RETURN
2060 REM*****************************
2070 REM*****************************
```

P96 Factorial

In statistics we frequently wish to calculate objects of the form:

N * (N-1) * (N-2) * ...... * 3 * 2 * 1

For example, if we want to know the number of ways of arranging the letters in the word COMPUTER, then:

We have 8 ways of choosing the first letter;
We have 7 ways of choosing the second letter;
We have 6 ways of choosing the third letter;

and so on.

Thus in total we have:

8 * 7 * 6 * 5 * 4 * 3 * 2 * 1 = 40320

ways of arranging the letters of the word COMPUTER.

Such objects are known as factorials, and are defined as follows:

N! = N * (N-1) * (N-2) * ..... * 3 * 2 * 1

Where ! is the symbol for factorial.

COMMANDS

Key in the program and RUN.

Follow the instructions.

```
10 REM FACTORIAL
20 REM *********
30 REM
100 CL$=CHR$(147):REM TO CLEAR SCREEN
110 POKE 53280,6:REM BLUE BORDER
120 POKE 53281,1:REM WHITE SCREEN
130 PRINTCHR$(144):REM BLACK INK
```

P96 Factorial

```
140 PRINT CL$:PRINT
150 PRINT TAB(13)"!!!!!!!!!!!!!!"
160 PRINT TAB(13)"  FACTORIAL  "
170 PRINT TAB(13)"!!!!!!!!!!!!!!"
180 PRINT:PRINT
190 PRINT TAB(4)
    "THIS PROGRAM MAY BE USED TO"
200 PRINT TAB(4)
    "EVALUATE THE FACTORIAL OF A"
210 PRINT TAB(4)
    "POSITIVE INTEGER LESS THAN OR"
220 PRINT TAB(4)"EQUAL TO 33."
230 PRINT
240 PRINT TAB(4)
    "THE PROGRAM USES THE FORMULA:"
250 PRINT
260 PRINT TAB(4)
    "N!=N*(N-1)*(N-2)*....*3*2*1."
270 PRINT
280 PRINT TAB(4)
    "THE LIMITATION OF 33 IS BECAUSE"
290 PRINT TAB(4)
    "OF THE LIMITED RANGE OF NUMBERS"
300 PRINT TAB(4)
    "WHICH CAN BE HELD INSIDE A"
310 PRINT TAB(4)"COMPUTER."
320 PRINT:PRINT
330 PRINT TAB(4)
    "PRESS ANY KEY TO CONTINUE."
340 GET A$:IF A$="" THEN 340:REM
    NO SPACE BETWEEN INVERTED COMMAS
350 REM****************************
360 PRINT CL$:PRINT:PRINT:PRINT
370 PRINT TAB(4)
    "PLEASE ENTER A POSITIVE WHOLE"
380 PRINT TAB(4)
    "NUMBER LESS THAN OR EQUAL TO 33."
390 PRINT:PRINT
400 PRINT TAB(7):INPUT
    "WHAT IS YOUR NUMBER";N%
410 IF N%>33 OR N%<1 THEN 350:REM
    NUMBERS OUTSIDE RANGE IGNORED
420 REM****************************
430 F=1
440 FOR K=1 TO N%
450 F=F*K
460 NEXT
```

```
470 REM*****************************
480 PRINT:PRINT
490 PRINT TAB(7)
    "THE FACTORIAL OF";N%;"IS:"
500 PRINT
510 PRINT TAB(6)F
520 PRINT TAB(7)
    "----------------------"
530 REM*****************************
540 PRINT:PRINT:PRINT
550 PRINT TAB(7):INPUT
    "WANT ANOTHER NUMBER (Y/N)";Y$
560 IF ASC(Y$)=89 THEN 350
570 END
580 REM*****************************
590 REM*****************************
```

P97 Greatest Common Divisor

This program uses the Euclidian Algorithm to compute the greatest common divisor of two natural numbers.

COMMANDS

Key in the program and RUN.

Enter numbers as positive integers.

```
10 REM GREATEST COMMON DIVISOR
20 REM ***********************
30 REM
100 CL$=CHR$(147):REM TO CLEAR SCREEN
110 POKE 53280,6:REM BLUE BORDER
120 POKE 53281,1:REM WHITE SCREEN
130 PRINT CHR$(144):REM BLACK INK
140 PRINT CL$:PRINT
150 PRINT TAB(6)
    "/////////////////////////"
160 PRINT TAB(6)
    "  GREATEST COMMON DIVISOR  "
170 PRINT TAB(6)
    "/////////////////////////"
180 PRINT:PRINT
190 PRINT TAB(4)
    "THIS PROGRAM USES THE EUCLIDEAN"
200 PRINT TAB(4)
    "ALGORITHM TO COMPUTE THE GREATEST"
210 PRINT TAB(4)
    "COMMON DIVISOR OF TWO NATURAL"
220 PRINT TAB(4)"NUMBERS."
230 PRINT:PRINT
240 PRINT TAB(10):INPUT
    "FIRST NUMBER";X1
250 PRINT
260 PRINT TAB(10):INPUT
    "SECOND NUMBER";X2
270 REM***************************
280 X1=ABS(INT(X1)):A=X1
290 X2=ABS(INT(X2)):B=X2
```

```
300 IF A<B THEN T=B:B=A:A=T:
    REM A IS THE LARGER NUMBER
310 REM*****************************
320 REM THE FOLLOWING IS THE EUCLIDIAN
        ALGORITHM:
330 R=A-(INT(A/B))*B:REM REMAINDER
340 Q=INT(A/B):REM QUOTIENT
350 A=B:B=R
360 IF R<>0 THEN 310
370 REM*****************************
380 PRINT CL$:PRINT:PRINT:PRINT
390 PRINT TAB(9)"THE GREATEST COMMON"
400 PRINT TAB(9)"DIVISOR OF"
410 PRINT
420 PRINT TAB(8)X1;"AND"
430 PRINT
440 PRINT TAB(8)X2;"IS:"
450 PRINT
460 PRINT TAB(8)A
500 PRINT:PRINT
510 PRINT TAB(9):INPUT
    "ANOTHER RUN (Y/N)";Y$
520 IF ASC(Y$)=89 THEN 140
530 END
540 REM*****************************
550 REM*****************************
```

P98 Polynomial Multiplication

This program allows the user to multiply two polynomials together.

Example

Multiply (2*x*x + 3*x + 2) by (x + 1)

If this has to be done by hand we proceed as follows:

$$\begin{array}{r} 2x^2 + 3x + 2 \\ \underline{x + 1} \\ 2x^2 + 3x + 2 \\ \underline{2x^3 + 3x^2 + 2x} \\ 2x^3 + 5x^2 + 5x + 2 \\ \underline{} \end{array}$$

This can be a rather time consuming exercise when the polynomials become large. This program takes all the work out of it.

The CBM 64, in common with most other micros, cannot express polynomials in a very satisfying manner, but bear with this and the algorithm can be very useful.

COMMANDS

Key in the program and RUN.

Follow instructions, keying in the parameters as prompted.

```
10 REM POLYNOMIAL MULTIPLICATION
20 REM ************************
30 REM
100 CL$=CHR$(147):REM TO CLEAR SCREEN
110 POKE 53280,1:REM WHITE BORDER
120 POKE 53281,1:REM WHITE SCREEN
```

```
130 PRINT CHR$(144):REM BLACK INK
140 PRINT CL$:PRINT
150 PRINT TAB(7)
    "POLYNOMIAL MULTIPLICATION"
160 PRINT TAB(7)
    "*************************"
170 PRINT
180 PRINT TAB(4)
    "THIS PROGRAM CAN BE USED TO FIND"
190 PRINT TAB(4)
    "THE RESULT OF MULTIPLYING TWO"
200 PRINT TAB(4)
    "POLYNOMIALS TOGETHER."
210 PRINT
220 PRINT TAB(4)
    "THE POLYNOMIALS ARE OF THE FORM:"
230 PRINT
240 PRINT TAB(4)
    "P(X)=A(0)*X^0+A(1)*X^1+A(2)*X^2"
250 PRINT TAB(9)"+....+A(N)*X^N"
260 PRINT
270 PRINT TAB(4)
    "Q(X)=B(0)*X^0+B(1)*X^1+B(2)*X^2"
280 PRINT TAB(9)"+....+B(N)*X^N"
290 PRINT
300 PRINT TAB(4)"AND THE RESULT IS:"
310 PRINT
320 PRINT TAB(4)
    "P(X)*Q(X)=C(0)*X^0+C(1)*X^1+C(2)"
330 PRINT TAB(14)
    "*X^2+..+C(M+N)*X^(M+N)"
340 PRINT:PRINT
350 PRINT TAB(7)
    "PRESS ANY KEY TO CONTINUE."
360 GET A$:IF A$="" THEN 360:REM
    NO SPACE BETWEEN INVERTED COMMAS
370 REM******************************
380 PRINT CL$:PRINT:PRINT:PRINT
390 PRINT TAB(4)
    "YOU ARE REQUIRED TO ENTER ONLY"
400 PRINT TAB(4)
    "THE DEGREE AND THE COEFFICIENTS"
410 PRINT TAB(4)
    "OF EACH POLYNOMIAL."
420 PRINT:PRINT
430 PRINT TAB(7)
    "PRESS ANY KEY TO CONTINUE."
```

P98 Polynomial Multiplication

```
440 GET A$:IF A$="" THEN 440:REM
    NO SPACE BETWEEN INVERTED COMMAS
450 REM*****************************
460 PRINT CL$:PRINT:PRINT:PRINT
470 PRINT TAB(9)
    "WHAT IS THE DEGREE OF"
480 PRINT TAB(9):INPUT"POLYNOMIAL 1";N%
490 IF N%<0 THEN 450
500 DIM A(N%)
510 FOR K=0 TO N%
520 PRINT
530 PRINT TAB(9)"COEFFICIENT";K;"=";
540 INPUT A(K)
550 NEXT
560 REM*****************************
570 PRINT CL$:PRINT:PRINT:PRINT
580 PRINT TAB(9)
    "WHAT IS THE DEGREE OF"
590 PRINT TAB(9):INPUT"POLYNOMIAL 2";M%
600 IF M%<0 THEN 560
610 DIM B(M%)
620 FOR K=0 TO M%
630 PRINT
640 PRINT TAB(9)"COEFFICIENT";K;"=";
650 INPUT B(K)
660 NEXT
670 REM*****************************
680 DIM C(N%+M%)
690 FOR J=0 TO N%
700 FOR K=0 TO M%
710 C(K+J)=C(K+J)+B(K)*A(J)
720 NEXT:NEXT
730 REM*****************************
740 PRINT CL$:PRINT:PRINT:PRINT
750 PRINT"THE RESULT OF MULTIPLYING"
760 PRINT
770 FOR J=N% TO 0 STEP-1
780 PRINT A(J);"*X^";J;"+";
790 NEXT
800 PRINT CHR$(157)CHR$(32):
    REM DELETE LAST +
810 PRINT:PRINT"BY":PRINT
820 FOR K=M% TO 0 STEP-1
830 PRINT B(K);"*X^";K;"+";
840 NEXT
850 PRINT CHR$(157)CHR$(32):
    REM DELETE LAST +
```

```
860 PRINT:PRINT"IS":PRINT
870 FOR L=M%+N% TO 0 STEP-1
880 PRINT C(L);"*X^";L;"+";
890 NEXT
900 PRINT CHR$(157)CHR$(32):
    REM DELETE LAST +
910 REM*****************************
920 PRINT:PRINT
930 PRINT TAB(10):INPUT
    "ANOTHER (Y/N)";Y$
940 IF ASC(Y$)=89 THEN CLR:
    CL$=CHR$(147):GOTO 450
950 END
960 REM*****************************
970 REM*****************************
```

P99   Secant Method

This program can be used to find a root of a function of a single variable. The Secant Method can be interpreted geometrically as follows:

Consider the diagram:

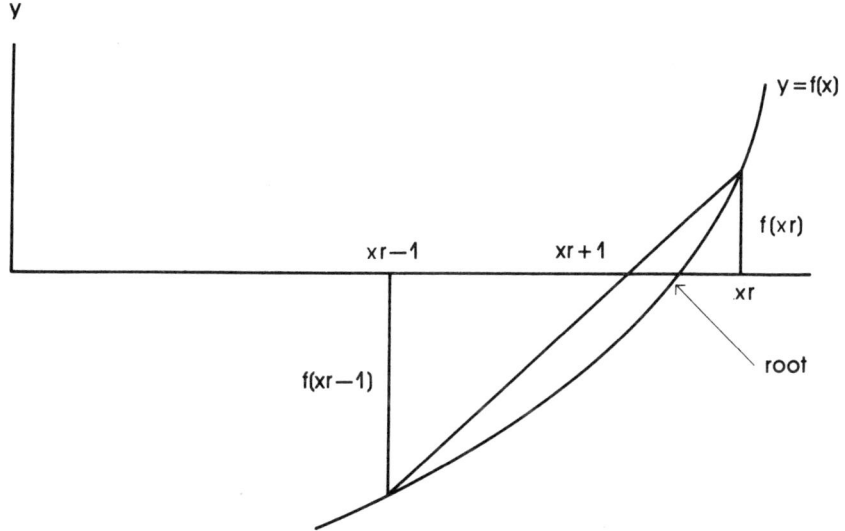

If xr and xr-1 lie on either side of a root we can draw the secant between the points (xr-1,f(xr-1)) and (xr,f(xr)). The secant cuts the x-axis at the point xr+1. Let xr+1 be the new approximation.

Then by similar triangles:

$$\frac{x_{r+1} - x_{r-1}}{-f(x_{r-1})} = \frac{x_r - x_{r+1}}{f(x_r)}$$

$$\therefore \quad x_{r+1} = x_r - f(x_r) \frac{(x_r - x_{r-1})}{f(x_r) - f(x_{r-1})}$$

The same relationship can be formed even if both approximations lie on the same side of the root.

COMMANDS

Key in the program and RUN.

Enter function and initial approximations when required.

Enter accuracy when prompted.

```
10 REM SECANT METHOD
20 REM *************
30 REM
100 CL$=CHR$(147):REM TO CLEAR SCREEN
110 POKE 53280,6:REM BLUE BORDER
120 POKE 53281,1:REM WHITE SCREEN
130 PRINT CHR$(144):REM BLACK INK
140 PRINT CL$:PRINT:PRINT
150 PRINT TAB(13)"SECANT METHOD"
160 PRINT TAB(13)"*************"
170 PRINT:PRINT
180 PRINT TAB(4)
    "THIS PROGRAM USES THE SECANT"
190 PRINT TAB(4)
    "METHOD TO FIND THE ROOT OF AN"
200 PRINT TAB(4)"EQUATION."
210 PRINT
220 PRINT TAB(4)
    "NOTE THAT THE METHOD WILL ATTEMPT"
230 PRINT TAB(4)
    "TO FIND A ROOT WITHIN AN INTERVAL"
240 PRINT TAB(4)
    "EVEN IF NO ROOT EXISTS."
250 PRINT:PRINT
260 PRINT TAB(7)
    "PRESS ANY KEY TO CONTINUE."
270 GET A$:IF A$="" THEN 270:REM
    NO SPACE BETWEEN INVERTED COMMAS
280 REM******************************
290 PRINT CL$:PRINT:PRINT
300 PRINT TAB(4)
    "THE METHOD REQUIRES THAT YOU"
```

P99 Secant Method

```
310 PRINT TAB(4)
    "INPUT THE FUNCTION, THE RANGE OF"
320 PRINT TAB(4)
    "X VALUES WITHIN WHICH THE ROOT"
330 PRINT TAB(4)
    "LIES AND THE REQUIRED ACCURACY."
340 PRINT:PRINT
350 PRINT TAB(7)
    "PRESS ANY KEY TO CONTINUE."
360 GET A$:IF A$="" THEN 360:REM
    NO SPACE BETWEEN INVERTED COMMAS
370 REM*****************************
380 PRINT CL$:PRINT
390 PRINT TAB(4)
    "TO INPUT THE FUNCTION PLEASE"
400 PRINT TAB(4)
    "TYPE IT IN DIRECTLY AFTER"
410 PRINT
420 PRINT TAB(4)"580 DEF FNA(X)="
430 PRINT
440 PRINT TAB(4)"THEN PRESS RETURN."
450 PRINT
460 PRINT TAB(4)
    "AFTER YOU HAVE DONE THIS TYPE IN"
470 PRINT
480 PRINT TAB(4)"RUN 580"
490 PRINT
500 PRINT TAB(4)
    "THEN PRESS RETURN. USE THE CURSOR"
510 PRINT TAB(4)
    "CONTROL KEYS TO POSITION THE"
520 PRINT TAB(4)
    "CURSOR DIRECTLY AFTER THE = SIGN"
530 PRINT:PRINT
540 PRINT TAB(4)"580 DEF FNA(X)="
550 PRINT:PRINT
560 STOP
570 REM*****************************
580 REM THIS LINE IS REPLACED BY THE
    FUNCTION ENTERED
590 REM*****************************
600 CL$=CHR$(147):PRINT CL$:PRINT:PRINT
610 PRINT TAB(8):INPUT
    "FIRST POINT-   X=";P1
620 PRINT
630 PRINT TAB(8):INPUT
    "SECOND POINT-  X=";P2
```

```
640 PRINT
650 PRINT TAB(8):INPUT
    "ACCURACY (+ OR -)";AC
660 PRINT:PRINT
665 REM*****************************
670 R=0
680 R=R+1
690 F1=FNA(P1):F2=FNA(P2)
695 IF F1=F2 THEN PRINT TAB(8)
    "CAN'T FIND ROOT":GOTO 760
700 P3=P2-F2*(P2-P1)/(F2-F1)
710 P1=P2:P2=P3
720 IF ABS(P2-P1)<AC THEN GOSUB 1000:
    GOTO 760
730 IF R<40 THEN 680:REM CAN'T USE FOR-
    NEXT LOOP DUE TO GOTO INSTRUCTIONS
740 GOSUB 2000
750 REM****************************
760 PRINT:PRINT
770 PRINT TAB(8):INPUT
    "ANOTHER RUN (Y/N)";Y$
780 IF ASC(Y$)=89 THEN 380
790 END
900 REM
910 REM           ***************
920 REM           *
930 REM           * SUBROUTINES
940 REM           *
950 REM           ***************
960 REM
1000 REM ROOT FOUND WITHIN LIMITS
1010 PRINT TAB(8)"ROOT IS";P2
1020 PRINT
1030 PRINT TAB(8)"AT ITERATION"
1040 PRINT TAB(8)"NUMBER";R
1050 RETURN
1060 REM*****************************
1070 REM*****************************
2000 REM ROOT NOT FOUND
2010 PRINT TAB(8)"ROOT NOT FOUND AFTER"
2020 PRINT TAB(8)"40 ITERATIONS."
2030 PRINT
2040 PRINT TAB(8)"IF ROOT EXISTS NEAR"
2050 PRINT TAB(8)"THE RANGE ENTERED,"
2070 PRINT TAB(8)"IT LIES BETWEEN:"
2080 PRINT
2090 PRINT TAB(7)P1
```

```
2100 PRINT TAB(8)"AND"
2110 PRINT TAB(7)P2
2120 RETURN
2130 REM*****************************
```

P100   Method of Bisections

The Method of Bisections is based on the use of sign changes to find a root of a function.

Consider the following diagram:

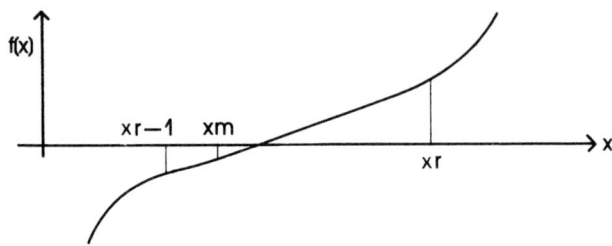

If we have two points, xr and xr-1, such that f(xr) and f(xr-1) have different signs, then there is a root between xr and xr-1. We then evaluate the function at the mid point, xm, between xr and xr-1. If xm=0 then we have a root. If SGN(f(xm)) does not equal SGN(f(xr-1)) then the root lies between xm and xr-1. Otherwise the root lies between xm and xr.

That is the idea behind the Method of Bisections, which is used in this program.

COMMANDS

Key in the program and RUN.

Enter the function and the end points of the interval straddling the root when prompted.

Enter the accuracy desired.

P100 Method of Bisections

```
10 REM METHOD OF BISECTIONS
20 REM ********************
30 REM
100 CL$=CHR$(147):REM TO CLEAR SCREEN
110 POKE 53280,6:REM BLUE BORDER
120 POKE 53281,1:REM WHITE SCREEN
130 PRINT CHR$(144):REM BLACK INK
140 PRINT CL$:PRINT:PRINT
150 PRINT TAB(9)"METHOD OF BISECTIONS"
160 PRINT TAB(9)"********************"
170 PRINT:PRINT
180 PRINT TAB(4)
    "THIS PROGRAM USES THE METHOD OF"
190 PRINT TAB(4)
    "BISECTIONS TO FIND THE ROOT OF"
200 PRINT TAB(4)"AN EQUATION."
210 PRINT
220 PRINT TAB(4)
    "NOTE THAT THE METHOD WILL ATTEMPT"
230 PRINT TAB(4)
    "TO FIND A ROOT WITHIN AN INTERVAL"
240 PRINT TAB(4)
    "EVEN IF NO ROOT EXISTS."
250 PRINT:PRINT
260 PRINT TAB(7)
    "PRESS ANY KEY TO CONTINUE."
270 GET A$:IF A$="" THEN 270:REM
    NO SPACE BETWEEN INVERTED COMMAS
280 REM*****************************
290 PRINT CL$:PRINT:PRINT
300 PRINT TAB(4)
    "THE METHOD REQUIRES THAT YOU"
310 PRINT TAB(4)
    "INPUT THE FUNCTION, THE RANGE OF"
320 PRINT TAB(4)
    "X VALUES WITHIN WHICH THE ROOT"
330 PRINT TAB(4)
    "LIES AND THE REQUIRED ACCURACY."
340 PRINT:PRINT
350 PRINT TAB(7)
    "PRESS ANY KEY TO CONTINUE."
360 GET A$:IF A$="" THEN 360:REM
    NO SPACE BETWEEN INVERTED COMMAS
370 REM*****************************
380 PRINT CL$:PRINT
390 PRINT TAB(4)
    "TO INPUT THE FUNCTION PLEASE"
```

```
400 PRINT TAB(4)
    "TYPE IT IN DIRECTLY AFTER"
410 PRINT
420 PRINT TAB(4)"580 DEF FNA(X)="
430 PRINT
440 PRINT TAB(4)"THEN PRESS RETURN."
450 PRINT
460 PRINT TAB(4)
    "AFTER YOU HAVE DONE THIS TYPE IN"
470 PRINT
480 PRINT TAB(4)"RUN 580"
490 PRINT
500 PRINT TAB(4)
    "THEN PRESS RETURN. USE THE CURSOR"
510 PRINT TAB(4)
    "CONTROL KEYS TO POSITION THE"
520 PRINT TAB(4)
    "CURSOR DIRECTLY AFTER THE = SIGN"
530 PRINT:PRINT
540 PRINT TAB(4)"580 DEF FNA(X)="
550 PRINT:PRINT
560 STOP
570 REM*****************************
580 REM THIS LINE IS REPLACED BY THE
    FUNCTION DEFINITION.
590 REM*****************************
600 CL$=CHR$(147):PRINT CL$:PRINT:PRINT
610 PRINT TAB(8):INPUT
    "FIRST POINT-   X=";P1
620 PRINT
630 PRINT TAB(8):INPUT
    "SECOND POINT-  X=";P2
640 PRINT
650 PRINT TAB(8):INPUT
    "ACCURACY (+ OR -)";AC
660 PRINT:PRINT
670 REM*****************************
680 FOR R=1 TO 40
690 T=(P1+P2)/2:K=P1
700 IF SGN(FNA(T))=SGN(FNA(K)) THEN
    P1=T:GOTO 720
710 P2=T
720 IF FNA(T)=0 THEN PRINT TAB(8)
    "SOLUTION IS";T:GOTO 780
730 FG=1:IF SGN(FNA(P1))=SGN(FNA(P2))
    THEN FG=0
```

```
740 IF ABS(P1-P2)<AC AND FG=1
    THEN GOSUB 1000:GOTO 780
750 NEXT
760 GOSUB 2000
770 REM***************************
780 PRINT:PRINT
790 PRINT TAB(8):INPUT
    "ANOTHER RUN (Y/N)";Y$
800 IF ASC(Y$)=89 THEN 380
810 END
900 REM
910 REM          ***************
920 REM          *
930 REM          * SUBROUTINES
940 REM          *
950 REM          ***************
960 REM
1000 REM ROOT FOUND WITHIN LIMITS
1010 PRINT TAB(8)"ROOT LIES BETWEEN"
1020 PRINT
1030 PRINT TAB(7)P1
1040 PRINT TAB(8)"AND"
1050 PRINT TAB(7)P2
1060 RETURN
1070 REM***************************
1080 REM***************************
2000 REM ROOT NOT FOUND
2010 PRINT TAB(8)"ROOT NOT FOUND AFTER"
2020 PRINT TAB(8)"40 ITERATIONS."
2030 RETURN
2040 REM***************************
2050 REM***************************
```

P101 Trapezoidal Rule

This program uses the Trapezoidal Rule to evaluate a definite integral of the form:

$$I = \int_a^b f(x)dx$$

Thus the program requires as input:

  f(x)
  a and b

A definite integral can be considered to be the area under the graph of a function. The trapezium rule approximates this area by a series of trapeziums, as in the following diagram:

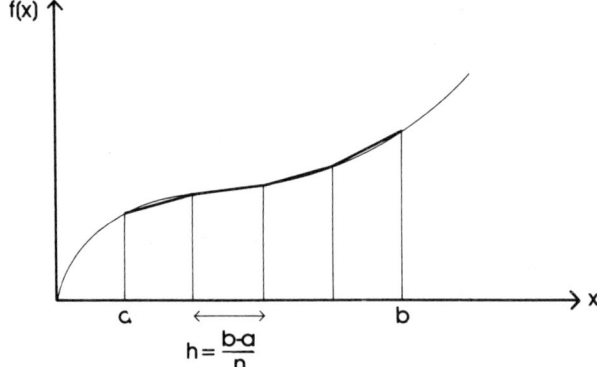

P101 Trapezoidal Rule

COMMANDS

Key in the program and RUN.

Follow the instructions.

```
10 REM TRAPEZOIDAL RULE
20 REM ****************
30 REM
100 CL$=CHR$(147):REM TO CLEAR SCREEN
110 POKE 53280,6:REM BLUE BORDER
120 POKE 53281,1:REM WHITE SCREEN
130 PRINT CHR$(144):REM BLACK INK
140 PRINT CL$:PRINT
150 PRINT TAB(11)"TRAPEZOIDAL RULE"
160 PRINT TAB(11)"****************"
170 PRINT
180 PRINT TAB(4)
    "THIS PROGRAM USES THE TRAPEZOIDAL"
190 PRINT TAB(4)
    "RULE TO EVALUATE A DEFINITE"
200 PRINT TAB(4)"INTEGRAL."
210 PRINT
220 PRINT TAB(4)
    "YOU ARE REQUIRED TO ENTER:"
230 PRINT
240 PRINT TAB(8) "1. YOUR FUNCTION OF X."
250 PRINT
260 PRINT TAB(8)"2. THE RANGE OF VALUES"
270 PRINT TAB(11)"OF X OVER WHICH YOU"
280 PRINT TAB(11)"WISH TO EVALUATE THE"
290 PRINT TAB(11)"INTEGRAL."
300 PRINT
310 PRINT TAB(8)"3. THE NUMBER OF SUB-"
320 PRINT TAB(11)"INTERVALS."
330 PRINT
340 PRINT
350 PRINT TAB(7)
    "PRESS ANY KEY TO CONTINUE."
360 GET A$:IF A$="" THEN 360:REM
    NO SPACE BETWEEN INVERTED COMMAS
370 REM******************************
380 PRINT CL$:PRINT
```

```
390 PRINT TAB(4)
    "TO INPUT THE FUNCTION PLEASE"
400 PRINT TAB(4)
    "TYPE IT IN DIRECTLY AFTER"
410 PRINT
420 PRINT TAB(4)"580 DEF FNA(X)="
430 PRINT
440 PRINT TAB(4)"THEN PRESS RETURN."
450 PRINT
460 PRINT TAB(4)
    "AFTER YOU HAVE DONE THIS TYPE IN"
470 PRINT
480 PRINT TAB(4)"RUN 580"
490 PRINT
500 PRINT TAB(4)
    "THEN PRESS RETURN. USE THE CURSOR"
510 PRINT TAB(4)
    "CONTROL KEYS TO POSITION THE"
520 PRINT TAB(4)
    "CURSOR DIRECTLY AFTER THE = SIGN"
530 PRINT:PRINT
540 PRINT TAB(4)"580 DEF FNA(X)="
550 PRINT:PRINT
560 STOP
570 REM*****************************
580 REM THIS LINE WILL BE REPLACED BY
    THE FUNCTION DEFINITION.
590 REM*****************************
600 CL$=CHR$(147):PRINT CL$:PRINT:PRINT
610 PRINT TAB(6):INPUT
    "LOWER VALUE OF X-RANGE";A
620 PRINT
630 PRINT TAB(6):INPUT
    "HIGHER VALUE OF X-RANGE";B
640 PRINT
650 PRINT TAB(6):INPUT
    "NUMBER OF POINTS";N%
660 IF N%<2 THEN N%=2:REM PREVENTS
    SILLY ENTRIES FROM BREAKING PROGRAM
670 REM*****************************
680 PRINT:PRINT
690 H=(ABS(B-A))/N%
700 LO=FNA(A)/2
710 HI=FNA(B)/2
720 X=A:K=0
730 FOR J=1 TO N%-1
740 X=X+H
```

P101 Trapezoidal Rule

```
750 K=K+FNA(X)
760 NEXT
770 IT=(LO+HI+K)*H
780 PRINT TAB(8)"INTEGRAL =";IT
790 PRINT TAB(8)"--------------------"
800 PRINT:PRINT
810 REM*****************************
820 PRINT TAB(8):INPUT
    "ANOTHER RUN (Y/N)";Y$
830 IF ASC(Y$)=89 THEN 370
840 END
850 REM*****************************
860 REM*****************************
```

P102 Simpson's Rule

Simpson's Rule is rather more complicated than the Trapezoidal Rule. Here we use a quadratic curve, rather than a straight line, between the end points of the interval. This leads to the following rule:

$$\int_a^b f(x)dx \simeq \frac{h}{3}\Big[f(x_0) + 4f(x_1) + 2f(x_2) + 4f(x_3) + 2f(x_4) + \ldots + f(x_n)\Big]$$

where $x_0 = a$, $x_n = b$ (n is even), $x_i = a + i * h$.

COMMANDS

Key in the program and RUN.

Enter the function as instructed.

Enter a and b when prompted.

Enter an even number of points as requested. If you enter an odd number, 1 will be added.

```
10 REM SIMPSON'S RULE
20 REM **************
30 REM
100 CL$=CHR$(147):REM TO CLEAR SCREEN
110 POKE 53280,6:REM BLUE BORDER
120 POKE 53281,1:REM WHITE SCREEN
130 PRINT CHR$(144):REM BLACK INK
140 PRINT CL$:PRINT
150 PRINT TAB(12)"SIMPSON'S RULE"
160 PRINT TAB(12)"**************"
170 PRINT
```

P102 Simpson's Rule

```
180 PRINT TAB(4)
    "THIS PROGRAM USES SIMPSON'S"
190 PRINT TAB(4)
    "RULE TO EVALUATE A DEFINITE"
200 PRINT TAB(4)"INTEGRAL."
210 PRINT
220 PRINT TAB(4)
    "YOU ARE REQUIRED TO ENTER:"
230 PRINT
240 PRINT TAB(8) "1. YOUR FUNCTION OF X."
250 PRINT
260 PRINT TAB(8)"2. THE RANGE OF VALUES"
270 PRINT TAB(11)"OF X OVER WHICH YOU"
280 PRINT TAB(11)"WISH TO EVALUATE THE"
290 PRINT TAB(11)"INTEGRAL."
300 PRINT
310 PRINT TAB(8)"3. THE NUMBER OF SUB-"
320 PRINT TAB(11)"INTERVALS (THIS MUST"
330 PRINT TAB(11)"BE EVEN)."
340 PRINT:PRINT
350 PRINT TAB(7)
    "PRESS ANY KEY TO CONTINUE."
360 GET A$:IF A$="" THEN 360:REM
    NO SPACE BETWEEN INVERTED COMMAS
370 REM****************************
380 PRINT CL$:PRINT
390 PRINT TAB(4)
    "TO INPUT THE FUNCTION PLEASE"
400 PRINT TAB(4)
    "TYPE IT IN DIRECTLY AFTER"
410 PRINT
420 PRINT TAB(4)"580 DEF FNA(X)="
430 PRINT
440 PRINT TAB(4)"THEN PRESS RETURN."
450 PRINT
460 PRINT TAB(4)
    "AFTER YOU HAVE DONE THIS TYPE IN"
470 PRINT
480 PRINT TAB(4)"RUN 580"
490 PRINT
500 PRINT TAB(4)
    "THEN PRESS RETURN. USE THE CURSOR"
510 PRINT TAB(4)
    "CONTROL KEYS TO POSITION THE"
520 PRINT TAB(4)
    "CURSOR DIRECTLY AFTER THE = SIGN"
530 PRINT:PRINT
```

```
540 PRINT TAB(4)"580 DEF FNA(X)="
550 PRINT:PRINT
560 STOP
570 REM******************************
580 REM THIS LINE WILL BE REPLACED BY
    THE FUNCTION DEFINITION.
590 REM******************************
600 CL$=CHR$(147):PRINT CL$:PRINT:PRINT
610 PRINT TAB(6):INPUT
    "LOWER VALUE OF X-RANGE";A
620 PRINT
630 PRINT TAB(6):INPUT
    "HIGHER VALUE OF X-RANGE";B
640 PRINT
650 PRINT TAB(6):INPUT
    "NUMBER OF POINTS";N%
660 IF N%<4 THEN N%=4:REM PREVENTS
    SILLY ENTRIES FROM BREAKING PROGRAM
670 IF N%-(INT(N%/2))*2<>0 THEN N%=N%+1:
    REM ENSURE N% IS EVEN
680 REM******************************
690 PRINT:PRINT
700 H=(ABS(B-A))/N%
710 FI=FNA(A)/2
720 LA=FNA(B)/2
730 X=A:EV=0:OD=0
740 FOR J=1 TO N%-3 STEP 2
750 X=X+H
760 OD=OD+FNA(X)
770 X=X+H
780 EV=EV+FNA(X)
790 NEXT
800 X=X+H
810 OD=OD+FNA(X)
820 IT=(FI+LA+4*OD+2*EV)*H/3
830 PRINT TAB(8)"INTEGRAL =";IT
840 PRINT TAB(8)"--------------------"
850 PRINT:PRINT
860 REM******************************
870 PRINT TAB(8):INPUT
    "ANOTHER RUN (Y/N)";Y$
880 IF ASC(Y$)=89 THEN 370
890 END
900 REM******************************
910 REM******************************
```